JOURNALISM AND SOCIETY

Praise for the book

'Every serious student of journalism should read this book. Combining sophisticated analysis with an accessible writing style, Denis McQuail has succeeded in producing a work of scholarship that shows what journalists do and what they should do.'
Stephen Coleman, Professor of Political Communication, Institute of Communications Studies, University of Leeds

'This luminous book sets a new standard for the textbook genre. Brilliant in contents, crystal-clear precision where every sentence counts, rigorous with ideas, it teaches the world mind. For a half century we have spoken earnestly of journalism's responsibility to society instead of to business and government. Now this concept is given sophistication unmatched, by the best scholar of media theory of his generation.'
Clifford Christians, University of Illinois

'This is going to be a must-read in journalism and communication classes. McQuail quality as we know it.'
Christina Holtz-Bacha, University of Erlangen-Nuremberg

'Journalism, as a profession, evolves, becoming increasingly complex and diverse. Especially now we need to be reminded where it came from, how it works, and where it stands in society. Denis McQuail provides the indispensable gateway.'
Mark Deuze, University of Amsterdam

'At a time when the journalistic profession is fundamentally challenged by technological transformations and new business models, Denis McQuail reminds us of the continuing social and political relevance of journalism in and for democratic societies. The grand old man of communication theory presents an overarching social theory of journalism that goes beyond the usual Anglo-American focus and develops a truly global scope, reflecting both his own previous work as well as that of many others. The master of synthesis offers an excellent overview of the position and mission of journalism in an information society that opens up the field of journalism and journalism studies for both students and scholars.'
Jo Bardoel, Professor of Journalism and Media, University of Amsterdam (ASCoR) and Nijmegen, the Netherlands

'In *Journalism and Society* Denis McQuail is at his best. He presents a very insightful revision of the sociological reflection on journalism and society, discussing the important implications of the new communication technologies for journalism of the 21st century. The declared aim of the book is to identify and describe the principles of journalism most widely recognized. McQuail goes well beyond, providing sound theoretical foundations of a new sociological paradigm of public communication in deeply transformed media and information environments. At the same time the book is a firm guide in the understanding of the principles of a profession that is a core activity of modern societies. A must-read book for students, academics and journalists.'
Gianpietro Mazzoleni, Professor of Sociology of Communication, University of Milan, Italy

'This book deals with the eternal question of how journalism is linked to society. Its nine chapters cover all pertinent aspects of journalism, including its freedom and responsibility, as well as issues such as the power of the press and the future of the press as an institution in the age of internet. All this is done with an analytical insight of the encyclopedic authority behind *Mass Communication Theory*. Also, pedagogically it is an exemplary textbook with each chapter including boxes to summarize the points, a conclusion to wind up, and selected further readings to support homework. I cannot think of a better staple food for students of journalism at all levels.'
Kaarle Nordenstreng, Professor Emeritus of Journalism and Mass Communication, University of Tampere, Finland

Los Angeles | London | New Delhi
Singapore | Washington DC

Los Angeles | London | New Delhi
Singapore | Washington DC

SAGE Publications Ltd
1 Oliver's Yard
55 City Road
London EC1Y 1SP

SAGE Publications Inc.
2455 Teller Road
Thousand Oaks, California 91320

SAGE Publications India Pvt Ltd
B 1/I 1 Mohan Cooperative Industrial Area
Mathura Road
New Delhi 110 044

SAGE Publications Asia-Pacific Pte Ltd
3 Church Street
#10-04 Samsung Hub
Singapore 049483

Editor: Mila Steele
Editorial assistant: James Piper
Production editor: Imogen Roome
Copyeditor: Kate Harrison
Proofreader: Jill Birch
Marketing manager: Michael Ainsley
Cover design: Jennifer Crisp
Typeset by: C&M Digitals (P) Ltd, Chennai, India
Printed and bound by CPI Group (UK) Ltd,
Croydon, CR0 4YY

First published 2013

Library of Congress Control Number: 201294

British Library Cataloguing in Publication da

A catalogue record for this book is available from British Library

ISBN 978-1-4462-6679-3
ISBN 978-1-4462-6680-9 (pbk)

To the memory of Hans Kleinsteuber, 1943–2012, a good friend and colleague and a free and generous spirit.

Contents

Preface

This book is intended as an introduction to the social theory of journalism. It covers a wide range of issues, but with a particular focus on the expectations of society from journalism and, in turn the latter's own perception of its public roles and responsibilities. It also examines the factors in society that have shaped journalism, both enabling and limiting it in its aims and scope and also in its effects. This overall perspective is one that attaches a high value to the contribution of journalism to society, especially by way of an attachment to truth, justice and freedom. The benefits are not guaranteed and not always delivered. However, the potential outweighs the failings that are often entailed in an institution that is not primarily altruistic and has to earn its own way in the world. It may even be the case that we cannot have the benefits of journalism without the offence and criticism it often provokes and the harm it can cause. The larger, normative, purpose of the book is to lend support to the efforts of journalism to perform its essential public roles, by way of voluntary accountability and protection from damaging market and political pressures.

The book had its origin in a small-scale project to write a short primer on contemporary social theory of journalism for use by students at the University of Yekaterinburg, as proposed by Dmitri Strovsky. Unfortunately, the project could not be completed as planned, but I am grateful for the stimulus to begin on this path, and later also to Takesato Watanabe, of Doshisha University, for further encouragement in the project. For the rest, I have too many debts to acknowledge individually, although, I owe much to colleagues and friends associated with the study of normative media theory over a number of years, including Jay Blumler, Jan van Cuilenburg and others at the University of Amsterdam, not forgetting the 'soul brothers' (Cliff Christians, Kaarle Nordenstreng, Bob White and Ted Glasser). My own interest in journalism, especially newspapers, began in a childhood fascination with news at a time of world-shaking events (the 1940s). But it was later given professional shape by my experience as a research adviser to the UK Royal Commission on the Press, 1974–7, with particular reference to news content and standards (thanks, Paul). This interest remained with me but my attention gradually shifted to normative issues and to the potential for implementation in policy. While my personal experience of journalism is quite limited, I have tried to take a broad view, without being able to claim any universality. But journalism today has many shared features of practice and theory across different countries and cultures and there is an increasing amount of comparative research to draw upon. There is at least a basis for reaching a number of generalisations on the matters dealt with here. In the time since the ambition of the book was enlarged beyond its first purpose, I have received much support in the rewriting from Sage and, in particular, from Mila Steele.

The whole structure and practice of professional journalism has come under great strain as a result of changing technology and market conditions. Change is also bringing new opportunities for more democratic public communication, along with less creative destruction. After reviewing the issues and evidence for the present purpose and from the perspective of society, I am still much inclined to stress the continuing relevance of the professional values and roles that have evolved and the enduring need on the part of society to support these, if need be, by way of structural provision.

Denis McQuail, Eastleigh, Hampshire

1 What is Journalism? How is it Linked to Society?

Introduction

This is a book of theory, specifically theory of the relation between journalism and society. It is written primarily from the perspective of society (rather than journalism), although it draws on the views of journalists as well as on research findings about journalism. The main focus is on the claims of society and the goals, rights, duties and responsibilities of journalists. Although the treatment is mainly explanatory and analytic, the outcome lends support to the case for an independent, professional and effective institution of a free press. This should be regarded as an indispensable element in a just and open society and beyond in the world. It is also unlikely that it can be achieved without some positive support from society, as well as from the press itself.

The term journalism is defined below but needs clarification in relation to other similar terms. Sometimes reference is made to 'the media' or 'mass media', or possibly 'news media', thus to the entire 'media system' or a large sector of it. The word 'press' is also encountered as an alternative (also explained below) that usually serves as a more abstract and formal description of much the same set of activities. Additionally, 'journalism' is often used as if synonymous with 'news' or even with the 'newspaper'. The relation between the various terms can be explained approximately as follows, since it is more than just a matter of words.

The widest frame of reference is that of 'mass media', both as an industry and a new social institution in its own right. Within this frame we can speak of the 'press' which occupies its own institutional terrain and acts to represent and stand for the interests of news media and, albeit informally and incompletely, to regulate some aspects of the work of journalists. Note that the 'press'concept is not limited to print media, as the word might suggest. Journalism is the core activity that the press stands for. It is also the word most commonly used to describe the occupation. Finally, we can mention the 'news' – the main product of journalism that is sometimes used interchangeably with other terms. The 'newspaper' enters the picture because most employed professional journalists probably still work for newspapers and the newspaper model of the news genre has largely been carried over to other media. However, other types of print media, especially magazines, have historically been important vehicles for information, opinion and comment about society. There is thus no consistency in usage, but this book will try and keep to a formulation in which 'journalism' is always the primary referent, but with an understanding that it is not coterminous with 'news' and not just a genre of the 'newspaper'.

Origins of journalism

In everyday terms, journalism refers to the activities and outcomes of those professionally engaged in collecting, analysing and publishing 'news'. In turn, news can be defined as factual accounts and explanations of current or recent events of wider relevance to a given public, usually characterised by their geographical location (city, region, nation, etc.). It is important not to reverse this connection and identify journalism only in terms of 'news' since there is a strong case for including other kinds of 'account' of social reality within the scope of journalism. Of course each of the main terms used in this definition needs further explanation, but this will suffice for the moment.

Journalism in this sense is strongly associated with the invention of printing and with the particular printed form of the newspaper, which first made its appearance in the early seventeenth century. Its emergence is clearly related to what has come to be called a 'modern' society and with the development of towns and international commerce as well as political changes. Compared to earlier forms, such societies were more free and individualistic, more secular and dedicated to material progress based on commerce and the application of science and technology. They have a looser social organization, with a high degree of division of labour but with interdependence of their elements. The fore-runners of print journalism are diverse and include: written accounts of events (sometimes distant in time), chronicles of dynastic, ecclesiastical or national developments, log-books and records, letters and journals kept by travellers, diplomatic despatches and presumably reports of spies and agents.

The prototype of the newspaper was the printed or handwritten newsletter that reported significant events and circumstances of relevance for trade, commerce and politics. These letters circulated along the postal and trade routes of Europe in the first instance and then more globally. They could be read aloud and handed on or copied, and were often intended for wider public diffusion. The contents of private letters, public announcements and also word of mouth reports were compiled into summary miscellanies, printed and sold as both entertainment and useful information.

Journalism in these forms existed well before there were professional journalists or editors, since news would usually be collected by printer-publishers from a variety of sources.

Although the original forms of journalism were disparate, it quite soon acquired certain distinguishing features, on the basis of common practices and public expectations that have persisted. The main characteristics of journalism as it gradually emerged in the form of the newspaper are summarised in Box 1.1.

Box 1.1 Defining features of early journalism

- Having reference to, or relevance for, recent or current events
- Factual, informative in form
- Public and open in terms of content and audience
- Independent of official authority
- Regular appearance in print
- Secular and miscellaneous in subject matter (not political or religious in purpose)
- Content selected mainly on grounds of potential interest to reader.

Once invented, journalism was found to be: indispensable for commerce; appealing to readers; and the basis of a profitable small business for printers. It also drew the attention of authorities governing cities, regions or nations. For them it could be seen as useful both as a means of control and influence and as a potential source of intelligence. State and city authorities in Europe sometimes published their own official newspapers or gazettes with a somewhat different purpose than commercial ventures, but with some overlap in content. Journalism was also liable to supervision or censorship as a potential cause of dissent or unrest, with much variation from one jurisdiction to another. Later, regular print publications (whether in newspaper or magazine form) came to be an important vehicle for movements towards political reform or revolution, national independence or freedom for religious minorities. Civic virtues and regional identities sometimes also gained journalistic support. The 'normative' dimension of journalism was well established before the commercial newspaper became dominant in the 'mass media age'.

In Europe and North America during the seventeenth and eighteenth centuries, journalism increasingly became a vehicle for the propaganda of established authorities and interests, and also a key instrument in the activities of opposing factions in political and religious struggles, reform movements and challenges to authority. As its role expanded, especially in relation to politics, it began to acquire an institutional character and formed the basis for what came to be known as 'The Press' in the nineteenth century (see below). Largely because of this development, the Press as an institution, with journalism as its core activity, has acquired a close association with aspirations for freedom and democracy. This strengthened the claim of journalism to have its own freedom.

As this brief history shows, journalism originated in the 'West' and became established as a genre and institution of society before newspapers really existed in Asia and the rest of the world. For this reason, at least, it is justifiable to define it largely in terms of a western 'dominant model', or at least as a very influential prototype. This has even been characterised more narrowly as an 'Anglo-American invention' (Chalaby, 1996). Nevertheless, the present and future of journalism need to take account of a much changed world in which journalism is a global phenomenon with a range of different forms and cultures, depending on the national society in which it is practised and the chosen medium. The different circumstances of its environment often strongly affect many of the theoretical issues about journalism discussed in this book.

Even so, we can still claim that our initial definition is still, generally, valid for most of the world's journalism and the key issues are still much the same in a more global environment, especially when they relate to freedom of reporting, standards of quality, the goals of journalism, the ties to society, the nature of the profession, and the challenges presented by changing media systems and changing worlds.

The journalism–society link: levels of analysis and theoretical perspectives

Although the practice of journalism, viewed from within, does not require any theoretical justification or explanation, some form of theory inevitably develops out of the wider interaction of journalists and their social environment, especially as journalism becomes more complex and more significant in its potential consequences. Theory may not be needed by journalists themselves to guide their day-to-day activities but it is essential for certain other purposes. It plays a part in explaining, or in justifying, the actions of journalists when these become controversial, and in processes of accountability involving the law or professional self-regulation. In particular, the claim to journalistic freedom as a fundamental principle cannot be sustained without theoretical justification as well as pragmatic arguments.

Following this line of thought, for purposes of theory, we can distinguish between three levels of attention to the practise of journalism: the levels being those of: the society; the news organization; and the individual journalist. The key issues facing journalism, beyond the practice of the task itself, are those of freedom, obligation to others, and accountability for meeting any obligations that are acknowledged. Each of these is experienced differently in the three main contexts looked at, with different expectations, rules for conduct and potential for negotiation, resistance or enforcement.

At the level of the society, journalism becomes enmeshed in all large public events, by way of contacts with social, cultural and political elites and drawn by the interests of its own audiences. At this level, ideas about the rights and obligations of journalism tend to circulate in the form of pressures and demands from society and proposals and counter-proposals concerning accountability and control. At the heart of the matter is the assumption that journalism plays an important, possibly essential, part in the collective life of a community or nation. In consequence, the press itself has to be governed, organized and conducted according to the same fundamental principles that are supposed to govern the rest of society. In a democracy this refers to freedom of speech, equality of all citizens and the rule of law.

Journalism in some form is a necessary condition for each of these principles, since it is a primary medium of public expression and it provides all citizens equally with the same information and advice for forming opinions and making choices. Under modern conditions of large-scale society, there can be no real public space for debate without journalism and no opportunity for the many to participate in relevant society-wide processes of self-government. Publicity is also essential to a fair and efficient judicial system. The press institution provides the primary means of self-regulation of journalism and also a limited guarantee of some measure of responsibility and of accountability to society as a whole.

Box 1.2 The level of society: some reasons why journalism raises theoretical issues

- Journalism is involved in all major public events
- Prominent actors in society use journalism for their own ends
- Principal values of society transfer to journalism and are, in turn, supported
- Journalism provides the basis for society-wide public debate and participation
- The justice system depends on publicity from media
- Journalism exerts pressure for accountability and society exerts pressure in kind in return.

At the *level of the news organisation* (e.g. newspaper or media firm), patterns of systematic reporting and publishing that characterise the output of journalists are related to larger structures of the market and of the social system. Theory to account for the structure and behaviour of news media usually requires reference to political and economic circumstances, to public policies and forms of governance (especially as embodied in regulations and law and also to the working of the market, especially the media market itself). The main relevant factors are summarised in Box 1.3.

Box 1.3 Factors affecting the conduct and performance of journalism at the level of the news organization

- The legal and regulatory system in place
- The structure of ownership and control (public versus private; degree of ownership monopoly; foreign ownership, etc.)

- The links between media and politics (parties, politicians, movements, ideas)
- Market forces, practices and pressures
- The general influence of organisational requirements and work routines on reporting, processing and distribution of news.

It is evident that the relation between news and society is mediated according to some or all of the factors mentioned in Box 1.3.

At the *individual level,* the journalist is a person dealing directly with other individuals, especially those who are considered as sources or as objects of reporting. More distantly, and notionally, the journalist has some form of relation with audience members. Real audiences aside, it has been shown that journalists, faced with a large, disparate and anonymous audience are inclined to construct a preferred view of the kind of person they are addressing. The various relationships involved are often in some degree reciprocal, so theory is concerned not only with what the journalist thinks of others, but also what others think of journalists.

The central aspect of these relationships concerns the potential obligations (professional or personal) that the journalist might be aware of. Conventions and customs of the profession play a large part in turning theory into practice. Furthermore, journalists are attached to the wider society by obligations and constraints that are sometimes personally experienced as citizens, but also often embedded in a web of informal rules of the workplace and the role, giving rise to expectations about conduct.

A significant factor for individual journalists may be the conception he or she has formed of the main purposes and rationale of the role of journalist, insofar as this is not fully determined by the organisation and work specification. Role conceptions relate to the degree and kind of social engagement that is called for or allowed. The extent to which a person aspires to professional status is also relevant here. Theory has tended to focus most on the perception of these roles on the part of journalists. How do they see their primary task and what do they regard as criteria of good journalism in light of this? The definition and perception of roles has direct implications for other key issues, including the degree of freedom they might claim in their work and relations with potential sources of news, especially those in positions of authority or influence.

There are also ethical norms and other standards that guide journalists in their relationships with other individuals. Central tenets relate to: respect for the privacy and dignity of subjects; an awareness of the consequences of publicity; and honesty in the collection of information and dealing with sources. These and other such matters are familiar to journalists. Observance may be governed by the policy of the news organization or by adherence to professional codes, but may sometimes be left to individual choice or governed by informal pressure and the demands and routines of everyday activity.

Box 1.4 The perspective of the individual journalist as an influence on conduct and performance

- Relationship to the audience, real or imagined (close or distant, favourable or hostile, etc.)
- Personal conception of the role
- Adherence to professional norms and codes
- Personal background, values and opinions
- Experience of in-work training and socialisation.

Although most questions of journalism theory relevant to the wider society can be dealt with by reference to one or other of these three levels and corresponding perspectives, there is an additional perspective to take into account – that of the reader or audience. Media use as a field of human behaviour has been extensively studied and 'the news' has often figured centrally in audience inquiries. Most relevant to this book, apart from the details of actual attention to, interpretation of, and 'learning' from news, are questions about motives for news attention.

Inquiries have revealed a wide range of motivations and satisfactions sought or obtained, with many variations, but frequent elements in public perceptions of news go beyond the more obvious purposes of keeping up with issues of the day and being informed of events. These additional purposes include: gaining a sense of security from the continuous flow of information; acquiring status through knowledge; having the means of social interaction with others; the entertainment and 'human interest' value of much content; and the sense of acquiring from regular news bulletins a framework for a daily routine or a ritual to follow.

Much actual use of news by large sections of the audience is thus not guided by motives related to essential informational needs of the person or the society. This fact co-exists with a widespread perception of news as generally a serious business. This ambiguous underlying reality of much news 'consumption' does help to make sense of audience choices and attitudes and also of the strategies of news providers to leaven 'hard' with 'soft' news. The much criticised news phenomenon of 'infotainment' may fail to meet high standards of information quality and is related to 'commercialisation', but it is not simply imposed from above on an unsuspecting and vulnerable public.

In general the findings of news audience research reflect and confirm more abstract theories about the social functions of news and journalism. They are also a reminder that 'news' is not only defined and characterised by its originators and that its significance and effects go beyond the informative aspect and are not very predictable. More to the point of the present book, a few key issues about journalism are highlighted from this point of view. These include the variable extent and basis of public trust in the suppliers of news (sources, media and journalists); and the variable degree of support from the audience for 'higher' journalistic purpose as opposed to forms of news that are sometimes regarded as trivial or even harmful. The larger question raised here concerns the extent to which journalism is constrained to reflect the reality of the culture of its society and the limits to influence this entails. The counter-currents to what is conventionally regarded as 'quality' journalism are strong.

Box 1.5 Audience perspectives on the news

- News is selectively and often casually attended to
- The perceived uses and satisfactions of news are very diverse
- The contents and consumption of news are seen as entertaining and diverting
- Social and cultural variations strongly influence attention and perception
- Trust and perceived credibility are very variable
- Audience beliefs about the rights and duties of journalists often deviate from established norms.

The main concerns of social theory of journalism

Journalism can be examined according to different types of theory (social, economic, literary, political, etc.) but the category of 'social theory' is most directly relevant to the public role of journalism and principles of the kind just introduced. Social theory is a mixture of *description* and *normative* prescription. As description, we are essentially treating journalism as conforming to a certain 'ideal type' of purpose and practice, but with differences according to time and place. Such an ideal form or model can be compared to the reality in a given national case and used as a tool of analysis and interpretation. The normative element refers to ideas about the ideal purposes of journalism and potential obligations to the wider society. It deals with the relative value of different goals and how these can or should be achieved, bearing in mind that in modern societies the 'press' is largely run as a business enterprise, not as a social service or for idealistic (or ideological) purposes.

Our aim is not to propose rules to be followed but to identify the guiding principles of journalism that are most widely recognised both internally and from the outside. The 'theory' we are seeking to describe either in empirical or prescriptive aspects, or both, is not fixed or universally valid, but open to alternative interpretations and formulations. Nevertheless, some coherence and consistency can be expected between societies that subscribe to the same values of civic and human rights and forms of political decision-making. The value of theory should lie in its potential to explain and assess the reality of journalistic work. It is an essential aid to criticism and self-awareness as well as to attempts at reform. The status accorded to journalism in the wider society depends on the values it subscribes to and how well it lives up to them. Efforts at improvement depend on there being a viable and respected body of social theory for diagnosis and prescription.

The main concerns of social theory of journalism are given in Box 1.6.

Box 1.6 Social theory of journalism: main concerns

- The nature of the 'needs of society' that are met by journalism
- The issue of whether or not journalism, despite its claims to freedom, has some obligations to society that it cannot ignore
- The nature and strength of any such obligations
- The means available to society to activate obligations or hold media to account for them
- The norms and standards that should apply to the practise of journalism, as it affects society
- Issues of control and accountability especially as they relate to freedom of expression and publication.

Diversity and diversification of journalism

Journalism itself is a social and cultural phenomenon linked to many other conditions and ultimately escaping clear and unambiguous definition. Nevertheless, we can identify some of its various manifestations and look at the pathways by which these have emerged. As noted earlier, journalism is only one of many different genres of writing with a bearing on the contemporary reality of society that were stimulated by the invention of printing and publishing.

An important strand of much early print publication was the wider concept of personal *authorship* that had been stimulated by the discovery of printing. For some versions of journalism, this has given it an expectation of originality, personal vision and intrinsic authority. The journalist as author should have the same rights of freedom of expression and of conscience as any other author. However, the mundane task of news collection and dissemination is not easy to reconcile with this principle. There are practical limits to the exercise of personal freedom, imagination and expression. Journalists are typically employed by organisations engaged in selling and distributing the products of their work. They are inevitably constrained by these circumstances.

The version of the occupation or role of journalist that has come to predominate, as distinct from the simple activity of printing and publishing bare accounts of actual events, reflects the tension between the many demands and expectations affecting journalistic work. The individual journalist of the eighteenth and nineteenth centuries in Europe or North America could sometimes lay claim to being an author or at least a writer, and not just a conduit from sources of information to typesetters. But the claim was not made by all or even many journalists and the public reputation and image of the profession was not usually very flattering. An inherent uncertainty about the status of the journalistic role remains with us.

Nevertheless, the literary and scientific dimension of authorship coupled with an involvement in the struggles for religious and political freedom did modify and extend the original idea of journalism as a neutral carrier of information about current events. One result can be seen in the emergence of different varieties or types of journalism, especially forms that involve the expression of strong opinions, the adoption of an adversary position, or the emergence of a 'watchdog' role. Contemporary journalism is characterised by a number of essentially different genres, carrying different expectations for the audience and society and often following their own distinctive ground rules.

This diversification is not simply a case of subject matter (for instance, the opinion-forming press or the press of sport, politics, business, art and culture or celebrity gossip). More important are distinctions according to place (local, regional, national), social class and education (quality versus tabloid journalism) or audience taste/interest and style of writing (sensational or restrained, literary and philosophical, etc.). Not least important was the fundamental difference between a profit-oriented newspaper press and one with ideal, political or ideological objectives.

In more recent times, differences according to medium (and technology) have added another significant dimension of variation. The print-based model of journalism has proved a powerful survivor and in many respects still remains more influential than audio-visual media (for instance, in setting the news agenda for the latter and in its closeness to power). In many countries, the newspaper never attained mass circulation and, where it did, it has been in decline. Even so, the communicative power of the word seems to exceed that of visual reporting because of its lack of ambiguity and with the advantage of permanence. However, film and television documentary have unique possibilities for impact and the primacy of words may be slowly giving way to the capacity of online media to combine all forms and genres, with immense practical advances in processing and distribution.

Box 1.7 Dimensions of variation in journalism

- Authorship versus employment
- Profession versus trade or craft
- Local versus national and cosmopolitan
- Profit versus non-profit
- General versus specialist
- Adversarial and active versus supportive or neutral
- Print versus other media
- Informative versus entertaining purpose.

The variations described are easily recognisable, and we can also discern a general tension between a view of the press as an institution primarily concerned with serving the public interest and one that is a branch of commerce or even of the entertainment industry. Whatever side one takes on the issues raised here, we are still dealing with much the same idea of what is basically expected of the press – namely the regular provision of relevant and reliable information about current issues and events. To that extent a large part of what the press ought to be doing is a matter of agreement and much the same body of social theory concerning the role of journalism can be applied.

However, there are large areas remaining for potential dispute, especially where it concerns not just the provision of information, but matters of interpretation, opinion and value judgments. These can strongly influence the selection of topics and events for journalistic attention as well as the manner in which stories are told. Sooner or later we come up against the view that a completely objective and factual journalism is not attainable. Theory can help to resolve this paradoxical feature of the work of journalism, by offering a more complex version of what can be achieved and an understanding of the limitations.

Journalism and changing technology: implications for society

Ever since the mechanisation of printing and the industrialisation of newspaper production, journalism has been changing in response to technological change. The early manual press supplied a limited class of readers, mainly in towns. Late nineteenth century developments led towards a 'mass market' audience, with journalism for all social classes. The new readers were thought to be less interested in politics and more interested in sport, gossip, human interest, crime and useful information for daily life. Broadcasting by radio and, later, television was slow to adopt a news and information function, but by the latter half of the last century television news had come to reach whole populations and was widely claimed by most to be their 'main source' of news. Accessibility, popularity of the medium and perceived reliability all played a part in achieving this position. The key consequence for society was that a majority was quickly and equally informed about the same events, in much the same version. This was interpreted as a basis for social cohesion and solidarity. It also encouraged governmental and other social actors to influence and control the medium, in ways that were not available for controlling the printed press. The dominant position of television news weakened as a result of increased competition from cable, satellite and other new channels, aided by deregulation and privatisation of media systems.

However, it was the rise of the internet in the late twentieth century that has most troubled the settled relations of journalism and society since then. The most significant features of internet journalism from this point of view are:

- its great diversity of forms and its accessibility to all would-be sources;
- its freedom from most controls, even from the benevolent guidance of a press institution and profession;
- its capacity for feedback and interactivity in relation to an audience;
- its relative delocalization;
- its non-institutionalized character; and
- its disconnection from other social institutions.

As a news medium, the internet is no longer closely linked to the existing structures of power and influence. It may even be considered potentially destabilising and socially fragmenting. It cannot be expected to recognise the same responsibility to society as earlier news media generally did, partly because of its more global character. Actual consequences are still uncertain, but it has certainly destabilised some features of the established media system, for instance, the once dominant position of the newspaper press.

Box 1.8 Implications of the internet for journalism–society relations

- Less easy to control, formally and informally
- More diversity of content, sources, style, audiences
- Less concentration of any 'power of the press' in a few hands
- More chance for the 'mass public' to evade hegemonic influence
- More chance for active social participation, at the same time as a reverse potential for disengagement on the part of individuals.

Defining journalism and the news today

Journalism was defined in general terms at the start of this chapter, but we can now give a more precise definition in the following terms:

> Journalism is the construction and publication of accounts of contemporary events, persons or circumstances of public significance or interest, based on information acquired from reliable sources.

Accounts of events can vary a good deal in form, although the most frequently occurring element is the factual report of an observed or recorded reality. The medium of report can also vary, including graphic, sound and visual means. A statement, speech, appeal, etc. by a public figure counts as an event in this definition. Often there is a secondary element that reports on the alternative perspectives on events, as far as can be known from witnesses, participants or interested parties. Thirdly, there may be commentary or opinion added by the journalist on a personal basis or as the view of a news organisation (i.e. of its owners or editors). The version of journalism outlined also strongly implies that journalism is *authored*, thus not just a collection of facts.

Journalism defined in this way is typically undertaken within a larger news organisation, by skilled or trained persons, following established and transparent rules and procedures. The main product of journalism (the factual accounts) is usually simply known as 'news', which has in itself become a central genre of mass communication. News has been characterised by sociologists (following Robert Park, 1940) in terms of the features shown in Box 1.9.

Most news conforms to a certain style and form that is readily recognised. The most obvious features are: its attempt to be timely and of the moment; its relevance to public concerns and the interests of its potential audience; and its central component of 'facts' that claim to provide accurate and reliable information about reality. A widely expected feature of news that goes with this is the stance of neutrality and objectivity, an attempt to avoid open value judgements and personal opinion in reporting. An extension of this is the general assumption that objective reporting will be independent of the interests of sources or other vested interests. Beyond these basic features are others, which are less obvious. One is that the 'reality' that is reflected is usually equated with an undistorted mirror image of what is actually going on in the society around.

The selection of some items out of many for attention cannot really reflect a reality that is for the most part not 'newsworthy'. It has to be guided by 'news values' – essentially ideas of what will interest an audience plus some assumptions about the meaning and significance of events. Finally it is evident that news is much more than information in the form of facts, but also a series of 'stories', with plots, characters, heroes and villains, happy or tragic endings, etc. The 'narrativity' of news is, inevitably, in some tension with the formal character of news. For good or ill, the above characterisation of news has shaped the internal and external perception of the nature of journalism. This association of meaning cannot be undone, nor its consequences evaded, although it is important not to forget other aspects of the journalistic task.

Box 1.9 Characteristics of 'news'

- Timeliness: having novelty and reference to or relevance for current events, but also being perishable
- Truthfulness: factual accuracy and completeness in essentials, plus verifiability
- Objectivity: neutrality of perspective and lack of conscious bias
- Independence: from sources, the objects of reporting, or vested interests
- Reflective, in a proportional way, of 'reality' as far as possible
- Relevance to expected audience interests and believed relative significance
- Predictability (consistency): in respect of type of event regarded as 'newsworthy'
- 'Narrativity': taking a story-telling form and structure.

The press as an institution

The term 'press', as already noted, is still often used as a collective word for the activities of journalists, editors and publishers, and generally for the organisations involved in producing news as defined above. It provides a short-hand reference to the whole complex of publication and circulation of ideas throughout society, without which democracy cannot work. Originally it only denoted print media, but has now been extended to electronic forms, at least in their journalistic activities. In general, an institution is a complex of activities and practices that are formally or informally regulated by the same set of broad purposes and by accepted rules of conduct that have developed over time. The press institution largely shapes the expectations that the wider society and its agencies have of news media and also provides a basis for mutual trust, as long as experience accords with the ideal claims made.

There is no formal organisation or office of 'the press' as such in any free country and no fixed rules of conduct. It has a much less concrete existence than the social institutions on which it reports, such as education, law, politics, business or the military. In part this uncertainty embodies and reflects the freedom that the press claims for itself and also its high degree of fragmentation. The institutional features of the press are correctly interpreted as potential means of social control.

Nevertheless, it is still helpful to think of the press institution as providing some coherence and guidance to essential activities of public information. Its 'membership' is largely determined by the aspiration of journalists and publishers plus the recognition accorded by the public and society at large. Despite the lack of a formal or fixed system of governance, the activities of 'the press' do entail a number of conventions and norms of conduct. These 'rules' generally support notions of wider responsibility and public accountability and, in turn, serve to foster the trust essential to the performance of a public informational role.

Membership of the press often brings with it certain informal rights and privileges in the collection of information about public events. Wide use is made by 'event organisers' of a process of 'accreditation' of journalists that serves as an entry ticket to news events, but it can equally serve to exclude. Generally, the term 'press' is only applied to the 'mainstream', professional, and established sector of the news media, especially newspapers and broadcasting. However, by now, news on the internet – especially where provided by established news media, news agencies and sources – is also often regarded as the voice of the press. Journalism that adopts a very adversarial or socially deviant attitude (as is permitted by press freedom) risks losing the benefits of public acceptance and at some point of non-conformity, its protected status and its 'accreditation'. This may occur as a voluntary choice, reflecting a deliberate choice for dissociation from the press 'establishment' but it may also result from pressure by authorities to conform.

One end served by the press institution is to help reconcile some of the inconsistencies and latent conflicts mentioned earlier. For instance, it establishes 'rules of the game' whereby newspapers can be financed by advertisers with vested interests in news content, while still claiming independence. Advertising has been an accompaniment to journalism since the earliest times, with an understanding that the two should be kept separate. In line with this, advertising material does not usually enjoy the same freedoms of expression as other content, where the 'rules of the game' apply. Similarly it helps to account for the co-existence of both idealistic and also material, profit-seeking, motives. The press institution is embodied in arrangements made within national societies, much influenced by culture and circumstances of time and place. However, there are also some universal features within the broad coverage of countries claiming to be democratic. Although the press institution has been described primarily as an entity of a national society, there has been a steady growth internationally of key features of the institution, especially by way of agreement on codes and values (see Appendix, §1 and the activities of trans-national global and regional associations of journalists, as well as of editors and publishers. The influence of groups active in supporting the rights and freedoms of journalists has also grown, by way of research and publicity. The international manifestation of the press institution is the more notable because it is not available as a means of control and is even a source of resistance and assistance against national level oppression.

Box 1.10 The press institution

The press institution:

- informally sets boundaries and provides an identity to the practice of journalism;
- has no formal constitution or organisational form;
- acts as an agency of professional self-regulation and accountability;
- is closely associated with 'mainstream' news media channels;
- secures some rights and privileges for journalists as well as some means of defence; and
- has the potential to be a means of control by society.

The idea of a press institution as outlined has been powerfully affected by new developments of technology and media structure. An immediate effect has been to break up or re-arrange the structure of media systems and to introduce new elements that take time to be institutionalized. There has been a distinct 'desacrilisation' of the established organs and functions of the press. They no longer have such high status or elevated goals, but provide services to the public and clients in a competitive market. There is also an opening up of information and opinion functions to anyone who wants access by way of new forms of online publication. These changes tend to undermine the already weak identity of 'The Press', although so far they have probably not made fundamental changes to its position in society, largely because the needs of society and of individuals in respect of public information are still much the same as before.

The 'power of the press'

Society is both the source and end destination of news, in such a way that journalism is inevitably involved in the exercise of power and not just the power of governments, propagandists and advertisers.

The often cited or alleged 'power of the press' lies in the many consequences sought or experienced by both 'senders' and 'receivers' of news, especially when effects relate to issues of public importance. In this context, 'power' can only mean 'influence' and persuasion, since information cannot in itself coerce. Sometimes the apparent power is a simple consequence of the volume of publicity, with no intention of influence involved. All agencies that operate in the public sphere are vulnerable to reactive effects caused by information circulated publicly and outside their own control.

The capacity to have influence stems from certain general circumstances of the operation of the press. Primary amongst these are: the *de facto* ability to 'control the gates' of communication to the public at large, deciding who and what will receive varying amounts of publicity; some control over the quality of this publicity – whether positive or negative; the dependence of many institutions of society on the news media as their main channel to the public but also the window through which they are themselves routinely perceived.

The effects at issue relate to public behaviour stimulated by news, or to attitudes and opinions formed on the basis of news information. The news media can affect choices in matters of consumption, voting and public reputation, whether intentionally or not. We should keep in mind, however, that the 'power of the press' is not an intrinsic property of the media, but largely the outcome of forces at work in the society that are mediated by way of the media. Aside from sheer reach, it depends on the degree of trust and respect accorded by the public to media sources. We need to look elsewhere for the true bases of social power and influence.

Whatever type or degree of power that can be attributed to the press, the situation of general dependence on flows of public information inevitably raises issues of the rights and responsibilities of journalists and leads to demands for accountability. Social theory of the press (ideas of what journalism ought or ought not to do) flows quite directly from the links of purpose, cause and effect that have been indicated.

Box 1.11 Power of the press: main types of effect

- Persuasion and change of attitude
- Formation of public opinion

(Continued)

(Continued)

- Influence on public image and reputation
- Effects on behaviour (e.g. voting, consumption, mobilisation to action)
- Setting the public agenda of issues
- Shaping public interpretations of events
- Informing the public and structuring 'public knowledge'
- Differential 'amplification' of news and images.

What society expects from journalism

A central feature of the case is that journalism (like the media in general) in a free society does not have any specific obligations to the state or any outside body, thanks largely to the doctrine of 'freedom of the press'. Journalists are certainly required to do no harm and obey the law, but they are not required by any outside authority to do any specific good. They are free to choose or avoid a variety of goals and tasks, within the scope of their occupation. The news media generally resent and resist attempts to prescribe any role for them in society, except as self-chosen.

Despite this, there is much in the history, constitution and conduct of the press institution that leads to the recognition of certain unwritten (and ultimately unenforceable) obligations to society. There are also many external pressures and also possible attractions towards service to society that cannot easily be ignored. Normative social theory of media relates both to self-chosen social purposes and also to claims from outside about how they should conduct themselves.

Amongst these external expectations, the strongest and clearest are those that stem from the presumed role of the press in democracies as a carrier of news and former of opinion and as a communicative link between citizen and government. The relationship of journalism to politics is a central feature of the case, since the claim to press freedom rests in part on the needs of democratic institutions. We can also point to deeply embedded conventions and customs in the history of journalism itself that makes such 'service to politics' quite normal, even central. Apart from anything else, the ongoing events of public significance which journalism is committed to report on are often political in one way or another and are also of relevance and interest to audiences for news.

The other major influences on normative expectations are the state and agencies of government on the one hand, and owners on the other. Although, in democratic theory, the former can have no absolute power over a free press, they are inevitably a potential source of rewards or punishments of various kinds (economic, status, regulatory, see Chapter 7). As a matter of course, well established press organisations pay attention to the wishes of government, if only out of self-interest. At times a symbiotic relationship of mutual assistance develops between the 'makers' and the 'merchants' of news. It is also normal for an adversarial relationship to develop; a conflict essentially over the power to control the flow of information and to 'define reality'. This is both a matter of keeping secrets and determining what is 'truth'.

At abnormal times of crisis, war or national emergency, there is a much higher likelihood that the news media will voluntarily cooperate with authorities, both by way of positive acts of news selection and access, and also by omission or self-censorship. Although such compliance may be temporary, it is also based on established lines of contact and cooperation as well as on foundations of patriotism and service to the national interest, that have a continuing influence in normal times.

The second major influence is that of owners and media business interests. The imperatives of large media corporations and market forces (more so than of governments) seem to many observers more threatening to freedom, with more idealistic goals subordinated to market discipline. The counter argument is that journalism has to be viable and earn a living, but profitability does not have to exclude other goals, even in an era of global mega-corporations. In fact, profitability can support independence and the ideals of journalism can still be pursued and may even be profitable. There are many different markets for information, not just a mass market, and ideal purposes also have a public following.

The practice of journalism is thus caught in a web of obligations and pressures of various degrees of strength and specificity. Social theory of journalism as presented in this book is both an attempt at codification of relevant norms and an assessment of the direction and strength of pressures encountered and how these relate to professional practice. It would be a mistake to suppose that journalism necessarily operates in a permanent state of tension or conflict with the rest of society, despite powerful strands in the press's own 'ideology' that proclaim a more or less permanent adversarial stance of journalists (albeit on behalf of the public) in the face of dominant social power.

Box 1.12 Expectations of society from journalism

- To circulate information on public matters to all
- To connect citizens to government and vice versa
- To support the routine work of the main institutions of society
- To respect the reigning values and norms of culture and society
- To serve the national interest
- To be available to help at times of crisis or emergency.

There is a potential contradiction between some expectations and the claim of the press itself to freedom and independence from state and government, or other vested interests. Most of the time this can be tolerated, but it does contribute to a dynamic climate of conflict in which journalism has to operate.

The self-image of the social role of the press

The newspaper press has often shown a voluntary dedication to the public good, and the titles traditionally chosen by newspapers have often reflected such public-spirited purposes. Box 1.13 lists some of the recurring verbal images or metaphors representing a public role, with examples of the newspaper titles that express these ideas – the titles date mainly from the high point of the newspaper at the turn of the nineteenth to twentieth centuries. The view that news media have a part to play in society is an inherent and important component of the image the press has of itself as an institution. The images either refer to some chosen task of the press, some normative quality, or both.

Box 1.13 Images and metaphors of the newspaper role in society, as expressed in typical titles

Task or quality (plus sample titles):

- Actuality and timeliness: The Times; Journal; Diary
- Bringer of information: News; Messenger; Intelligencer; Chronicle; Courier; Reporter
- Identification with a place: by carrying the name of a city, region, etc.
- International range of coverage: Globe; News of the World; Planet; Universe
- Speed: Express; Mercury; Despatch; Telegraph
- Wake-up call: Clarion; Bugle; Drum
- Harbinger of events: Herald; Crier; Leader
- Being of and for the people: Humanité; Labour; Tribune; Citizen; Worker; The People
- Being a public voice: Voice; Echo; Tribune; Word
- Acting as a guardian: Guardian; Argus; Sentinel
- Reliability and trust: Truth; Ledger, Record; Gazette; Tablet; Mirror; Trust
- Freedom: Independent and Free in titles; Liberation
- Observation and Scrutiny: Examiner; Inquirer; Observer; Monitor; Eagle
- Emblem and guide: Standard; Flag; Leader
- Enlightenment: Sun; Spark; Star.

We can say that the main organs of print journalism have traditionally chosen titles that express an aspect of the larger role of the press and that the foundations of social theory of the press have been laid by the press itself. Radio and television, in giving names to their news and actuality programme formats, have typically followed on the same path as newspapers by choosing from essentially the same stock of metaphors. The elements of 'theory' assembled in later chapters are thus largely an elaboration of ideas that originate with the press itself (publishers, printers, editors and journalists), in some kind of informal negotiation with the public and with those who want to reach the public (politicians, advertisers, educators, entertainers, etc.).

There is a diversity of meanings and emphasis that finds expression in a diversity of types of publication and types of journalism, as noted earlier. Even so, there is also a certain degree of convergence on what is likely to be most widely regarded as good practice. It is this modal form that has been institutionalised in what some consider as a profession in its own right (see Chapter 4).

The pressures and demands from outside are not all equal in force and conditions of society vary in even more fundamental ways (economic, social, cultural, etc.). It is primarily for this reason that there are alternative versions of the social role of the press, with particular reference to differences between liberal and socialist ideology, various degrees of statism or corporatism and different levels of economic and social development. In general, internal norms relating to the core practice of journalistic work have actually varied less than the external systems of governance applied to the 'press'.

Conclusion: questions to be addressed

The following chapters will develop the points made in this introduction, with particular reference to the social role of the press and the implications for journalistic standards. Account has to be taken not only of variations between social and cultural contexts but also of economic conditions and practical circumstances. Amongst the pressures towards convergence of practice, special weight has to be given to the impact of technology.

The following questions cover the main themes of the book as a whole and are placed here to give an idea in advance of its range and purpose. A set of more specific questions is posed at the start of each chapter to serve as an agenda and guide to readers.

Functions and purposes of journalism in relation to society

- How are they perceived by society?
- How are they defined by the media themselves?
- How far is a journalistic obligation to fulfil these functions acknowledged?
- How do journalists themselves perceive their own role amongst the choices available?

The public interest in journalism

- What are the main elements of a public interest that journalism is expected to promote and how can it be known or expressed?
- How can it be served by journalism?
- How far does journalism carry an obligation in this matter?

Social (normative) theory of the press

- Is there sufficient common ground on which to base a 'social theory of the press'?
- How universal is or can it be across different media systems?
- What are the main sources of limitation and variations?

Journalism as a profession

- What does it mean to classify it as such?
- If so classified, what does this entail in the way of rights and duties? If not a profession, why not?
- How far does it conform to criteria of other professions?
- Does it matter one way or the other?

Freedom and accountability

- Do journalists have special rights to freedom?
- Where are limits set?
- What are the main threats to freedom of the press, e.g. political, economic, cultural, etc?
- What means of accountability are compatible with 'Freedom of the Press'?

Power of the press

- What is the basis for alleged power?
- How far can it be directed or controlled?
- How far can journalists be held accountable either for the effects of their work or its quality? What forms of accountability are appropriate for the purpose?

Theory and actuality of performance

- To what extent is there a gap between social theory of journalism and the reality of practice and outcomes?
- How can such shortfalls between theory and reality be explained?
- In the light of performance, what remains of expectations of service to the public interest?
- In what sense and how far can journalism be considered as a 'mirror of society'?

Changes in technology and media systems

- What are the consequences of ongoing changes for the press institution and normative relations of journalism to society?

Further reading

Berkowitz, D. (ed.) (1997). *The Social Meanings of News*. Thousand Oaks, CA: Sage.
Christians, C., Glasser, T., McQuail, D. Nordenstreng, K. and White, R. (2009). *Normative Theories of the Press*. Champaign IL: University of Illinois Press.
Graber, D., McQuail, D. and Norriss, P. (eds) (2005). *The Politics of News: News of Politics*, 2nd edition. Washington, DC: Congressional Quarterly.
Preston, P. (ed.) (2009). *Making the News: Journalism and News Cultures in Europe*. London: Routledge.
Thussu, D. (2007). *News as Entertainment*. London: Sage.
Wahl-Jorgenson, K. and Hanitzsch, T. (eds) (2009). *Handbook of Journalism Studies*. London: Routledge.

Online readings

Go to www.sagepub.co.uk/mcquailjournalism for free access to the online readings.

Bardoel, J. (1996). 'Beyond journalism: between information society and civil society', *European Journal of Communication*, 11, 3: 283–302.
Chalaby, J. (1996) 'Journalism as an Anglo-American invention', *European Journal of Communication*, 11, 3: 303–26.

2 Journalistic Responsibility to Society

Introduction

Since the early days of printing, publication has been driven by a variety of motives, including: profit and employment; a sense of public responsibility; advocacy of a cause, political party or ideology; an attraction to the craft of writing and printing. At the same time, publication has quite often been accompanied by restrictions as well as risks, because of potential harm to the interests of others or to the society in general. Against this background, a body of thought has gradually emerged concerning the rights (especially that of freedom to publish) and the obligations of journalists.

This chapter is primarily concerned with the various theoretical reasons or justifications for considering journalism to have some measure of public responsibility, despite guarantees of freedom. Although the two are not necessarily incompatible, there is an underlying tension between freedom and responsibility that is never far from the surface. Most of the relevant thinking about these matters has emerged during the last century, although the roots lie deeper. Certainly, the rise of truly mass media provided a stimulus to reflection, given a widely held conviction that under new circumstances of mass publication – not only mass newspapers, but also broadcasting and other media – that the media have a great potential for both good and harm. Given this, it is not surprising that the issue of public responsibility gained in salience and with it the question of what limits might be set to 'freedom of the press' in the name of the larger public good.

The following questions are addressed in this chapter and should be taken as a guide by the reader.

The Public Interest Concept

- How is it to be defined in relation to the press?
- How can it be determined?
- What are the main alternative versions of the public interest?

Responsibility and obligation

- How do they apply to journalism?
- What are their main forms or types?
- How are they derived from theories of the press and society?

Freedom and accountability

- How do different press theories deal with these issues?
- What limitations can be derived from theory?
- What forms of accountability are indicated for journalism?

Challenge and change in normative theory

- How does critical theory view journalistic responsibility?
- How does the internet fit into an existing framework of theory?
- Is there any overall structure of ideas about press responsibility?

Defining journalistic responsibility

Journalism is not a single or simple activity, in itself not easy to define and the same difficulty arises in dealing with the meaning of 'responsibility'. One version (McQuail, 2003:45) defines it as follows: 'any well-founded expectation based on law, custom or morality that the press should promote the public good and avoid harm'. This relates to: standards of quality (for instance, in respect of truthfulness, independence, fairness, decency, etc.); alleged harmful effects; and also to questions of positive obligation to serve some public purpose. Notions of media obligation to society are often weak or contested because of the claim to press freedom, and they vary from one national society to another. They can also be contradictory and ideologically motivated.

The term responsibility has various meanings when used in relation to mass media. One key distinction has been made according to the origin or driving force behind an obligation. Three main types of responsibility have been named (Hodges, 1986): those that are 'assigned' or imposed from outside; those that are 'contracted', or agreed between the parties concerned; and those that are self-chosen. In the case of journalism, there are relatively few externally assigned tasks, and these are mainly confined to broadcasting (e.g. providing impartial political access) or to matters of general law – essentially the duty to avoid causing harm of various kinds. In times of national emergency, more examples of assigned tasks are to be found. The range of 'contracted' obligations is wide, but most relate to specific or implied promises of service and quality made to audiences and clients in return for payment, or to regulators in return for licences; self-chosen obligations are also varied and to be found in editorial promises to serve audiences or public purposes according to conviction or professional ethics.

A primary public responsibility of journalism is to avoid any incitement to hatred or violence, or damage to reputation. Another comes under the heading of 'moral responsibility'. This can arise when there is no necessary cause and effect, but a foreseeable connection can be made between news publication (or omission) and some ill-effect, such as suicide, health problems or reputation. A different kind of responsibility is carried by professional journalists who agree to observe codes and canons of good practice.

Despite the freedom so often claimed and celebrated, there is evidently quite a wide universe of expectations that can lead to the media being called to account for their own quality, conduct and effects. At the core of this exploration are questions about the nature of the 'public interest' in what the media do. It is largely on this topic that the question of journalistic responsibility depends.

Box 2.1 Types of responsibility

- Legal and regulatory obligations
- Duties stemming from the occupational role
- Promises of service and level of quality
- Causal responsibility for (harmful) consequences
- Moral responsibility for unintended or long-term harm
- Responsibility as a professional.

Publication and the public interest

The concept of a *public interest* is both simple and also controversial in social and political theory. As applied to the mass media, its simple meaning is that they carry out a number of important, even essential, tasks and it is 'in the general interest' (or good of the majority) that these are carried out well and according to principles of efficiency, justice, fairness, and respect for current social and cultural values. At the minimum, we can say that it is in the public interest that the media should do no harm and not treat the major institutions of society with disrespect, but the notion entails many positive expectations as well as restrictions, and also various forms of accountability, ranging from law to voluntary self-regulation.

The broader notion of a public interest has a long history in society's arrangements for meeting its own essential needs. The most relevant root idea is that certain provisions and services that are essential for all can only be satisfactorily provided or regulated by some central public authority. This applies especially to such matters as transport (roads, bridges), defence, crime and punishment, weights and measures, currency standardisation. In these areas, uniform collective arrangements suited both authorities and most citizens, ensuring universal access and high standards. The range of 'needs' was gradually widened to include education and other channels of information provision for personal as well as public purpose. The postal system was often the first such public communication provision.

Journalism does not obviously fall into the category of essential needs, but it was the press itself that helped to promote the idea that it was indispensable to society, even though no monopoly or form of regulation was sought. At the core of the practice of journalism, as it developed into the 'Press', was the growing conviction that it should be free to publish varied versions of the 'truth'. The basic idea of a service 'in the public interest' as described did not extend far beyond the means of transmission, having no prescription as to specific purpose. In the mid-nineteenth century, the development of electronic communication by cable and wireless telegraphy followed the mail service in becoming a business that could be most efficiently run by public authorities, on behalf of all, although especially for the strategic purposes of the state. When broadcasting arrived in the twentieth century it was soon drawn into the sphere of public provision in many countries, with the USA as a main exception. The newspaper was caught up in a clash between would-be public regulators and defenders of the unfettered market, although no state monopoly for the press was seriously advocated in liberal social systems. However, there were certainly supporters of more regulation to prevent the abuses attributed to 'commercialisation' and monopoly ownership of the press.

The tensions and arguments between advocates of control or self-control of the press and defenders of the free market have continued until today, in modified terms. For libertarians the market, for all its faults, is the only reliable defence of the right to exercise true press freedom and therefore of the public interest. To interfere, on grounds of preventing abuse, would be to risk more than would be gained. In the end, it is argued, only the public as audience can decide what is in their interest.

The arrival of the internet as a new medium has enlarged the scope of the discussion. The internet began without any assigned purposes or regulation and became a mass medium (in terms of diffusion), seemingly by chance. It has become a public communication amenity, open to all and without the drawbacks of state control. However, it has increasingly developed as a set of large global private enterprises, with primary goals of profit. Its potential as a public service still exists but this feature has become more marginal, leading to demands for protection of some public open space for citizen uses. Meanwhile, it is increasingly becoming subject to various forms of state supervision, interference and legal encroachments.

The field of conflict described here is too complex to treat simply as an argument between defenders of a free market and advocates of more intervention on the public's behalf. A recurrent problem for those engaged in the debates on this issue is the difficulty of establishing in any consistent or objective way just what the 'public interest' in the press might be. In fact there is no such way to be found. The market solution seems least problematic because it embraces the majoritarian or democratic principle – essentially that of 'giving the public what it wants'. This seems to meet the criteria of clarity and ease of discovery, but it is far from a simple matter and it is not at all easy to ascertain 'what the public wants' in any objective way. For one thing, according to a good deal of research, the public quite often voices strong dissatisfaction with the press and other media and supports quite stringent limitations on freedom of publication, well beyond what is consistent with the principle of freedom of the press. The underlying cause is simply that the benefits of the press are varied and sometimes mutually incompatible, for instance the desire for social harmony and order and the pursuit of accountability, change and novelty. The position varies from country to country and issue to issue (for instance, political or moral questions).

Advocates of intervention on grounds of 'public interest' have no easier task if one rules out an appeal to some absolute value or an ideological principle and wishes to avoid paternalistic solutions that will not be accepted. In fact, there are quite a few alternative routes towards agreeing a more nuanced and practicable version of the public interest. Much press policy in the twentieth century has been guided by modest, flexible and realistic goals that are supported by democratic governments (Just and Trappel, 2012). These have focused mainly on structural interventions aimed to increase or protect diversity; access on a wide scale to good quality information; and limitations to concentration of ownership. This also opens the way for some forms of monitoring or review on the part of society and for pressure to adopt codes of practice and voluntary forms of accountability, such as press councils, or even statutory obligations.

In everyday journalistic practice, when disputes arise between news media and those on whom they report, the question that most often arises is whether a specific piece of contested reporting can be considered a matter of genuine public concern, affecting wider interests, or something in the private and personal sphere (e.g. of a scandalous or sexual character) that is only designed to attract audience attention. The underlying thinking is that freedom to publish, even where it harms individuals, can be justified only where a true public interest can be argued to exist, but not otherwise. In this context, public interest refers to such matters as increasing transparency, exposing wrong-doing, holding political and economic power to account, expressing public opinion and protecting the interests of citizens, etc. However, this line is a very difficult one to draw, especially where it concerns political figures, celebrities or others prominent in public life, whose entire private life can have implications for public conduct.

The concept of public interest in this way of thinking becomes very narrow and legalistic in meaning and scope, far from its potential as a standard for assessing media performance and guiding policy. It does not provide a guide to the rights of others besides media owners and journalists (and the public as individual consumers, perhaps). An idea of the public interest is required that does more than reflect numerical appeal or settle a legal argument about where to draw the line. The possible 'public interest' of publishing a single specific item is different from the potential of a complex set of communication arrangements for a society.

Several different values and criteria need to be recognised, including the human rights of groups as well as of individuals and long-term consequences as well as immediate satisfactions. There are many different kinds of benefit or harm. There can be no blueprint or precise formula. Journalists have to make their choices according to circumstances and personal vision. More to the point perhaps is that the notion of public interest is best preserved for the overall framework and arrangements for meeting public communication needs, independently of any specific application.

It might also help to replace the term 'public interest' with the more open, potentially more encompassing term of 'common good', for such system arrangements. These include benefits such as universal provision, affordable access, secure and open 'public space' for expression, debate etc., plus support for cultural and educational goals. The potential human rights to more than just basic necessities have gradually come to be recognised in other spheres of communication and culture. Having said this, it remains the case that it is not primarily the task of journalists to serve any one version of the 'common good' or public interest. It is arguable that achieving the objective of a free and open circulation of reliable and relevant information and ideas throughout a society is a sufficient contribution to the eventual 'public good', if only it can be attained.

Box 2.2 Meanings of the 'public interest'

- What most interests the public as consumer
- What the majority determines
- Whatever achieves the greatest good for the greatest number (as determined by the market)
- What a given predominant value dictates (e.g. freedom, order, an ideology)
- What is of wider and long-term benefit to society (as variously judged)
- Whatever relates to public rather than private concerns
- The 'common good', as serving fundamental communication needs of the whole society and community as well as of groups and individuals.

The foundations of journalistic obligation

Journalism is a complex but also very pragmatic activity that responds to the circumstances and needs of the moment and changes according to social and technological factors. It is not driven by theory and is usually practised without much attention to issues of public obligation. Nevertheless, there are fundamental influences stemming from journalism's own history that have been captured in the reflections of different social theorists. The most relevant of these are summarised below. As will be seen, they are disparate and emphasise values that are sometimes mutually inconsistent. Ideas have changed over time, as the circumstances of journalism have changed, although later 'theories' do not necessarily replace earlier versions, but often co-exist or produce new adaptations.

No attention is given here to what has been called 'authoritarian theory', essentially the view that the press should submit to the will of the state or ruler. A version of such theory might be justified under certain extreme circumstances. In reality, this claim is still made and acted on quite widely around the world, but it has no support in the social theory of democratic societies, except under the most extreme circumstances. The range of theories looked at here are all potentially compatible with contemporary versions of codes of human rights such as the UN Charter and the European Convention on Human Rights (see Appendix §1).

Free press theory

At first sight theory of press freedom does not seem a promising source of ideas about possible *obligations* of media to society. This is certainly true of what has been called the 'libertarian' theory of the press (see Siebert et al., 1956) which recognises no limits to rights to publication (of those who possess the means to do so). The origins of 'libertarian' theory are usually traced to western Europe after the sixteenth century protestant Reformation, when state control of the press was opposed absolutely on grounds of reason, freedom of conscience politics and even theology. Later claims to freedom of the press (from censorship) that were included in various eighteenth-century formulations of the 'Rights of Man' were an essential part of general claims to freedom from autocratic government advanced by liberal and socialist reformist and revolutionary movements (see Appendix §1). The implicit promise was that a free press would advance the progress of society.

Throughout much of his early career, Karl Marx argued for the right and necessity of a free press as a basis for a democratic society, very much in line with then contemporary liberal thinking. A free press would be expected to expose the misdeeds of autocratic governments, hold them to account for misuse of power and give a truthful account of the conditions of the people. It would also transform material struggles into a broader emancipatory movement. Freedom of the press, in Marx's view, was not the right to run a business, but a right of the autonomous individual and a means to uncover the underlying truth about society (Hardt, 2003). Freedom of the press has since been included in all significant national and international statements of Human Rights (see the Appendix).

Support for freedom of publication is based not only on fundamental principles (the deontological view), but also on considerations of public benefit, measured by the calculus of human welfare. This is especially true of utilitarian theory as expounded by John Stuart Mill (1869/1956). The achievement of the 'greatest good for the greatest number' requires that government be guided by the wishes of all citizens, freely expressed. This is close to the majoritarian version of a public interest, as outlined above. Mill argued that progress and welfare depended on the free circulation of ideas by means of which truth and utility would be maximised. Thus freedom is, in some sense, not just a value but 'functional' for material welfare and progress. But these arguments also entail the view that the press has some moral obligation (as well as a right) to make active use for public good of the freedom it enjoys, and also not to abuse this right.

Advocates of a free press (there are few actual open opponents) divide sharply on whether its essential meaning is the absence of restraint (as in US First Amendment law and theory: Nerone, 1995) or, instead, a 'positive' view in which freedom should be conditional on the pursuit of the good of society as well as the self. It is also measured by the extent of real chances for access and publication being available in adequate degree. The first (negative) view very much favours economic freedom as the chief criterion and refers to the 'free market place of ideas', in which the press system is compared to an idealised market, in which all goods (here, ideas) are on offer and compete with each other openly for customers, with variations of quality and price. Free market conditions are held to ensure the best 'quality' of ideas for most people at affordable prices, with bad or unwanted ideas driven out. The public interest is served in this view by the 'hidden hand' of the market. Market failures (especially where competition ends in monopoly) are not ruled out but, by and large, its advocates see it as the most effective mechanism.

The alternative (positive view of freedom) supports public intervention designed to compensate for the inequalities and failures that develop in real markets and to achieve goals that the market does not serve. There are plenty of practical examples of measures adopted to improve the real chances of the public to receive informative benefits from the media. The benefits include more choice of alternative voices and higher quality of the information available. Policies for this have included inquiries into standards, subsidies for some newspapers, tax concessions, limits to press concentration and pressures for self-regulation. Above all, public broadcasting has proved the most effective means of widening the availability of good quality journalism.

Although there is little doubt that freedom of the press is closely correlated with other basic conditions of a free society and inconsistent with excessive state power and true democracy, it is also the case that journalism cannot operate properly in conditions of 'statelessnes' or in failed states (Waisbord, 2007). Journalism cannot cope with extreme insecurity and often violence, which result in self-censorship at best. Even an oppressive state can meet some essential conditions for journalism to fulfil some of its public roles.

The condition of 'freedom of the press' is widely agreed to be highly desirable, but not all agree on where and in what degree it is to be found. In the interests of promoting it, much effort has been made by varied bodies to estimate the relative degree of freedom actually present in different countries. There are many obstacles to doing so, especially as not all really agree on basic principles and actual performance always falls short of the ideal. A comparison of several international indices of press freedom by Becker et al. (2007) shows the variety of concepts applied and also of measures or ratings achieved, although the resulting rank order of most countries does come out at much the same according to different scales. The firmest data relate to laws designed to protect press freedom and the actual extent and diversity of available media. More subjective are ratings of state and other political pressures. Economic pressures are objectifiable, but not their consequences. Other key indicators relate to freedom of information, press professionalisation, plurality of sources, plus attacks on, or imprisonment of, journalists.

Although freedom for the press seems to be universally popular, especially where it is denied, there is evidence from many countries of a significant degree of ambivalence in public attitudes. This may relate to any of three main concerns: that the press should have respect for the decisions of legitimate governments and authorities; that the security and cohesion of a society should be protected; and that freedom should not be used in a way that causes harm. It is at least clear from this that the full meaning of press freedom also entails the principle of social responsibility.

Box 2.3 Main tenets of free press theory

- Publication is an extension of the human right of free speech and cannot be restricted before the event or punished afterwards
- Free competition will lead to the triumph of truth over falsehood

- The best means to achieve a free press is by way of the 'free market place of ideas', thus no restraint on ownership or sale and exchange of information
- Self-regulation is the only permissible form of control
- The main enemy of freedom is the state, hence the 'default' attitude of the press should be adversarial
- Although formally without limits, in practice there are many constraints on how the freedom can be exercised.

Journalism as meeting essential needs of society

It was not only the press that proclaimed its own value to society. During the nineteenth century, as the newspaper began to grow in economic and political importance, the new science of sociology offered a number of ideas on its place in the general scheme of social organisation and change. The focus was not on duties and obligations, but on the important 'functions' served, often indirectly and without organised purpose, by the publicising and informative activities of the press. Key ideas are to be found in the work of French and German thinkers, especially Emile Durkheim, Gabriel Tarde, Georg Simmel and Max Weber. Hardt (2003) has given an account of early German theories of the social function of the newspaper. These theories indicate various potential benefits of the press for a modern society, which has special needs arising from its extensive and interdependent nature and increased social fragmentation. The main ideas that emerged can be summarised in terms of the following key functions:

1. *Integration and cohesion*. In an urban industrial society, there is a loss of the traditional means of social integration, especially the church, family and locality. The newspaper can provide a substitute by circulating a common stock of information and views to more isolated citizens, allowing new patterns of allegiance to form on a more pluralistic basis. The (then rather new) idea of a nation, with a common language and shared interests was generally strongly supported by the emerging mass press. While society has changed, many of the features indicated are even more pronounced and 'the press' is even more important to a sense of belonging and means of cooperation.
2. *Maintaining social order* throughout a state is often served well by the mass media (initially the newspaper press), even without autocratic

direction. The flow of information can be managed and directed and journalism reflects back to the authorities the state of the nation and its discontents. The newspaper was characterised in one key phrase as 'the nerves of society', akin to the nervous system of the human body. In another phrase – 'the conscience of society' – the normative role of the press was encapsulated.

3 *Monitoring events and circumstances* affecting the society and providing warning of risks and impending dangers.

4 *The formation and expression of public opinion* is a key effect of the newspaper, reflecting popular views, rather than just those of elites and their opponents. In particular, it leads to a public awareness of the wider 'climate of opinion' in a society, even if not always with accuracy.

5 *Stimulation of change and innovation* was also recognised as an effect at an early point. The press acted to diffuse new fashions, ideas and consumer desires and in so doing stimulate commerce and mobility.

This form of sociological theorising was continued in the twentieth century, with the rise of social system and functionalist theory (see Lasswell, 1948; Wright, 1960). It continues to attract a following. A modern version of functional theory credits television with the power to promote a sense of belonging (on a global as well as national scale) through sharing vicariously in symbolically significant public events, such as royal or state occasions, state visits, major sporting events, public festivals, etc. (Dayan and Katz, 1992). The media have also been described as playing a key part in a number of social processes. These include: socialisation (transmission of norms and values); advancing social movements; and forging identities in political, national, ethnic and local cultural terms. Some specific functions ascribed to journalism are indicated in Chapter 4, below.

Modern social theory has emphasised the degree to which most experience of 'reality' is now mediated through mass media (Luhmann, 2000; Thompson, 1995) rather than encountered directly. Insofar as this is true, it signals an increase in the need for effective and reliable forms of mediation. These ideas are all applicable to contemporary mass media and indeed it is difficult to imagine a modern society being able to operate at all effectively without means of communication that permeate the whole society and transmit and exchange vast amounts of information.

Despite its claim be an objective account, or prediction, of the likely consequences of the mass media, sociological theory offers numerous pointers to the desirable, as well as the undesirable roles that media can and do play in social life. In that sense, like all functionalist thinking, it has a normative implication of social benefit to be found in the greater cohesion and smooth working of a 'social system'.

The press as Fourth Estate

The idea of press freedom is often assumed to be a basic foundation stone of democracy – a necessary condition for, and a mark of, a genuine democracy. This probably provides the clearest example of the way in which journalists meet essential social needs, in practice. There are several different traditions and forms of democracy (Christians et al., 2009) and the press is related to politics in different ways in different political cultures (Hallin and Mancini, 2004). Nevertheless, we can state certain basic informational requirements for the effective working of democracy, when this is understood as any form of genuine popular sovereignty. The main requirements are as shown in Box 2.4.

Box 2.4 Informational requirements of democracy

- Continuous availability and circulation of trustworthy information relevant to current issues and problems of society
- Similarly, information about political parties, their programmes and leaders
- Means of open and diverse expression of public opinion
- A public that is informed, interested and motivated to act on the basis of information
- Means of communication for connecting all actors in the space of politics.

The perceived *necessity* of journalistic support for democracy is reflected in the fact that the press institution is often allocated certain customary rights and privileges that ensure its access to public events and information. The unrestricted reporting of proceedings of public assemblies is a key task. It is also given some limited protection for search and disclosure and some protection of sources. The degree and form of such recognition of a key social role vary greatly from one society to another, but is generally justified in terms of the needs specified in Box 2.4 above. During the twentieth century, the traditional mass media of press and broadcasting usually provided quite effective means for fulfilling the requirements mentioned.

The term 'Fourth Estate' (or 'Fourth Branch') was often used in earlier times to characterise the role of the press in the process of democratic government (Schultz, 1998). In this view, the press is a source of power similar to that of other branches of government (executive, legislative, judicial), even if it has no formal status in any constitution. Essential elements of Fourth Estate theory are summarised in Box 2.5.

Box 2.5 Theory of the Fourth Estate

- The press is the main voice speaking up for the interests of the people as a whole
- Essential to this role is independence from government and courage to speak out
- A key task is the holding to account of government and other holders of power to the people, by way of publicity and advocacy
- The press provides a reciprocal channel of communication between government and citizens
- This implies a forum function for the expression of public opinion.

The political role of the newspaper press has changed a good deal since its early days but it is still hard to conceive the conduct of contemporary democratic politics without the extensive involvement of the news media. In fact, the activity and influence of the press, by most accounts, is now as great as it ever was, even if driven as much by professional news managers and image-makers as by journalists and editors. Despite many changes and for a mixture of reasons, news media in democracies still make some effort to live up to the Fourth Estate ideal. In many countries, the regulation of broadcasting still requires it to carry out key elements of the Fourth Estate role, as an independent source of information and guidance for voters.

The ideal itself is open to criticism. The self-assigned 'Fourth Estate' model over-privileges the powerful, established, media by comparison with ordinary citizens, especially where the media develop symbiotic links with political and economic power. It also tends to ignore the role of minority, underground and alternative media including many new online media that are outside the 'press institution'.

The 'mainstream' model of the press also emphasises the ideal of journalism as an impartial and reliable source of political information for all.

In an alternative version, the press is politically segmented and polarised, with each opposed political movement having its own means of publication. The partisan press has retained some hold in the reality of the media systems in Europe and elsewhere although it has largely disappeared in the United States, being incompatible both with commercial requirements and also with a journalistic professionalism which favours 'objectivity' and balance.

More widely, partisanship was found inconsistent with broadcasting, for similar reasons but also because of monopoly conditions and government regulation. Even so, there is still a strong theoretical case to be made for the continuation of politically committed journalism and it will not die out. Committed journalism is not in itself unprofessional when it is open and honest and respects basic criteria for truth. It is not the same as propaganda, as defined in Chapter 3 (Truth as a principle).

The idea of a 'public sphere'

There is a more recent formulation of the political role of the press, to be found in the notion of a 'public sphere', a term mainly derived from the work of Jurgen Habermas (1962/1989). According to Dahlgren:

> Habermas conceptualised the public sphere as that realm of social life where the exchange of information and news on questions of common concern can take place so that public opinion can be formed … since the scale of modern society does not allow more than relatively small numbers of citizens to be co-present, the mass media have become the chief institution of the public sphere. (1995:7–8)

The original public sphere described by Habermas referred to the actual places where bourgeois intellectuals (from the eighteenth century onwards) discussed and developed ideas for political reform. The typical locales were coffee shops and the pages of newspapers, which were the contemporary equivalent of an imagined Athenian Agora or market place. Physical access to such space is free and freedom of speech and association are assured. The more significant metaphorical space lies between the sphere of government and state action and the 'basis' of societies where the personal lives of citizens are conducted. This image also captures the role of the press in society. Necessary conditions for the operation of a public sphere include, then as now, besides the means of publication, a sufficiently educated, informed, or interested body of citizens and the potential for an informed and freely expressed public opinion.

Revived ideas of a public sphere also depend on the concept of *civil society* as a preferred form. A condition of civil society is one of openness and plurality without severe conflict or constraint within a framework of rule by law, where there are many more or less autonomous and voluntary 'intermediate' agencies and associations between the citizen and the state. These provide the focus for participation and identification and also insulate the individual from the oppressive power of a central state in the last instance or the pressures of a 'mass society'. The ideas described seem to offer a suitable framework for embedding the contribution of new media such as the internet which allow much more information and ideas to flow between citizens, experts and politicians and between citizens themselves (Papacharissi, 2002 and see Chapter 8). The new media also facilitate new forms of (virtual) 'assembly' and organisation in support of causes.

Box 2.6 Contributions of journalism to the public sphere

- Maintaining and managing a space for public debate
- Circulating opinions and ideas
- Extending freedom and diversity for the public
- Connecting citizens with governments
- Giving opportunities to voices of organised civil society (NGOs) to speak out
- Mobilisation towards civic engagement.

Social responsibility theory

By the start of the twentieth century, the increasing 'massification' and commercialisation of the press combined to raise doubts about the working of the liberal model of press freedom, left to its own devices. Socialists and radicals laid the blame at the door of monopoly capitalism, which often controlled the established press, allegedly in the interests of a ruling class. Conservative critics blamed a decline in standards and ethics on the combined effect of unfettered commercialism and on the low cultural level of the new mass reading public.

Such reactions led in the United States to the Commission on Freedom of the Press, set up in the early 1940s as a private initiative to inquire into the failings of the US press and into possible remedies (Hutchins, 1947). The essential task was to ensure that the press would somehow earn its right to freedom by delivering on the unwritten contract made with the people to inform fully and freely. Its main outcome was what has come to be called 'social responsibility' theory.

According to the Commission's report, press freedom is only a 'conditional right'. The press was asked to accept the task of performing a 'public service of a professional kind' and not just to meet the immediate demands of its own readers. In a later publication, Peterson (1956) set out the basic terms of the 'social responsibility theory of the press', which went some way beyond the requirements of the various professional codes of journalism that were already current in the United States. Aside from the fulfilment of the informative role, the press was asked to contribute to the cohesion of society and the representation and expression of its diversity.

Important features of the newly formulated theory included the view that freedom from restraint is not enough, there also has to be freedom to pursue positive goals: 'to be real, freedom must be effective' (Peterson, 1956:93); and there must be the 'appropriate means of attaining those goals'. Social responsibility theory also held that 'government must not allow freedom it must actively promote it' (ibid.:95). The main author of the 1947 Commission Report, Hocking, wrote that 'government remains the residuary legatee of responsibility for an adequate press performance' (see Nerone, 1995:86). This gives some theoretical legitimation to public intervention in the press, despite the claims of press freedom.

The idea of 'social responsibility theory' was not welcomed in the US press industry but it did reinforce a growing trend towards professionalisation and self-regulation of the press. It also reflected the more socially conscious atmosphere of American society after the experience of the Depression and in keeping with progressive thinking that gained ground in time of a national war effort. The same ideas were influential in Europe at a time when press systems were being reformed or reconstructed on democratic lines after World War II.

Despite the limited scope for application to the press, such theory is still invoked on behalf of greater press self-regulation and public accountability. It gives support to journalistic professionalism and a justification for instruments such as press councils or similar complaint procedures that are widely found, even if weak in their power to control the alleged excesses and failings of the press.

Public service broadcasting, as found in various countries, is still the most prominent example of the deliberate application of social responsibility theory to mass media, including journalism. From limited beginnings, and at first avoiding journalism, it has since then come to offer a distinctive philosophy of media provision (including journalism) that still stands as an alternative to the free market model, although in a much modified form. It is distinctive, because it was implemented through law, regulation and financial support without violating constitutional principles of press freedom, which were initially applicable only to printed forms. Its main principles are summarised in Box 2.7.

Box 2.7 Social responsibility theory as embodied in public service broadcasting

- Universality and diversity of provision
- Democratic accountability to the public
- Responsibility for meeting general and special needs as assigned
- Commitment to quality not determined by the market
- Possible subordination to national needs as determined
- Commitment to protect certain norms and cultural values
- In journalism, a position of political neutrality
- Non-profit financial structure.

Journalistic work within broadcasting is often carried out according to ground-rules that approximate to social responsibility theory and differ from those that may apply in commercial print media, although basic professional commitments are the same (see Appendix §4). In most democracies, the public standing and credibility of broadcast news has typically been somewhat higher than those of other news sources (BBC, 2007).

Social responsibility theory has declined in the scope of its remit and as a force for policy-making in a much more market-based era, facing more competition and with a great diversity and volume of all forms of media that defy any simple form of public regulation. While still extensive and keeping wide public support, public service broadcasting is vulnerable to lack of support from governments and political parties as well as to pressure from commercial competition. Social responsibility theory is not necessarily incompatible with for-profit financing, although it normally entails some restrictions on commercial freedom (e.g. by way of licensing conditions or some form of regulation).

A different version of what is essentially social responsibility theory may be found under conditions of economic and social development, where media resources are limited like everything else. Some important development goals require the wide and effective transmission of ideas and information, plus a necessary degree of social consensus. Journalists in such circumstances may be expected to support national development efforts and, if necessary, surrender some of their professional autonomy. There is evidence, from contemporary surveys of journalists, that many do accept some obligations to society on grounds of fundamental needs and are willing to subordinate claims to complete freedom of publication in the 'public interest', as determined by government or its development agencies.

Box 2.8 General theory of social responsibility as applied to mass media

- Ownership and control of news media can benefit from being a public trust
- There is an obligation to be truthful, fair, objective and relevant to the public served
- Editorial freedom should ultimately be subject to some form of public accountability
- Codes of conduct and professional ethics should be agreed and observed
- Under conditions of extreme emergency or danger, news media can accept control or direction. This also applies in long-term conditions of development.

Critical theory

Although social responsibility theory originally derived from criticism of the commercial press, it largely represented conventional and 'establishment' views of the social obligations of the news media. A 'responsible' press was not likely to be fundamentally threatening to a legitimate government, whatever its shortcomings. During the 1960s and 1970s, much more radical criticism, inspired by neo-Marxist and other radical ideas, was directed at mass media in general (see, Hardt, 1991). In its strongest forms, it portrayed established media as the informational and cultural arm of a capitalist-bureaucratic state apparatus, with little possibility of reform or democratisation from within.

The news media were described as exercising a 'hegemonic' power (Gramsci's term) that maintained a misleading social consensus, although without openly 'making propaganda'. According to Stuart Hall (1977), news typically established a hegemonic view of the world by 'masking' or ignoring certain aspects of reality; by fragmenting class solidarity and interests; and by promoting an imagined unity and false consensus of society. A more recent version of critical theory has drawn on evidence of mainstream US media closeness to elite concerns and the direction of US foreign policy. This 'propaganda model' has been proposed (Herman, 2000), according to which news passes through a series of 'filters' that work to this end. The filters include: the interests of owners; 'newsworthiness'; advertiser tolerance; cost of news collection; possible cost of defending publication; ideological compatibility.

Critical theory does not seek to provide alternative guidelines about media responsibilities. Even so, it does make sense of the evident limitations of most news and helps to explain how (and why) news journalism is inclined to support the status quo, intentionally or not. Much empirical research on news content during the 1970s and since has validated a social critical theory view of the dominant news output. Despite its destructive intention, critical theory does explicitly or implicitly presume that media (in a reformed state) should be of service to society, albeit a different society purged of injustice, inequality and false consciousness.

The internet has not escaped the attention of critical theorists, despite its early image as a home to alternative and free public access for all voices, alongside its liberating potential. It has also become a new branch of the global media industry, subject to similar economic and social demands and constraints, as apply to other sectors. According to Fuchs (2009), there are new forms of commodification of the audience and of content, and the countless voices that are now heard, still lack any political power and can simply be ignored by elites.

Box 2.9 Main features of critical theory

- Mass media are predominantly owned and controlled by sectional interests of class society

- News and journalism are inevitably skewed towards support of the interests of a capital-owning class
- Liberal ideas of 'freedom of the press' do not secure true freedom for the many
- The responsibility of journalism, within the limits of the system, is to try and expose the true situation
- The only adequate solution is to reverse power roles and make media genuinely free.

Minority media theory; democratic-participant theory

One branch of critical theory came to espouse the promise of the first 'new media', especially because of the potential for small-scale, grass-roots communication in channels independent from dominant mass media. The guiding principles are of participation, interactivity, smallness of scale, local identity, cultural autonomy and variety, emancipation and self-help. The main beneficiaries would be groups within the larger society, based on a variety of criteria, including ethnicity, immigration, local community, special needs or interests, beliefs etc. These ideas about new and small-scale media originated before the internet age in rich, media-abundant and 'mature' democratic societies, although they seem most relevant to societies where there is still a struggle for basic rights.

The term 'rebellious communication' has been coined (Downing, 2001) to refer to media that pursue emancipatory and political ends in situations of oppression. Such media operate in a positive way in the critical tradition. They include those serving a political cause – ranging from female emancipation to the overthrow of oppressive or bourgeois regimes – and include manifestations of 'alternative' publication such as *samizdat* in the former Soviet Union, grass-roots micro-media in developing countries or in situations of authoritarian rule or foreign occupation. They are often stimulated by, and help to generate, 'new social movements'. However, such media are often short-term expedients in particular circumstances and do not offer an enduring model to follow when 'normal' conditions (e.g. of freedom) are restored.

Box 2.10 Democratic participant media theory

- Main purpose is to serve the interests of minorities of all kinds
- Small-scale, local, grass-roots media are preferable (to mass media)
- Media should serve participation and interactivity in general
- Journalism may have to adopt an underground or illegal role.

New movements in journalism

While critical theory had little direct impact on journalistic practice, there were significant trends amongst many professional journalists to develop and protect professional values as a form of service to society, based on meeting essential information needs. There was a reaction against the increased commercialisation and monopolisation of the newspaper press, especially in the United States. One new version of theory was based on the social theory of 'communitarianism' that advocated a more solidaristic and ethical form of society, one that stresses locality and the mutual interdependence of citizens. 'In the communitarian model', according to Nerone (1995:70–1), 'the goal of reporting is not intelligence but civic transformation ... the news media should seek to engender a like-minded philosophy among the public. A revitalized citizenship shaped by community norms becomes the press's aim. News would be an agent of community formation'. Communitarian theory of the press is in some respects quite radical. In some other respects it can also be portrayed as anti-libertarian. It is certainly a theory which emphasises active democracy and widely shared moral obligations of a social as well as personal nature.

Related in some way, but much more pragmatic and limited in its implications is new thinking about 'civic' or 'public' journalism (Glasser, 1999; Schudson, 1998) which originated within the practice of journalism itself. Its main thrust was a return to a more engaged form of journalism, to closer relationships between media and their audience, but also the 'community'. The (news) media are asked to do more to engage their audiences and be involved in their local communities in relevant ways. A basic premise is that journalism has a *purpose*, which is to improve the quality of civic life by fostering participation and debate. Schudson (1998) describes it as based on a 'Trustee model' rather than a Market or Advocacy model: 'in the Trustee model, journalists should provide news according to what they as a professional group believe citizens should know' (ibid.:136). Journalists themselves are 'professionals who hold citizenship in trust for us'. Some theorists of public journalism emphasise the role of journalism as facilitating a broad 'conversation' in society rather than simply providing information.

Public journalism parts company with the tradition of neutrality and 'objective' reporting, but it is not a return to an older tradition of partisanship and political advocacy. When expressed as a theory it has some affinities with versions of the public service broadcasting role, although it certainly does not look to government, law or regulation for support and has thus also parted company from old-fashioned social responsibility theory. It is voluntaristic and compatible with the free market, although also potentially fragile and ineffective. It might seem that public journalism has been overtaken by events in the form of a decline in the traditional newspaper market and the arrival of new possibilities for achieving the same ends by a variety of new media.

Box 2.11 Tenets of public or civic journalism

- Engage with the local community
- Discover and respond to audience needs and interests
- Pursue goal of improving quality of civic life
- Foster public discussion (conversation)
- Voluntaristic and self-financing, but not profit driven.

Internet news theory

Theorising surrounding the significance of the internet as a news medium has been influenced by many of the ideas discussed here. The new possibilities of online news have been welcomed as essentially liberating and also offering a means of inter-communication at a local and group level (see, for example, Castells, 2001). These ideas often underlie the aspirations of contemporary 'citizen journalists' – those especially who use the internet to publish and exchange news and views that may be an alternative to what is found in mainstream media.

No clear theory about internet journalism and its possible responsibilities has been formulated and there are conflicting views. Early speculation envisaged a break with the past of 'top-down' monopolistic news flow and the emergence of a new kind of public sphere marked by abundance of information, multiple flows, complete freedom and enhanced citizen participation with a potential for a richer form of democracy. This would highlight much discussion and exchange and be an antidote to the alleged harm of alienation from politics as a reaction to manipulation and cynicism. Looking back after a decade or two, the changes to be observed are not so dramatic, although important in some places and circumstances. Some observers have reported more 'normalisation' of the internet than 'revolutionising' of mass media.

As far as normative expectations relating to democracy and society are concerned, views are divided. One theorist (Dahlberg, 2011) discerns four main 'positions' in respect of new media:

1 'libertarian/individualist';
2 participant (or deliberative) democracy;
3 'fragmented communitarianism';
4 autonomy and Marxism.

The first embraces the liberal-market view of self-interested competition, without social obligation of any kind. The second endorses a revived version of existing ideals of more interaction and citizen engagement (a benevolent form of normalisation); the third option welcomes an escape from an older order of national consensus, elite dominance and mass politics in favour of a form of society that emphasises localism, community and interest group involvement, with many and varied forms of cooperation. The last stands for a mixed and fragmented version of critical social theory and practice. The internet opens the way in any or all of these directions, with different implications for normative commitments by a largely different set of journalists. A large and unresolved issue concerns the potential (or responsibility) of the internet for social fragmentation or integration, both of which seem to be promoted by the new media.

In general, new thinking about new media veers away from ideas of *responsibility to society as a whole* and also from measures for enforcing it, especially as the internet has no institutional existence. The editorial functions of online media are largely absent or minimal, so their potential obligations are unclear. There is much uncertainty about the position of the journalist in the internet context, with no consistent definition of the role (see Chapter 8).

Looking for a structure in social theory of the press

Not surprisingly, there is no single coherent message to be derived from these varied theoretical sources. The ideas outlined extend in time from the late eighteenth to the late twentieth centuries, during which there have been profound changes both in media and social contexts. The 'communication needs' of society and the means for meeting them are not fixed but vary according to historical and cultural conditions. Even so, we can discern the outlines of a structure of sorts in the materials presented. At the simplest level of analysis, there is a fundamental opposition between two orientations – one that emphasises individual rights to freedom above all and another that gives priority, or equal weight, to public or collective welfare. In shorthand terms these could be called 'libertarian' and 'democratic' respectively, if we accept the claims of protagonists.

At the same time, the two opposed 'camps' are far from homogeneous in their occupants. Amongst the 'libertarians' can be found radicals, anarchists, extreme conservatives and free marketeers of varying degrees of pragmatism. The other side includes media professionals, social democrats, left-critical theorists, community activists, media bureaucrats, paternalistic conservatives and moderate reformers. It is evident that other dimensions are involved besides the one outlined. They include: left versus right leaning; public versus private sector advocates; essentialism versus utilitarianism; ideology versus pragmatism; chance versus determinism.

There are too many possibilities for any simple or elegant solution to be found. However, for present purposes of examining questions of responsibility and accountability of journalism to society, three main variants of press theory can be discerned as follows.

1. *Market liberalism (the 'free market-place of ideas').* This holds that the free market is the best solution to the issues at hand as well as safeguarding individual rights to publish and to receive. The market will reveal most clearly what media services are really needed, on the basis of demand. It will also accept the need for some regulation but only in the interests of efficient and fair operation of the media market. In spirit it is generally utilitarian and individualist, claiming to achieve the 'greatest good for the greatest number' with the minimum of intervention. Its advocates hold it to be apolitical.
2. *Professionalism.* Questions of responsibility should be handled by reference to the press institution and competent self-regulatory processes.

Responsibility and accountability are accepted in principle, but must not impinge on professional autonomy. In general, this heading covers both 'Fourth Estate' theory and public journalism. 'Social responsibility' notions are present in some degree, but subordinate to professional autonomy and a freedom to choose goals and standards without any external interference.

3 *'Democratic' theory*. This encompasses a range of possibilities for identifying and meeting public interest requirements from mass media. However, there is also a broad internal division here between somewhat traditional interventionist and statist approaches (approximately) and those identified above as 'democratic-participant' that emphasise maximum participation from grass-roots, interactivity and freedom, but with a broad purpose, not of 'serving society' but of creating new and more truly democratic forms of political communication and politics. The inevitability of a political role of the press in society is emphasised, although there are alternative versions of how this should be handled. The alternative, decentralised, open model is clearly well served by the internet and requires not intervention, but protection of the new freedoms to communicate.

Beyond these main options, there are a number of variants, with varying degrees of social non-conformity or even revolutionary potential, perhaps captured by Dahlberg's category of 'autonomy plus Marxist', although Marx would not be amused.

Conclusion

Despite its lack of coherence, the thinking outlined in this chapter provides the necessary frame of reference and concepts for defining the potential responsibilities of journalism to 'serve the public interest' from different points of view. We can recognise certain enduring values of public communication in the western tradition that shape current notions of these responsibilities. These relevant 'publication values' are explained in the following chapters and can be found in many formulations in laws, codes of ethics and practice, public policy goals and editorial manifestos. There is also plenty of evidence of a developed public opinion concerning the rights and responsibilities of news media. The following chapter provides an outline and discussion of the specific qualities that are most relevant to journalistic practice from the perspective of society.

Further reading

Dahlgren, P. (1995). *Television and the Public Sphere*. London: Sage.
Habermas, J. (2007). 'Political communication in media society', *Communication Theory*, 16, 4: 411–26.
Hardt, H. (2003). *Social Theories of the Press: Early German and American Perspectives*. Malden NJ: Rowman and Littlefield.
Keane, J. (1991). *The Media and Democracy*. Cambridge: Polity.
Nerone, J. (1995) *Last Rights: Revisiting Four Theories of the Press*. Urbana IL: University of Illinois Press.
Peterson, T. (1956) 'The social responsibility theory' in Siebert, F.R. et al. (eds), *Four Theories of the Press*. Urbana, IL: University of Illinois Press, pp. 73–104.
Schultz, J. (1998). *Reviving the Fourth Estate*. Cambridge: Cambridge University Press.
Strömbäck, J. (2005). 'Democracy and norms for journalism', *Journalism Studies*, 6, 3: 331–45.
Zeno-Zencovitch, V. (2008). *Freedom of Expression*. London: Routledge.

Online readings

Go to www.sagepub.co.uk/mcquailjournalism for free access to the online readings.

Becker, L., Vlad, T. and Nusser, N. (2007). 'An evaluation of press freedom indicators', *International Communication Gazette*, 69, 1: 5–28.
Dahlberg, L. (2010). 'Reconstructing digital democracy: an outline of four "positions"', *New Media and Society*, 13, 6: 855–72.
Klaehn, J. (2002). 'A critical review and assessment of Herman and Chomsky's "Propaganda Model"', *European Journal of Communication*, 17, 2: 148–82.
Papacharissi, Z. (2002). 'The virtual sphere: the internet as public sphere', *New Media and Society*, 4, 1: 9–27.

3 Principles of Journalistic Performance

Introduction

The theories outlined in Chapter 2 are closely linked to a number of normative principles that have a wider currency than any one particular theory. The values involved are often applied in journalism as guidelines to be followed, or are used to assess the quality of journalism, for different purposes. Here, the emphasis is on a potential contribution to the society or the public interest. The ideas to be discussed do not all carry equal weight and each version of a 'social theory of the press' tends to have a different emphasis. The values outlined are not the only ones relevant to what is considered 'good' journalism, especially as judged from the practical point of view of gaining and keeping audiences, or of meeting various other standards of professional quality.

These values have their main origin in the history of western society in the 'modern' era, rather than in journalism itself. They are referred to here as 'publication values' because of their relevance to a particular act and process of open expression and wide dissemination of information, opinion and ideas. What is published cannot be unsaid and this can have unpredictable consequences for others when it reaches the public arena.

The main questions for this chapter to answer are as follows:

Public communication values

- What are they?
- How can they be measured or indexed for assessment?

Truth in journalism

- What standard to apply, how to achieve?
- What are the main component criteria?

- How can the criteria be recognised in practice?
- What are the limits to what is possible in meeting truth criteria?

Freedom in and for journalism

- How can it be embodied in practice?
- How can different degrees of freedom be recognised?
- What are the benefits for society?

Equality and diversity

- How are these expressed in publication?
- What are their benefits in communication?
- How can freedom be recognised?

Solidarity and order

- What forms do they take in journalistic work?
- What are the expected benefits? Why valued?

Basic publication values affecting the public interest

The relevant values are rather abstract ideas that need to be 'translated' into criteria of quality that can be recognised in the work of journalists and used in assessing quality. There are four main underlying principles according to which journalists *ought* to operate (in an ideal world) according to widely held views. These can be described in summary terms as follows:

1 *Truth*. This refers to the aim or expectation that journalism will provide a trustworthy and sufficiently full account of relevant aspects of the reality of current events and circumstances 'without fear and favour'.

2 *Freedom*. As applied to journalism, this relates not just to the condition of independence but to the use actually made of freedom by journalists in choosing what to report and in the manner of doing so. This extends to a readiness to engage in controversial matters if necessary and to criticise those with social and economic power, on behalf of the public.

3 *Solidarity.* Journalism in its choice of topics and *sources* can encourage greater social identity and participation for groups and communities, provide sympathy and active support for minorities and victims. Or it can fail on any of these points. Solidarity also involves support for the unity and cohesion of the larger society and for the public interest.

4 *Order and cohesion.* Here the focus is on the potential effects of news on disorder, crime and insecurity. Broadly, the news media are expected to support rather than hinder the legitimate agencies of social control, especially in circumstances of criminality, public emergency or danger.

Although these four general principles are often invoked, they do not represent fixed purposes for all journalism or absolute standards of quality. These depend on the context, on the preferences of audiences as well as the free choices made by the media. There is a great variety of journalistic forms and of purposes and the same set of values and criteria does not apply to all media, or even to one form such as 'the newspaper'. There is little point, for instance, in blaming allegedly 'sensationalist' or tabloid newspapers for not being more like the 'quality' papers that they do not aspire to be. Nor can local and regional journalists be criticised for neglecting international news.

The assessment of journalistic performance can also be carried out according to the different perspectives (as outlined in Chapter 1), each reflecting different interests and objectives. The main differences of perspective are those of: 'society'; the organisation; media professionals; and the public or audience. The interests of 'society' are mainly expressed by governments or other authorities and agencies of 'civil society' and relate both to positive obligations and prohibitions, often found in various media laws and regulations. The central criterion is service to a public interest, however conceived. Public opinion also plays a part in this matter.

The media organisation applies criteria of efficiency and of success in the market (for advertising or audience). The editor or journalist judges performance according to professional and creative criteria. Here too there is variety, but the emphasis is likely to be on exclusivity and originality of news, quality of writing or filming, depth and credibility of information. Finally the specific 'audience', also a part of the 'public' of civil society, is mainly here conceived in the role of consumer, applying widely different criteria of personal taste, utility or satisfaction to news channels and output. The specific criteria of quality derived from the four basic values are outlined in the following sections. Firstly the meaning of the four principles is explained in more detail.

Truth as a principle

The value of truth has long been invoked as a support for claims to freedom of publication. The claimed sources of truth in pre-modern times included: divine revelation; the authority of a church or religious belief; the authority of rulers; and the personal wisdom and reputation of authors, both ancient and new. The humanistic and scientific renaissance of the fifteenth to seventeenth centuries extended ideas of truth to encompass both the truth as determined by individual conscience and also to scientific truth as established by evidence and theory. The meaning of truth as an accurate report of reality or as a faithful reproduction of texts emerged and was reinforced by the requirements of science, law, government and commerce. The development of printing (texts, uniform and permanent) played an important part in reinforcing and elevating this version of truth. Early newspapers would never have established a key position without a strict attention to a notion of truth as verifiable facts. They would either have been forbidden or found of limited use.

Since then, the idea of any single authoritative and verifiable truth has been undermined by several tendencies. These include the recognition of competing versions of the truth as embedded in conflicting political and religious beliefs or simply as a result of different experiences and perceptions of reality. The rise of liberal pluralism has promoted the rights of individuals to express and defend their own versions of truth. Liberal theory has even defended the freedom to publish what is known to be untrue, as long as it does no direct harm to others and is open to challenge. In particular, economic liberalism gives all versions of truth an equal right to enter the 'market-place' of ideas, where truth can be determined according to demand and perceived utility.

In our own time, truth in journalism has come to be primarily identified with neutral, reliable, verifiable reporting and with expert analysis and interpretation. The main tests of truth are variously found in its application to reality, reference to other sources, personal observation, past experience, or common sense. Truth in journalism is widely identified with the practice of 'objectivity', which emphasises neutrality and balance on the part of a reporter and a limitation as far as possible to verifiable 'facts' of any case (see below, Chapter 5).

It is this limited version of truth that informs most 'social responsibility' theory of the press. Even critical theory makes an appeal to some notion of verifiable reality and seeks to expose any 'bias' and 'distortions'. Despite this 'secularisation' of the value of truth, there remains a significant core element of journalistic values relating either to the voice of conscience, the possession of strong beliefs or the speaking out of unpalatable truths, often with some risk attached. The reference here is mainly to committed, investigative or campaigning journalism. Because of this variety of versions and degrees of truth, it is not easy to reach any absolute judgement about the truth of any particular news report.

The most relevant indicators of journalistic truth, and thus the criteria by which 'truth value' can be recognised, are summarily presented in Table 3.1.

TABLE 3.1 Criteria of journalistic truth (based on McQuail, 2003:76)

Qualities of content	Qualities of 'author' or conduct
Accuracy	Integrity
Reliability	Authenticity
Verisimilitude	Personal truth
Balance	Courage
Comprehensibility	Transparency
Relevance	

The entries in Table 3.1 are divided according to those that relate to qualities of content and those relating to conduct (i.e. to the actions and intentions of the journalist). The former are often to be found specified in internal journalistic codes or in the activities of external assessors. The latter are less often specified but are sometimes embodied in professional routines and procedures and otherwise in discussions of the ideals of journalism. All of these criteria are in some degree open to an objective assessment. They can be briefly described as follows.

- *Accuracy and reliability* refer to: intrinsic qualities of a text, including correspondence with an original text, a given source, or another news account; having an authoritative or expert origin; avoidance of 'transmission errors'; observance of rules of language; and conforming to thc 'factual' form of presentation. All features of texts that contribute to their reliability can be referred to, including the potential for verification and the status of sources. Reliability is a matter of perception and experience, but it is usually related to objective characteristics of an informational text. Accurate and reliable texts normally also meet criteria of completeness (for the purpose at hand) and relevance. For accounts to be accepted as 'true', they should offer sufficient relevant information to be understood as intended.

- *Verisimilitude* captures the notion that a message claiming to be true should conform to an apparent reality that is observable to others. Different 'true' accounts should be mutually consistent and match the experience and observation of 'receivers', where the evidence is available.
- *Balance*. This criterion recognises the subjectivity and uncertainty of all perception and interpretation and looks for an acknowledgement and representation in accounts of different perspectives and interpretations that are most likely to be relevant to understanding.
- *Comprehensibility* expresses the need of the audience to understand. Conditions for effective communication are mainly thought to comprise: 'readability' (accessible language, clarity of expression), concreteness of subject matter, attractive and helpful presentation, completeness and relevance.
- *Relevance* is an aspect of truth, obliging reporters to concentrate on matters of believed significance (by varying criteria) and on key aspects of events, without omission or digression. Relevance is related to the usefulness of the information, as well as to the quality of being interesting to an audience.
- *Integrity* refers to the good faith of the source or sender as well as of the reporter to take care in collecting, selecting and editing. Favouritism, buying information or selling access and support are examples of bad journalistic practice and lack of integrity.
- *Authenticity* is a related principle, referring primarily to cultural aspects of media texts. 'Texts' of all kinds can be considered to be more or less true to the principles and practice of the culture of those who create, receive or participate in media content or are represented in it.
- *Personal truth*. Aside from ideologies and belief systems, individuals may have personal visions of what is right and true, which only they can validate. The recognition of such personal versions of truth and the importance of free expression in respect of them, in whatever chosen form, is an important element of western culture and a component in the notion of human rights.
- *Courage* is a publication virtue related mainly to integrity and conscience, displayed by those who expose truths that are uncomfortable for a society or its authorities, guided by conscience, professionalism or social concern. It extends to accepting risk of punishment or harm for telling the truth. As with personal truth, there is no objective test of this quality, but it is usually recognisable by its intrinsic merit to those who care about or value it.

- *Transparency* refers to a clear identification by an author of position, interest or values, candidness and openness of purpose. Anonymous communications, hidden propaganda or bribery by sources are at the opposite end of the range.

This set of criteria can in principle be applied as appropriate to a wide range of *journalistic* 'texts' in whatever form. However, the *truth* of a message is not a property of the text or the procedure adopted, but is a construct that depends on the perception and intention of original sources, observers and reporters, the recipients of communication and (where relevant) the participants in events reported. In practice, the conditions for attaining any complete 'truth' in relation to ongoing human affairs are not really attainable and some more or less agreed conventions of what to regard as 'truthful communication' have been developed, including a notion of the 'good faith' of the journalist. This may also depend on the degree of trust in the larger news organisation or medium.

These remarks lead to a consideration of the various forms and characteristics of 'untruth' in media that are most relevant to assessing performance. Three particular forms have been singled out as problematic, as follows.

- *Bias.* This describes a systematic (although not necessarily intended) tendency to deviate consistently from a neutral line. It happens in various ways, especially by selective attention, selective omission, one-sided interpretation or by making implicit negative or positive judgements. It can emerge not only in the text but also in visual images, sounds and other presentational features.
- *Propaganda.* Here the reference is to conscious and systematic efforts to use the means of public communication to advance an ideological cause or material interest of the sender or source, often by covert means (for instance by omission, distortion or misinformation) and without regard for anyone else's truth or the true interests of the recipient. Propaganda is deficient according to most of the 'indicators of journalistic truth' listed above. Journalists rarely make propaganda on their own initiative but they can be conduits for the propaganda of others, whether knowingly or not. The heavy reliance by news media on press releases and official information makes it impossible to avoid all 'propaganda'.
- *Ideology.* The ubiquity and even inevitability of 'ideology' in news reports has often been remarked on by analysts and 'readers' of news. It refers to an implicit normative direction given to reports, drawing

on some belief or value system that is not explicated or called in to question. It has its origin and basis in the history and culture of the society from which news originates or for whom it is intended as well as in a particular journalistic culture. Critical theory regards ideology as systematic and not accidental or innocent. More objective assessments of news content see it as an unintended consequence of news 'framing' and other news values. Prominent examples of (quasi-) ideologies include: patriotism; anti-communism; 'freedom and democracy'; anti-terrorism; environmentalism. It has been claimed that ideology is 'the main source of deviation in news reporting from a standardized base in more or less objective news values' (Westerstahl and Johansson, 1994:77).

Many aspects of the 'information quality' of journalism, according to the truth criteria outlined above, are combined within the notion of *news objectivity*. A key element in the practice of objective journalism is 'factuality', as such – the provision of information in a form that is precise, verifiable and not tainted by opinion. However, as Westerstahl (1983) made clear, objective news reports always have an evaluative as well as a factual dimension. The very act of selecting topics and the related 'facts' for notice in the news is guided by implicit judgements of value and significance. The criterion of 'balance' recognises the difficulty of eliminating value judgements from accounts of reality. News journalism can deal with this by seeking to report alternative perspectives on events, from relevant sources and standpoints. It can also try to avoid value-laden or sensational forms of presentation.

The criterion of 'relevance' is especially important, in this respect, to journalistic objectivity. Relevance can be judged according to different criteria, including past journalistic selection, scale and intensity of events, external authority or expert opinion, public opinion, audience interest or the potential consequences of events for the audience.

The concept of objectivity and its critique are discussed in more detail in Chapter 5.

Freedom as a principle

The value of freedom in communication needs little explanation or justification beyond what has already been said. It is widely seen as the single necessary condition for realising most other benefits of public communication. It figures in virtually all theory, although with different degrees of emphasis. Most 'western' political and media theory, even in its critical versions, is agreed on the centrality of freedom of publication. It is indispensable for resisting encroachments by state or other power; it contributes to inquiry and discovery as well as to social and cultural progress. Aside from the conditions of media structure and work, journalistic freedom should be promoted by the relative autonomy of the reporter or editor to choose the subject matter of reporting. The value of freedom should be expressed by way of the honesty of reports and the courage that might be required to uncover and publish the truth.

Freedom is a condition, rather than a criterion or attribute of journalism and we cannot objectively determine the degree of freedom from content alone. However, it is possible to trace connections between the degree of freedom available to the press and some outcomes in publication which then serve as an indicator or sign of independence. The main conditions of freedom of journalism are *structural*: absence of compulsory licensing, of advance censorship, of any obligations to publish, or of restrictive laws punishing publication after the event; the availability of (and realistic access to) the means of publication (diversity of 'channels' and absence of monopoly); absence of other hidden pressures or controls that inhibit publication, including pressure from governments and politicians and economic restrictions. Independence also means freedom from excessive pressure from owners and managers.

The link between freedom to publish and desirable outcomes in publication is summarised in a simplified way in Figure 3.1.

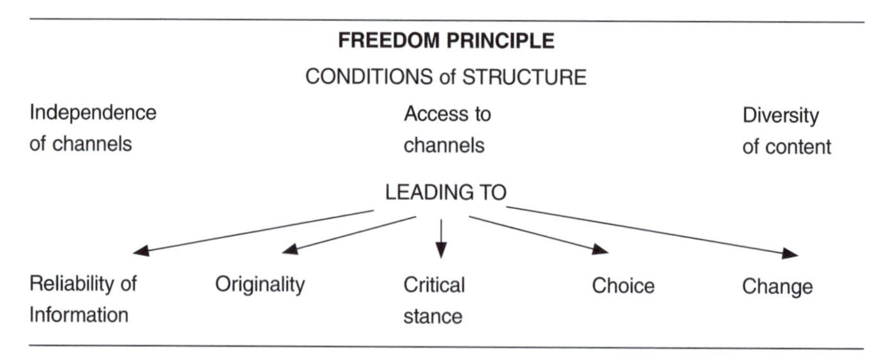

FIGURE 3.1 Freedom: from structure to performance (based on McQuail, 1992:167)

The expected benefits flowing from journalistic freedom for citizens and society include, especially, those shown in Box 3.1.

Box 3.1 Benefits of journalistic freedom

- Offering the means to scrutinise and criticise those with political and economic power
- Providing information necessary to form sound opinions and a critical outlook
- Aiding active participation in political, social and cultural life of the society
- Promoting of cultural and social innovation
- Providing access channels for diverse voices and purposes, and corresponding news coverage
- Enabling investigations of failure, injustice and wrongdoing of all kinds.

We can, in principle, objectively assess the relative 'freedom' of journalism or willingness to use it, according to the presence or absence of these features in news content. Other indicators of use of freedom tend to be negative, for example, reactions of anger or alarm at criticism on the part of authorities when subject to press criticism, moves to suppress particular news items or ban journalists, etc.

There is no guarantee that the benefits of freedom indicated in Box 3.1 will be delivered since media are free to perform 'badly', within some limits. The strategic interests of media owners may not be served by criticism of governments and powerful interest groups. Their financial interests may not benefit from too much originality, investigation or diversity in content (which tends to be expensive). Governments may have more to lose in the short term than to gain from freedom used in the ways indicated. Advertisers generally prefer uncontroversial and predictable environments for their messages. Even audiences may shy away from the conflict, controversy and criticism associated with journalistic 'freedom in action'.

The pursuit of the theoretical fruits of freedom of publication can also come into tension with the requirements of media as a profitable industry, for instance by alienating significant sources of income, information or influence. In practice, a good deal of the tension is taken care of by an informal division of labour and role within and between media. This then allows specialisms of channel and genre to develop which are devoted to critical, investigative and innovative journalism. There are also informal settlements and understandings that police the frontier between control and freedom and between media and the 'outside' world.

However, there is no way to eliminate the conflicts associated with the practice of free publication. There are frequently heard complaints that the media abuse their freedom, whether by harming individuals or social groups, undermining order or offending against morals, decency or public opinion. The 'invasion of privacy' and potential damage to reputation are often cited as an argument against complete freedom to publish. On the other hand, there are also allegations that media fail to use their freedom well and submit, for base motives, to the various pressures and inducements mentioned above. They become lap dogs rather than public watchdogs, conformist and consensual. Since no significant constituency is obviously injured or much offended by the selective silence and inactivity of the press, this rarely leads to any complaint, claim or challenge.

Equality, diversity and solidarity as principles

Equality is quite closely related as a value to that of freedom and also to the principle of justice (equality of all citizens before the law and of rights to the same benefits of citizenship of a given polity). What it means for journalism needs some explanation. On a purely abstract level we can say that all persons have an equal right to express themselves to others and to the society, and to receive the expressions of all others even if they lack the means to do either. The implication of equality for journalists is that they should at least treat their sources, those they report on and their audiences with equal respect, even if equality and universality of access cannot be offered. This is not to say that journalists or the press in general owe particular allegiance to an ideal of social or economic equality. But the business of publication, by its very openness and commitment to objectivity, rules out deliberate discrimination, except by the normal processes of market segmentation. There are also quite strong populist elements in the ideology of the press that have always celebrated its close links to the general public and its service to their interests.

The question of equality of 'representation' in news concerns the amount and diversity of attention paid to different sectors or groups in society. An individual, idea or group etc. cannot normally claim any specific right to be 'represented', whether or not equally, nor to control the terms on which access is given. However, the quantity and quality of representation in news is potentially problematic for those who miss out on news attention. Complete lack of representation in media (invisibility) is often regarded as detrimental, although less so than unwanted representation on unfavourable terms.

Most media 'blindspots' of this kind (and even most bias) are the unintended result of applying normal news selection criteria. Even so, there are grounds in fairness for claiming proportionate visibility and representation on terms acceptable to the objects of media attention. In other words, the powerless in society are looking in some measure for the same kind of respect or circumspection that journalists tend to give to the powerful. Again, this claim is quite in keeping with the mythology or ideology of journalism that has tended to celebrate the stand taken by reporters on behalf of the 'little people' of society.

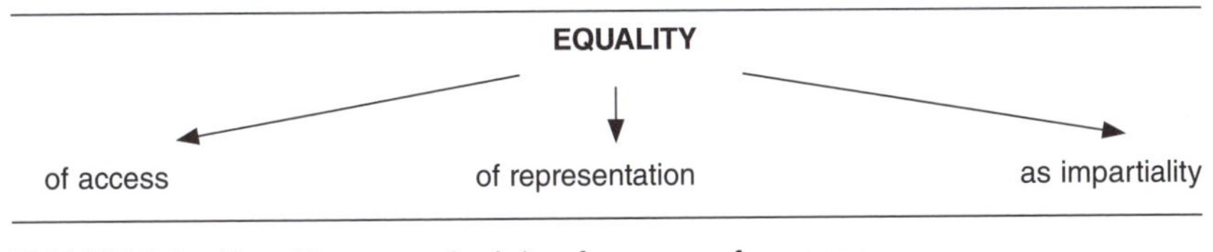

FIGURE 3.2 Equality as a principle of news performance

Diversity

Equality is therefore connected with *diversity*, itself a primary benefit to be expected from the condition of freedom of the press. A free press should tend to give access to all who wish to communicate in public, and thus to a wide range of voices in society, if not equality in volume, at least in kind. Diversity will be limited only by the relative strength of demand for different 'voices' and the potential of audiences to support media in economic terms. Diversity has been a widely valued principle of public communication in societies that make a virtue of their *pluralism* (thus most contemporary democracies). Its value has been highlighted by the dangers of press concentration and monopoly and the most frequently occurring public policy measures for media are directed towards its promotion (e.g. by laws against concentration ownership or by subsidies for competing media).

The more there is equal or 'fair' access for individuals or groups (communities, beliefs, cultures) as owners, senders or referents, the greater the likely overall diversity of the media system and provision and the more likely is the public to have a relevant range of choice. A pluralistic society is then likely to communicate better 'with itself', reducing tensions and strains. It is a particularly important value in the context of democratic politics, where competition for popular support between different voices and parties requires a diverse dissemination of information and views.

There are alternative standards for recognising or assessing diversity in news journalism, with two main alternatives. One is with reference to a reflective or representative form of diversity, such that the representation achieved in the news corresponds with the 'real-world' distribution. Essentially, this is a fairness principle, with media access expected to be proportional to the distribution in the society as a whole. This means that majorities will get more if not most attention and access, with consequent difficulties for minorities in challenging the status quo. The main alternative is the equality or open access principle for all, according to which all have an equal claim on access and representation.

In practice, this has little chance of realisation. Taken literally, it would lead to absurdities and be impossible to implement. It would seem far from fair to most people. Nevertheless, in some circumstances, it is an appropriate standard. For instance, in a number of countries there are regulations about media access at election times, such as a cap on political campaign spending or even a rule allocating broadcasting space to all recognised political parties. Such regulations are becoming less common and less effective as media have expanded. Most of the problems that arise under the heading of diversity relate to the broad conditions of a media *system* and do not directly face individual journalists, although news editors need to take account of them.

In the course of their normal operation, the media implicitly promote identity and a sense of belonging to any of several social units within the national society. Media are mainly territorially based and address specific national, regional and linguistically defined publics. Within this primary identification (and sometimes cutting across it) are other potential identifications based on social, cultural and other circumstances (race, gender, religion, etc.). The internal identity of many such social and sub-groups can be strengthened or weakened, depending on whether or not they have their own (minority) media of communication and on how such groups are treated in the 'majority' media of the whole society.

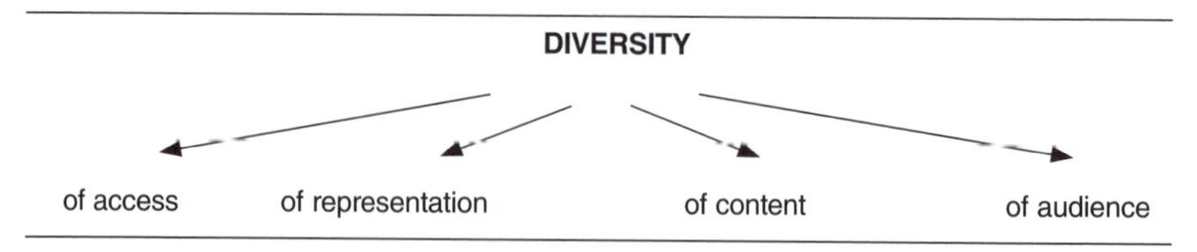

FIGURE 3.3 Diversity as a criterion of news quality

The theoretical benefits of diversity for society as a whole and for its constituent groups can only be fully realised under two additional conditions.

One relates to the range of content and reference, another to the audience. In respect of the first, a diverse news provision would deal with all potential topics of relevance and significance (home and foreign, sport and business, politics and human interest, and so on) plus differences of style and presentation to suit various tastes. For diversity it is important that the various 'constituencies' in society have some exposure to each other, especially majorities to minorities, and that all are reached by some content in common. The diversity of audiences is generally considered to contribute to a more socially cohesive society, a condition now threatened by the rise of new, more individuated and segmented media.

Solidarity

The value of solidarity is a stronger and more explicit expression of an attachment to social equality, based on somewhat mixed foundations, ranging from patriotism and attachment to a 'national interest' to a concern for groups and individuals that might be marginalised, victimised or excluded. In their study of investigative journalism, Ettema and Glasser (1998) name solidarity as one of the three primary values supporting this form of reporting. Investigative journalism has other impulses, not least the wish to attract audiences interested in scandal and the private lives of celebrities.

Social solidarity can be promoted at the level of the national society by the reporting of economic and cultural (or military) achievements or, conversely, of crisis or disaster that tends to bring people together. Solidarity is often manifested by way of patriotic symbols and messages. The news consistently reports external (world) events from the standpoint of a 'national interest'. A somewhat different notion of solidarity applies to attempts to be inclusive within the national boundary. This applies to positive treatment of minority groups and also to sympathetic reports of problems and hardships suffered by fellow-citizens, in respect of health, welfare or natural disasters (the 'social empathy function' of media that extends understanding and help). This may be expressed in campaigning to expose evils and promote reform.

The process may also be shaped by a sub-text that distinguishes between the 'deserving' and the 'undeserving' of our sympathy. There is a potential for conflict between the patriotic concept of solidarity and that relating to sympathy for the excluded. The latter may be portrayed as potential threats to general welfare (if engaged in crime or disorder or seen as a social and economic burden). A more pressing contemporary example is provided by the situation of large immigrant groups that may have sympathies and ties to other countries and cultures (for instance, Islam in the western case). Some minorities simply become targets for popular prejudice that some news media are tempted to amplify.

The case of minorities within a national society that require support for their own culture, identity and needs has already been mentioned. In this case the criterion of solidarity relates to how well media directed to such purposes meets their goal. From an international point of view, news media can also be seen as either undermining or promoting a more global awareness of shared concerns. Foreign events are generally reported according to a frame of reference of potential risk, danger or advantage for the domestic public, who form the audience. Even so, there is some evidence that larger concerns, such as a need for peace and an awareness of environmental hazards and support for development goals, that transcend purely national interest have gained some ground in international news reporting. The main applications of the solidarity principle are summarised in Figure 3.4.

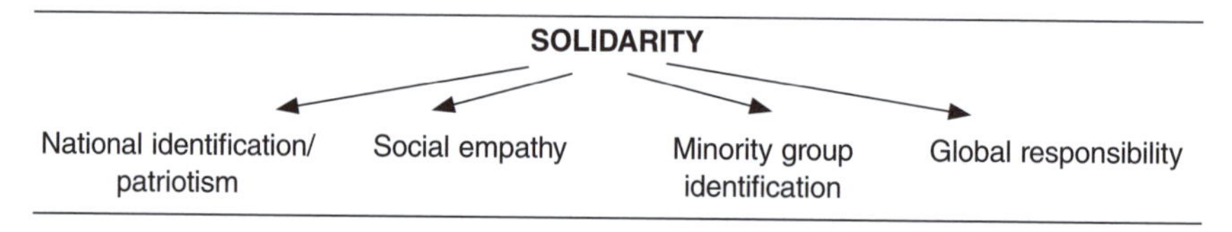

FIGURE 3.4 Dimensions of the solidarity principle

Order and cohesion as principles for journalism

Several distinct, but interrelated, values are covered by this heading. One is that of the unity and cohesion of a whole society, or some less extensive community. In this meaning it is reflected in the role of the journalist as a patriotic citizen and a supporter of local and regional interests, language, identity and culture. This has largely been explained. It is worth recording that reliable survey evidence in a number of countries shows that the need for 'social harmony' and stability may be valued by the public over total freedom of the press (e.g. BBC, 2007).

Secondly, journalists are expected to respect prevailing cultural values and to avoid giving offence to morals, religion or sensibilities of their audience. The direction of influence of this impulse tends to be conservative, supporting consensus and tradition, but it also entails sympathy for the weak and vulnerable.

Thirdly, there is a value of 'order' in the narrow sense of absence of disorder in the form of crime, unrest, breakdown of law, warfare.

According to this value, journalism is likely to support forces of 'law and order' and legitimate authorities. Certainly, journalism does often come in for criticism for indirectly encouraging some forms of disorder by giving 'undue' attention or spreading news of violent incidents. Open sympathy for crime or violence is not normally at issue, although when unrest has a political character there is scope for journalists to side with the 'troublemakers' and to criticise the 'forces of law and order'.

Expectations deriving from principles of social order and cohesion cut across most distinctions of genre, embracing all informative, cultural and entertainment publications and are not only a matter for journalists. The main sub-principles can be described as follows.

Law and order

In respect of law and order, the media should provide privileged access to legitimate authorities that deal with issues of crime and justice, security and defence, public order, crisis and emergency. These channels should connect responsible authorities with the general public, allowing information, advice, warning, instruction, etc., on issues of security and order to flow 'downward', as it were, but also to convey information, reactions and public opinion 'upwards'. More generally, the predominant messages of the media in both news reporting and cultural content is to discourage and symbolically punish crime and anti-social behaviour and reward 'pro-social' attitudes and activities. These principles do not put greater obligations on journalists than on ordinary citizens, but they do indicate an area of potential responsibility for editors and journalists.

Civic duty

Democratic political systems usually presume that news media will respect established procedures and also the persons of politicians and others in authority. Help is expected in the general servicing of the information and communication needs of the main institutions of government, politics and law. Although rules are largely unwritten in these matters, privileged access will often be expected for mainstream political figures and views, reports of parliament and other elected bodies. Politically moderate or majority views will have preference over those from marginal or 'extremist' sources. Conflicts will be dealt with in a judicious and balanced way. Unwritten rules of 'political correctness' (avoidance of terms of offence to minorities) will usually apply on sensitive issues. Generally, news media exhibit patterns of local loyalty and national patriotism.

Public decency and morality

Most news media also operate according to unwritten as well as written rules of conduct in matters of potential offence to public mores, which are never precisely knowable in any case. The general expectation is that the media will follow the reigning consensus about what is acceptable in the publication of potentially sensitive content dealing mainly with sex and violence or both, and ranging beyond into topics of sickness, death and the occult. In some places, religion and blasphemy are still sensitive areas of publication.

Standards of conduct for journalists

Quite a number of the qualities thought desirable in journalism can be placed under the general idea of what is right and proper conduct in the given conditions of time and place, without any call for formal regulation or accountability. This applies especially to news perceived to have some risk of harm to individuals and society at the receiving end. Some additional matters have not been mentioned that have mainly to do with ethical issues for journalism. The most relevant features of journalistic conduct that need to be mentioned are summarised in Box 3.2. This topic is discussed in more detail in Chapter 7 (and see also Appendix §3).

Box 3.2 Guidelines for conduct of journalists

- Be honest in acquiring information and in selecting news for publication.
- Respect privacy and dignity of those involved in or affected by news events. This extends to respect for communication privacy of public figures.
- Anticipate and avoid harmful (unintended) effects for third parties or for an audience as a result of publication.
- Follow such codes of professional ethics and conduct as are applicable.
- Listen to responses (negative as well as positive) from an audience and those affected by publication.
- Accept responsibility for publication.

Conclusion

The criteria of quality of journalism outlined in this chapter are directly related to the various aspirations and expectations attaching to journalism in their broader social role. This account is not complete and there are alternative approaches to identifying relevant qualities, for instance, by looking at the needs of media clients or the demands and interests of audiences. Aside from this, there is a set of norms and ethics usually proposed and self-policed by journalists themselves or the larger institution of journalism. The issues arising in that respect usually have more to do with protecting the status of the profession than with serving society, although there is a strong connection between both, especially on matters of potential harm. This includes the causing of offence, invading privacy and dignity, causing actual harm to individuals, even if unintentionally. These matters are mainly dealt with in Chapter 6.

Finally, it is necessary to point out that this review of criteria of performance does not take much account of some of the qualities that are most highly prized by professional journalists. The criteria discussed are derived from social and media theory that largely originates outside the media. Many of the normative prescriptions are recognised or adopted by journalists, especially those relating to truth and freedom of reporting. Even so, the standards formulated here are more about social ideals than everyday journalistic practice.

Journalists themselves, and the news media in general, have a different set of priorities, shaped by the pressures of competition and the search for audiences and income. As a result, the qualities most emphasised are likely to be the intrinsic interest and appeal of news stories and the speed and exclusivity of coverage. These in turn are likely to mean a focus on prominent personalities, very recent events, dramatic stories, plus the availability of pictures and inside stories. Such qualities do not really stem from any theory, but from experience and common sense, and may have little to do with the larger public roles of journalism. However, the qualities valued by journalists underlie the effectiveness of the press at actually informing the public and gaining their attention. They also provide the motivation to expose the actions of the powerful and warn the public quickly of risks and dangers. It remains to say that there is no unified journalistic outlook on purpose and quality, but a well-attested diversity of goals, ranging from high-minded social purpose to success in a chosen media market.

Further reading

Lemert, J.B. (1989). *Criticising the Media*. Newbury Park, CA: Sage.
McQuail, D. (1992). *Media Performance: Mass Communication in the Public Interest*. London: Sage.
Trappel, J., Niemen, H. and Nord, L. (eds) (2011). *The Media Democracy Monitor*. Bristol: Intellect.
Zaller, J. (2003). 'A new standard of news quality: burglar alarms for the monitorial citizen', *Political Communication*, 20, 2: 109–30.

Online readings

Go to www.sagepub.co.uk/mcquailjournalism for free access to the online readings.

Bourdana, S. (2010). 'On the values guiding the French practice of journalism', *Journalism*, 3: 293–310.
Broersma, M. (2010). 'The unbearable limitations of journalism. On press critique and journalism's claim to truth', *International Communication Gazette*, 72, 1: 21–34.
Deprez, A. and Raeymaeckers, K. (2010). 'Bias in the news? Belgian press coverage of the First and Second Intifada', *International Communication Gazette*, 72, 1: 9–20.
Deuze, M. (2005). 'Professional ideals and ideology of journalists reconsidered', *Journalism*, 6: 442–64.
Westerstahl, J. (1983). 'Objective news reporting', *Communication Research*, 10, 3: 403–24.

4 Towards a Framework of Analysis for Journalism

Introduction

Here we look more closely at journalism as an occupation with a variety of specific goals and work tasks that are carried out within the press institution according to certain ethical and practical rules. The purpose is to better understand the various motives and goals of those who work in journalism. For this we need to go beyond the description of journalism practice. The ultimate purpose is to be able to answer questions about the potential of journalism to have wider influence in society, to make comparisons between countries and media systems and to assess the direction and trends of change resulting from technological and media industry developments. We also aim to shed light on some of the fundamental divisions that characterise the occupation, especially the potential conflict between serving ideal goals for the 'society' and the purpose of making profit by providing a service to a variety of customers and clients.

Despite their long history, the press and journalism have never received the same degree and depth of attention paid to more weighty and older institutions and occupations, such as medicine, the law, politics, the church, the military or business. The press had not been completely ignored by early sociologists and political scientists (especially in France and Germany) who recognised the key part played by communication in processes of social, political and economic change. As the power of the 'people' in the political process made itself felt, the 'news' and the opinions and ideas spread by newspapers became central to political events and also to reform and even revolution. Journalism itself played an equally important part in nationalist movements and in conflicts between nation states, where public opinion was mobilised for wars of defence, expansion or aggression.

In more recent times, the role of journalism in all spheres has expanded, and a great deal of research has been carried out with several different theoretical perspectives on journalism emerging. The central ideas they contain provide us with a starting point for the present analysis of the occupation and key points are summarised in the following pages.

The occupation of journalism can be seen in the larger context of the news organisation, which itself forms part of the loosely structured 'press institution', which in turn informally regulates links and potential obligations to the wider society. Here we focus on issues that journalists face arising from their location in society as well as in relation to practical tasks of 'news production'.

The main questions to be asked are as follows:

Overall framing of the journalism occupation in relation to society

- How is it viewed in the perspective of the main social science traditions?
- What degree of autonomy should or can journalism have in relation to society?

Journalism as a profession

- What are the main criteria of a profession?
- How far does journalism meet these criteria?
- What is the central skill or mystery, if any?

Journalism culture and ideology

- Is there an 'ideology of journalism'?
- How far is there a shared occupational culture, whether national or international?

Occupational roles of journalism

- What are the main roles available within the occupation?
- What are the main role conflicts and tensions?
- In what sense is it a 'public occupation'?
- What signs of change can be discerned?

Alternative approaches

Not surprisingly, theoretical approaches to the issues raised here have themselves been strongly influenced by the different academic disciplines in which they have their roots.

Political science

Political scientists have focused most attention on relationships between journalism and the political system, but this opens up wider issues about the relationship between journalism and power in society. Quite a large share of routine news content, including news about the economy, social problems and foreign affairs is of significance for the political system. In the democratic competition for power, it has become essential for competing leaders and parties to demonstrate competence and success in many of these matters. Governments in office need to employ the 'soft power' of information and persuasion to gain compliance. Oppositional and reform movements seek recognition and favourable treatment 'in the news', sometimes by way of staged events, demonstrations, etc., as well as publicity.

For undemocratic rulers it is no less important to manage the supply of news but the means of direct control are always to hand. In liberal societies, there is continual rivalry between political contenders to 'set the agenda' of the news in their own best interest. This also implies the need to compete with journalists for control of the 'gates' of communication between politicians and citizens. The issue of politics–journalism relations is central and, in most cases, the outcome is a mixture of conflict and cooperation, with political actors trying to manage the way things appear in return for information released from political and government sources. Other agencies in society do the same. The balance of advantage is often unequal and/or unpredictable, but generally follows lines of power and money. However, not all influence is for sale. The picture is complicated by the fact that some journalists and some news sources are active supporters or opponents of political parties and ideologies as well as participants in civic affairs and not just neutral gatekeepers or observers.

Sociology

Sociological research and theory relating to journalism has its origins in the United States in the 1930s and 1940s, but only flourished in the 1960s and later. The main aims of this more recent branch of sociology were to uncover the dynamics of power and cooperation within the newsroom and between the newsroom and the larger organisation. In keeping with general US practice, the media organisation or firm was found typically to place economic and management goals ahead of the professional or social aspirations of journalists, with consequences for content and some resulting tension when the requirements of economy and organisational routine clashed with the creativity and originality valued by the news reporter, writer and editor.

The journalistic workplace was characterised by Tunstall (1971) as typically a 'non-routine bureaucracy', referring to the need for predictable output to meet a steady demand, despite the equal need to respond creatively to the new and unexpected. Sociology also focused on the different motivations and goals that characterise the work of journalists. We can see this in the choices made amongst alternative roles and the relative priority attached (see below). In reality, most news organisations are characterised by mixed goals, with some agreement on necessary conditions for success, especially in keeping the interest of an audience and being up-to-date and, if possible, being first in making news public.

Another line of sociological analysis has been to consider whether the occupation can be accounted as a true 'profession', such as law, medicine, etc. This has meant firstly establishing some agreed version of 'traits' that characterise a profession (or just professionalism) and looking at the case of journalism to see if these traits can be recognised (see below). This approach has an attraction for associations of journalists which aspire to the status that goes with the title of profession. It also accords with the goal of raising standards of journalism. As we will see shortly (in the following section), this approach also helps to reveal some of the strengths and weaknesses as well as the aspirations of journalism practice, even if no single or definitive answer to the question has emerged.

An influential theory of journalism (field theory) is that based on the work of the sociologist Pierre Bourdieu and brings politics and economics into the picture as well. It treats journalism as one of a number of more or less autonomous 'fields' of activity that constitute the total social sphere. The most relevant neighbouring fields are those of politics, economy and the academy (true at least in France, probably not everywhere). Bourdieu defined a field as a 'microcosm which has its own rules, which is constituted autonomously and which cannot be understood from external factors' (quoted in Benson and Neveu, 2005:32). Although a field is a social-cultural entity, the approach recognises that any individual journalist has a specific position in the field and this position depends on the newspaper or channel for which he or she works, and the place of this organisation in the overall sector and the wider media market and its relation to the political system. Within the journalism field, there are further sub-cultural divisions. For instance, Bourdieu singled out 'market journalism' (preoccupied by ratings and competition) as a type with different rules than, say, the journalism of political and social influence. The consequences for some forms of news 'bias' are evident and, all in all, it is a poor basis for a claim to being objective. Thinking along these lines is consistent with the view that much news and information actually receives an 'advertising subsidy' from advertisers or PR sources. Field theory opens up a fruitful method for analysing the role of the journalist in a given context (Benson and Neveu, 2005).

Economics

There is no unified economic theory of journalism, but many studies point to a set of powerful economic forces that are at work to influence what journalists do. These forces are of different kinds, ranging from the overriding commercial purposes of media firms, through issues of the cost of news gathering, to the career ambitions of individual journalists. News has to be offered that appeals to the interests of audiences with varying purchasing power and criteria of news significance vary accordingly. A broad prediction on most such issues can be read from the influential body of political-economic theory that formed part of 'critical theory' (see Chapter 2). The core thesis was that all media output would have an underlying purpose of serving the interests of media owners, the capitalist system and the 'status quo', within the limits of what the market would tolerate.

Despite its general plausibility, this does not explain, in much detail, how the process works or how to account for variations and exceptions, although much of the actual behaviour in selecting, reporting and processing news can be traced back to economic causes rather than idealistic motivation (Fengler and Russ-Mohl, 2008). An empirical study of television news by McManus (1994) resulted in an economic model of how the market shapes news, especially because of the need to maximise either paying audiences or attention to be sold to advertisers. The central proposition of the model is that the probability of a given news item being selected would be:

- Inversely proportional:
  - to the harm that the information might cause to major advertisers;
  - to the cost that might be incurred by publication;
  - to the cost of reporting it.

- Directly proportional to the expected breadth of appeal to the audience that advertisers will pay to reach.

At the present time, the competition between print and online journalism is largely determined by such economic factors. In general, economic theory explains conduct and content of journalism by way of structural (media market or system) rather than personal factors.

Social-cultural

Quite a few studies of journalists have reported the existence of a range of different 'news cultures', both within and between national settings. These differences involve different values and standards that journalists learn in a process of newsroom socialisation. They lead to variations in authority structures of newsrooms as well as in actual performance, well beyond questions of style and presentation. They relate to news competitiveness, degrees of 'sensationalism' or personalisation, methods of collecting information and relation to sources and external pressures and demands (Deuze, 2002; Patterson, 2005, and below, Chapter 6). Quite apart from this, journalism is a cultural product, shaped by the cultural context of the surrounding society, according to region, tradition, taste, life-style, etc.

The relevant cultural issues (perhaps the most relevant) do not relate just to the current cultural climate of the profession or newsroom, but extend deeply into the history of the national societies in which journalists operate. These factors cast a very long shadow because they affect fundamental matters including relations of deference and expected submission in relations between journalists and authority, as well as the place of journalism either as practice or publications in the national culture. Fundamental tensions may persist from pre-democratic times between the state and media and a large cultural gap may exist between elite and popular tastes for the products of journalism.

Box 4.1 Main perspectives and issues arising

- Political: Control of access to news 'gates' and of a news agenda
- Economic: Market versus professionalism and public ideal
- Sociological: Organisational and work routines versus creativity and originality

- The extent to which journalism has autonomy as a field of social action
- Social-cultural: Influence of news cultures and 'ideology' of journalism
- Influence of personal factors and social situation
- Deep (national) historical roots.

Each of the perspectives outlined has a capacity to uncover some essential aspect of journalism, but on its own each can be limiting in respect of influences dealt with. In addition, no perspective on its own focuses clearly on the self-defined task of the journalist. For this reason, we choose to develop a framework based on the idea of journalism as a profession, in aspiration or achievement, despite the flows in such an approach to the study of an occupation. Many of the ideas outlined already can be seen to fit in the discussion.

On journalism as a profession – a unifying approach

Here the notion of a profession is treated as a hypothesis to be applied to journalism, in order to ask in which respects it does (or could) qualify for this label and in which respects not.

In fact there is no firm concept of what counts as a profession that can act as a standard of comparison. Ideas of what would count as the ideal for a profession of journalism are probably more divided than is the case with other occupations. We do not need to imply any judgement about the value of professionalism one way or other and it may even be misleading to rank occupations by this nebulous standard. However, it has become a common practice and reflects 'commonsense' judgements. The key test is the presence or absence of certain occupational characteristics. These are derived from features often attributed to a small number of 'classic' professions, especially medicine and law, to which have been added various scientific or highly skilled specialist occupations. The word 'professional' is often used simply to mean paid and expert rather than amateur, unqualified or voluntary work. There are different versions of relevant criteria, but the five points that seem to be most relevant for journalism are as shown in Box 4.2.

Box 4.2 General criteria of a profession

- Having a core skill requiring high levels of training, skill and judgement plus access to a systematic body of knowledge
- Making a claim to monopoly of the service involved that is largely accepted by society
- Possessing a certain degree of freedom as an occupation, with personal autonomy of judgement for the practitioner
- Having and following a set of distinct norms of professional conduct
- Having an ethic of service to the society or to a 'public interest'; a claim to be occupying a position of public trust, with corresponding responsibility and accountability.

There is another professional characteristic that is sometimes recognised as important and has relevance for the case of journalism. This concerns the attitude of detachment and neutrality (implying both impartiality and impersonality). It calls for an equal and fair treatment of sources and objects of reporting, in the same way as a doctor or lawyer will treat any patient or client on the same terms and with the same attitude. Professionalism calls for a rational and unemotional approach to work.

There are quite a few occupations that have some but not all of these features and others that are sometimes described as 'professional', without fully meeting any of these criteria. The number of occupations aspiring to the status of a profession has also increased along with the greater complexity and specialisation of organised work. This has tended to dilute the meaning of the term and make classification more uncertain and less significant. Journalism does have the potential to meet all five of the criteria in some degree and some circumstances, but it is far from accepted as a 'classic' profession with a corresponding claim to social status and public respect. Each of the criteria also presents some particular problems for journalism.

An obvious stumbling block comes from the absence of any fixed body of essential knowledge or skill that is unique to journalism, despite the existence of many training programmes and the greater complexity of journalistic work in the new media environment. Individuals are still employed as journalists with no such training where they have some special talent and it is impossible to say for certain which esoteric skill might be needed to carry out any of the various work tasks mentioned below. Professional bodies of journalists do not normally decide whether a person is qualified or not in a technical sense. In any case, the boundaries of the occupation are not usually controlled, meaning that there is no effective monopoly (none is claimed). The employing news organisation decides for itself who to select. The skills typically claimed by journalists are either very general and basic, rules of thumb, or matters of flair and intuition that cannot be reliably transmitted by training. Moreover, the definition of journalism that we started out with does not only apply to paid employees.

More fundamental, perhaps, than the lack of clear boundaries, is the conflict between the aspiration (if there is one) of journalism to professional monopoly and the right that everyone has to make public their own observations and accounts of events for whatever purpose and in whatever way we choose. In some countries, a journalist belonging to an accredited news organisation can claim certain privileges and rights (e.g. access to closed places and information, protection of identity of sources, less risk of libel action). Uncertainty about the position of the journalist in this respect has been accentuated by the rise of citizen journalism in the form of blogs and other internet-based forms of communication to the wider world.

The lack of full control of entry to the work of journalism is one aspect of lack of professional autonomy. Personal autonomy is no more secure. Most journalists do not control their own work in any detail, decide what topics to cover as news or how to cover them. They are not free to reveal their own opinions, contrary to the policy of the employing organisation. Most decisions about the content of work are decided by managers and editors in news organisations. Hallin and Mancini (2004:35) note that the autonomy of the journalist is not necessarily that of the individual but of the 'corps of journalists taken as a whole'. They also say that there is considerable variability across media systems. The so-called 'internal freedom' of journalists does not extend to a right to free expression by way of the employing news organisation, although it may support conscientious objection to certain tasks. Potential conflicts are usually avoided by selective or self-selective recruitment.

While many efforts have been made to develop and enforce agreed codes of conduct and ethics for journalism, the coverage is far from complete and agreement on core values across media and national boundaries is limited. The potential for any external enforcement is quite low, left largely to self-government by the particular branch or national institution. There is only a limited ethic of obligation to a particular client, such as we find in other professions. The audience served by news is too diffuse and unknown. Some examples of codes are given in the Appendix, §3 and §5.

However, a study of 31 European codes showed a fair amount of agreement on two matters – the need to show accountability on a broad front (to sources, public, employers, and the state) and the wish to support professional identity (Laetila, 1995). The advertiser who buys space that finances the news is prevented by the norm of news independence from receiving special consideration. Journalists (unlike other professionals) do not normally accept a responsibility for harmful consequences of their reporting, unless they are the result of clear failures or a deliberate act.

This rejection of any general liability for 'effects' can be justified by the need to protect freedom of publication (not to mention of the journalist) from powerful interests that might well be offended even by legitimate and true news accounts. There will always be some pressure to suppress information on grounds of potential harm and the acceptance of liability would be a path towards self-censorship, since truth is not always a sufficient defence. Neither the individual journalist nor the collective body of journalists can usually claim much autonomy or right to self-determination vis-à-vis ultimate owners and controllers of the media.

The claims of journalism to be of service to society or the public interest are often valid but not beyond question. As we have seen, there is rarely an agreed version of the public interest and news media do not usually recognise such a notion. Journalism covers very different kinds of news content ranging from sensational gossip to weighty financial and political reporting and commentary. Some media regard gossip as just as much in need of being made known, when it relates to public figures. Taken as a whole, journalism mixes the 'material' with the 'sacred' in ways that cannot easily be separated from each other. It is not really possible to divide the tasks of journalists along such lines or to reserve the title of profession for those that are more altruistic.

Even media that acknowledge a social responsibility to respect the public good as defined by the established authorities, may well feel an obligation to dissent on major issues, for instance, in the case of foreign wars or domestic repression. Others would put the matter more strongly and say that there is an inevitable tension between a supposed service to the public good (as defined from 'above') and the service to truth and freedom of publication. This view will be held by those whose ideal of conduct for the press is as watchdog on, and critic of, all those who exercise power in society. Serving 'society' from this point of view can entail seriously upsetting those in power.

Finally, the detachment and universality expected of the true professional is matched to some degree in the attitude of neutrality and the practice of objective reporting that is regarded by many journalists as essential to their work. However, as we see later, this is not a universal journalistic value and in some media systems highly regarded journalism (and journalists) can be influenced in their reporting by personal or partisan commitments (Patterson, 2005). This reflects the existence of alternative, competing, versions of the journalistic role that may have to be accommodated within the same press institution. In their study of press–politics relations, Hallin and Mancini (2004:37) contrast a 'professionalised' model of the press with an 'instrumentalised' version. The latter means 'control of the media by outside actors – parties, politicians, social groups or movements, or economic actors seeking influence'. This situation is not uncommon and not alien to the historical role of the newspaper. The rise of the 'professional' model is not only driven by public service ideals or the triumph of other professional values, it is also a matter of good business and expanding markets. As noted earlier, it has sometimes been identified as an 'Anglo-American' model of journalism (Chalaby, 1996).

Box 4.3 Weaknesses in the claim to be a profession

- Uncertainty over central skill and body of knowledge
- No control of entry to or boundary around the practice of journalism
- Autonomy to practice is limited
- Lack of a fixed or agreed code of conduct or institution of enforcement
- Public service role subordinate to profit
- Limited acceptance of responsibility.

Despite these and other qualifications, it is still instructive to take the notion of a profession as a starting point of reference in assessing what journalists do and what they are expected to do and in making comparisons. As with most occupations, individual journalists do not usually have to concern themselves with the wider social role of the press institution, but concentrate on the application of their particular skills in concrete situations. However, this carries a real risk that, lacking any sense of wider purpose, journalism surrenders integrity and autonomy and along with this, the respect and trust of the public. This, in turn, undermines the credibility of journalistic information and is ultimately destructive. Nearest to the truth, perhaps, is that journalism is such a mixed occupation that some individuals and news organisations meet professional criteria, while others (probably a majority) do not and do not aspire to.

Does journalism have its own 'ideology'?

Some students of journalism have concluded that journalism in the twentieth century came to develop its own ideology, not in the sense of a belief system but a set of values about what constitutes 'good journalism' and also informal rules for the sort of practices that will lead to it. For instance, Tuchman (1978) in her ethnographic study of television news concluded that 'professionalism' had come to be defined according to the operational needs of the news organisation itself, rather than the needs of public and society. The height of professional skill was thus measured by criteria of formal objectivity, being first with the news and attracting and keeping an audience as an end in itself. She described this as an 'ideology' of the occupation.

There is support for this view from other studies, although often in a context where ideology means a belief system with uncertain basis in reality. One could equally describe an idealistic vision of journalism as a service to society as an ideology. Although for most journalists, their work is a pragmatic activity, there is no doubt that some journalists do see it in vocational terms. Brodasson (1994) has written of the 'sacred side of professional journalism' and the term 'sacerdotal' has been applied to the attitude of journalists dedicated to a mission of public enlightenment. The 'mythology' around journalism that is often encountered in fiction (films, books and TV drama), as well as in memoirs of journalists, provides support for an image of a hard-headed but basically moral defender of the right.

It does seem that the term 'ideology' is being rather loosely used in this context and it would probably be rejected by most journalists.

However, contemporary journalism has developed far beyond its pen and paper beginnings, involving much technical skill and also creative judgement, plus sensitivity to political and other realities. This has strengthened the claim of journalism to a higher status of expertise and also authority on matters of news-gathering and disseminating. A more recent tendency is to use ideology in a neutral sense as a guide to the main ethical values of occupational practice (see Deuze, 2005; Hanitzsch, 2007).

Following the notion of a journalistic field introduced earlier, an overview has been suggested combining some of the ideas discussed and an empirical study of 1,800 journalists in 31 countries (Hanitzsch et al., 2011). In place of 'culture' or 'ideologies' the term 'journalistic milieu' is introduced – 'different groups of journalists who share similar understandings of the social functions of journalism'. These groups cut across national and organisational boundaries, although they reflect the larger contextual conditions under which journalists operate in different societies. The study presumed that differences of professional milieu reflected three general dimensions: one of interventionism or neutrality (in the affairs of society); a second of relationship to power (essentially either challenging or loyal); and third, degree of market orientation to the work and the public (regarded either more as citizens or consumers). Four main varieties of professional milieu emerged from the empirical study, under the headings: 'popular disseminator'; 'detached watchdog'; 'critical change agent'; and 'opportunist facilitator'. The last named is least familiar in western media theory and practice – involving support for official policies and positive image-making for political and business leaders. The varying distribution of types reflects different levels of development of democratic institutions and rule of law, as well as of the economy.

The sociologist Max Weber nearly a century ago (in 1918) referred to the journalist as belonging to 'a sort of pariah caste', somewhat like the artist in lacking a fixed classification (Weber, 1948). This view is still consistent with some features of the occupational self-image and divergent roles. Contemporary journalists are unlikely to be considered as 'outsiders' in society, but in certain circumstances they may have to behave as such in the interests of truth and aspiration to serve the public. For quite different reasons, however, public opinion often ranks journalism rather low in esteem and trust.

The occupational roles of journalism

Journalism can be accounted for in a descriptive way by reference to the different tasks, often of a specialist kind that are assigned or chosen. The main work of journalism can be divided into three or four phases: information 'discovery' and collection; processing into accounts for publication; provision of comment, interpretation or context; and actual publication or dissemination. The nature of the work varies with circumstances, but some kind of pattern is observable. The first phase is mainly the work of the reporter, who turns observations, records, interview material, etc. into reports. The second phase largely belongs to editors and sub-editors whose task is to select and adapt reports to fit a larger news product. At the third phase, editors ensure conformity to news policy, but columnists are also engaged. Presentation tasks vary according to medium, from design specialists to 'anchors', often familiar and popular or respected figures who can influence content and relations with an audience.

An alternative path towards understanding the nature of journalistic work is to consider journalism as an occupation that bundles together a number of different roles. The concept of a 'role', as developed especially by sociologists, takes account of two elements, one that we might call normative and another, empirical. The first refers to purposes and values that are supposed to guide actions and the second to actual work tasks and processes. The main values involved, as already largely explained (in Chapter 3), relate to: an orientation to a chosen public (as well as society as a whole) as primary beneficiary; and reporting in an independent way, with regard for truth, fairness and some courage.

The concept also incorporates the fact that the work of any occupation can be viewed from different standpoints, most relevantly those of: owners and managers; practitioners; intended beneficiaries or clients. In the case of occupations that have a public character, including journalism, a fourth perspective is often important, that of 'society', or of observers, critics and public opinion. For this reason, a role is more than a job description or a statement of the main tasks to be carried out. Ideas of purpose, duty, responsibility and relative value are also involved although they will vary from one context to another. Valuation will take account of utility as well as ethical, social or cultural criteria.

The role concept originates in 'functionalist' theory of human society (see Chapter 2) which tries to explain systematic features of society in terms of the essential needs they meet for survival and growth (especially needs for cohesion, cooperation, and ordered growth and change). The idea of a function implies an underlying rationale or purpose at a level above that of the individual. When applied to explain 'what journalism is for' in the larger scheme of things, it gives rise to a number of specific occupational roles that are recognised by journalists, although not all chosen or equally valued. The leading options are as shown in Box 4.4.

Box 4.4 Main choices of journalistic role

- Acting as a monitor of events in the world, on behalf of the needs and interests of a chosen audience or public and bringing them relevant and up-to-date information of use to the public in coping with risks, changes and opportunities
- Acting as a 'watchdog' for the public in respect of political or economic power and especially its potential misuse; this version is sometimes described as an 'adversarial' concept of journalism
- Playing an active part in social and political life by facilitating the work of key institutions (through publicity, informing, activating, etc.)
- Supporting the cohesion and the economic, social and cultural interests of nation, region or place served by a given medium
- Advocating a chosen cause or social movement or conducting a campaign; this is most frequently encountered as a 'partisan role'
- Collaborating with the established authorities to combat crime, disorder and threats to security.

These goals or purposes do not usually take precedence over the immediate practical tasks of news production and dissemination, but they influence decisions where a choice has to be made (which means all the time in some degree). As noted already, these items are optional guides to conduct or expectations, and there are some tensions and inconsistencies, for instance, between the monitoring and advocacy or between the adversarial and the collaborative purpose.

The various tasks as indicated do not say much about the scope a journalist might have in a given case. For instance, a 'reporter', can be no more than a messenger or 'postman', but equally be an active investigator, a documentary film-maker, or a searching interviewer. Such variation can be further characterised according to some general dimensions, including status in an organisation or society, public visibility, or freedom to express opinion.

Conflicts and mixed expectations

The primary source of purpose for most individual professional journalists is dependent on their particular location in the media system, since it is here that journalists are trained, socialised and employed. Not all the tasks and purposes mentioned above are regarded equally and there are many differences between types of media. There are also tensions and contradictions between several of the roles, which have been exposed in research investigating the role conceptions held by journalists themselves. The main oppositions to emerge are as summarised in Box 4.5.

Box 4.5 Oppositions and conflicts of role

- Adopting an active versus a passive role in relation to the surrounding society
- Concentrating on 'facts' versus seeking to interpret and advise by way of commentary and opinion
- Acting as a 'gatekeeper' or platform for voices in society versus being an 'advocate' for some cause or interest
- Serving the media organisation and advancing a career versus trying to follow a personal conception of the journalistic role and vocation
- Choosing between social (and non-profit) purposes and the criteria of the market place.

There is an underlying theme to this set of choices and they reflect the pull of divergent normative poles and different sources of reward for practising journalists, ranging from high public respect to high financial reward. These remarks reflect the diversity of what we call journalism and the variety of forms that news media can take, each with its own purpose, (self-)selected public and market niche. The arrival of new types of media, especially ones based on the internet, have added to the variety and clouded the issue of what journalism is and what it is for.

Although there are real differences underlying the oppositions shown in Box 4.5, there is room within the larger field of journalism in a developed media system for the co-existence of different types of journalism. However, not all are likely to enjoy the same professional or public status. The predominant ideal of newspaper journalism in the twentieth century was strongly weighted in favour of extensive information relating to current issues of national or international politics and business. Ideas of professional excellence were strongly influenced by the values of an educated administrative class accustomed to following rules of rationality and order and having an elite status. It is appropriate to think of this tendency as involving the 'institutionalisation' of a leading sector of the press and a consequent reduction in personal autonomy.

The values and practices of this 'prestige press' were adopted in some degree as a standard for public broadcasting and filtered down to other forms of journalism as alternatives to market populism. In the case of public broadcasting, the model of 'objective' journalism was especially suited because of its claim to political neutrality and general support for the mission of seeking to inform the general public on 'serious' matters. Further support for the neutral, objective, factually-informative model came from the growth of national and international markets for news, as delivered by world news agencies.

Most of the evidence that we have about how journalists see their own roles indicates an overall frame of reference in which the main choice lies between neutral reporting of ongoing events on the one hand and, on the other, some form of engagement or participation that puts the informational activity at the service of a cause, movement, political part or ideology. In the liberal democracies where most research has been carried out, there is a strong leaning towards the neutral pole with an emphasis on speed and accuracy in bringing information. However, there is also evidence of an aspiration at least for journalism to play a part in society by keeping some check on the activities of government and other powerful agencies in society and also to warn the public of risks and dangers of various kinds. Such ideas also respond and vary according to the prevailing social-political climate of the time.

This means that the informational task is never completely neutral, but is guided at the very least by a journalistic assessment of what issues really matter and what information might be most useful and relevant to the intended audience. A stronger version of this would support the role of the news media as a 'watchdog' on behalf of the public interest. Another specific (and yet more active) version of the core informational role of journalism is expressed by the notion of 'investigative journalism', applied to the (relatively rare or scattered) occasions where journalists actively pursue some line of enquiry on their own, rather than reporting the activities of other investigative agencies. This form of journalism is typically driven both by some specific instance of wrongdoing or scandal in public life and also by a general sense that it is the duty of the media to shed light on darker corners of society (Ettema and Glasser, 1998).

In order to better reflect the different degrees of engagement chosen by journalists, we need a more complex view of the structure of journalistic role conceptions, rather than the simple dichotomy mentioned above (neutrality versus engagement). Weaver and Wilhoit (1986) indicated three main alternative positions for a journalist to adopt, although they are not completely exclusive. First comes the task of informing and dissemination; second there is that of interpreting and investigating; and third there is an 'adversarial' role that covers the task of criticism and especially an attitude of distance or even suspicion towards government. However, this typology was based on the US situation and has only a partial application elsewhere. In particular it does not really take into account the perspective of journalists who work for public broadcasting authorities, as they do in many European countries, nor does it represent the position of the partisan press, in which both the organisation and the public expect journalism to take on a clear political colour.

These particular cross-cultural differences were revealed in comparative research in the US, Germany, the UK, Italy and Sweden (Patterson, 2005). Research from former communist countries, including Russia, adds further complexity, especially where the journalistic profession is composed of different generations, with different experiences of professional education and socialisation, as well as different operating environments and conditions (Pasti, 2005). There is an accumulation of evidence relating to Russian journalism that indicates a strong residue of former theories of journalism under socialism, plus a reluctance to play an unconstructive role in difficult national circumstances, plus a realistic reflection of existing political and economic conditions of all forms of journalism. In Russia and elsewhere, the attitude of journalists also reflects a state of public opinion that places a higher value on maintaining social harmony and peace than absolute observance of freedom of the press (BBC, 2007).

We are left in no doubt that conceptions of the role of journalist, globally, are both pluralistic and also reflective of the surrounding political culture and the stage of development of other institutions. There are also different 'news cultures' in different societies as a result of complex historical factors, that are not fully explained by objective influences.

Demand versus supply of news

The 'high professional' model of journalism briefly sketched was the version that found most favour with political and cultural elites, but it never achieved wide success in the (mass) market place, not surprisingly. The theory of social responsibility and numerous theorists of democracy have made a convincing case for the needs of citizens for an extensive supply of relevant and reliable information. Many efforts were made to provide for these needs, often by way of radio and television services following some requirements of 'social responsibility' and many journalists, aspiring to a central ideal of the profession. Many newspapers accepted a responsibility to go beyond what large audiences often seemed to want, even if one sector of the market usually chose to exploit popular taste for sensation, scandal, celebrity and excitement. At some point this division was unbridgeable. The role of 'populist disseminator' referred to above reflects the compromise position of most news media: they aimed at providing much reliable and relevant information, but within the boundaries of what would be of interest to their audience, and therefore, attended to.

Although journalists often claim to have a 'feel' for what will interest an audience and are guided by this, a great deal of audience research has been carried out into the news interests of the public. To no great surprise, this confirms that the typical news audience most of the time is not primarily interested in the political and economic events that make most headlines, especially when they relate to foreign news. News interests go primarily to what is close to hand, familiar, immediately relevant and especially to news content that is personalised, tells a story and has some 'human interest' value. Weightier and 'serious' news is not disregarded, but for most people can be confined to brief summaries and updates of the kind that are now a feature of all kinds of media in continuous use.

Debates about the adequacy of news supply and the source of failures to inform on a widescale are far from resolved. There are several ways in which they can be framed, for instance, in terms of the failings of 'market journalism' not only in terms of adequate quality and amount, but also corrupting popular taste by unbridled 'sensationalism'; or by pointing to social structure as an almost insurmountable cause of 'knowledge gaps' in society; possibly by a belief in the innately 'fallen state' of the popular masses – an old idea that may not be dead. In recent times, the debate has taken a new form by questioning the necessity of continuous and extensive knowledge of all sorts of 'serious' matters. As long as the news media keep watch, all will be well. This is the view of journalism as a 'fire alarm' that does not need to ring all the time (see below, Chapter 5, The monitorial role and democracy). The debate cannot be settled in any simple way but there is little doubt from evidence that different societies and media systems have achieved quite varied results in the levels of public information that democracy calls for.

Changing goals and types of journalism

It is increasingly unrealistic to treat the news media as a single institution or to speak of journalism as one distinct occupation. Diversification of news media and competition between them has intensified, both in respect of media types and between different channels and titles. Several different dynamics are at work. On the one hand, there are competitive pressures to make news and information more digestible and entertaining for an even wider audience. On the other hand, there is an impetus towards providing news for specialist and high value markets. Moreover, the internet is encouraging new forms of journalism, with contours not yet clear, but often rejecting formal organisation and with it any claim to professional status according to the traditional model. The consequences are very mixed, with competing goals and unclear prescriptions for quality and professionalism. However, it looks as if the direction of change favours divergent purposes. There is both more scope for localism and particularism as well as globalism; there is more acceptance of 'amateurs' under the name of 'citizen journalists'; the mode of neutral objectivity is still dominant, but alternative versions are gaining ground; the general purpose print newspaper has to contend with internet-based publications on all imaginable topics.

The many variants that have emerged can no longer be clearly distinguished by reference to the three traditional models of journalism suggested by Schudson (1998) under the labels 'advocacy', 'market' and 'trustee' (see above, Chapter 2), although the ideas are still valid. These stand, respectively, for: a press whose primary aim is to promote a cause or party, usually financed by the subscriptions of the chosen audience/public; a profit-driven press, that is self-financing; a press with public interest goals that may be financed by public funds, the audience or a non-profit foundation.

This classification, based on latter twentieth-century traditional media structures gives primacy to methods of finance and general editorial purpose as determining factors on journalism and the press. In doing so, it neglects other factors such as the new types of audience market, a greater variety of sources of income, changing forms of organisation of production and distribution, new technology of production and distribution and the changing news habits of audiences. No new typology can be offered, but journalism as an occupation is likely to change a good deal, leading in turn to revised audience expectations about performance.

There remains a great deal of uncertainty about where the application of new technologies will lead. The term 'convergence' highlights one set of consequences that became apparent at an early stage. The steady digitisation of all content breached long-standing boundaries between media based on type of communication channel (audio, audio-visual, print, etc.) and, in doing so, between established journalistic specialisms and their typical skills. These new channels can all deliver the same news content – the same journalistic product. The introduction of new channels – online, mobile telephony and others – has extended the choice of 'delivery platforms' and multiplied formats. However, the model of a centre–peripheral flow from a central pool of content, organised by one media firm, does not have to change fundamentally (Quandt and Singer, 2009). On the other hand, there is also a 'convergence' made possible by the interactive potential of online media, with a reduced separation between journalists and audiences and a mixing of sources, sometimes including the audience itself, plus many non-institutionalised sources.

If not a profession, at least a 'public occupation'?

Even leaving aside the changes mentioned, it does not help either to classify the journalism occupation as a profession, or to deny it this status. What is evident is that it belongs to a special category of occupation with functions that meet a variety of public needs (collective and individual). These relevant tasks are mainly carried out transparently and are open to public scrutiny and valuation. In the circumstances, it is appropriate to describe journalism as a 'public occupation'. It provides essential public benefits and frequently has some capacity to influence events. Consequently, it accepts a need to be publicly accountable for what it does, with a strong preference for self-regulation. It is more than a trade or craft and, even if not a profession in the classic sense, the work of journalists has been extensively 'professionalised'. It increasingly requires higher education and training; it aspires to certain standards of quality in respect of its product and its manner of operating; and, in its developed form as a channel of public communication, it does not belong to the realm of amateurs.

This assessment needs only to be qualified with respect to the diverse forms taken by journalism. It applies less and less as one moves away from the 'mainstream', institutional case. It might not apply to many examples of partisan media. It would be irrelevant to a dissident, underground or truly alternative form of journalism operating beyond the boundaries of the media market (and not always fully public in the senses mentioned). It may also be irrelevant to emerging forms of citizen journalism or personalised news-casting. In between are many different forms that make a claim of some kind to the label of 'journalism'. There is, however, evidence that the growth in itself of the weblog, made possible by the internet, does not necessarily challenge traditional journalism. It is quite strongly influenced in the form it takes by a wish to adopt traditional norms and practices (Singer, 2007). This suggests, in turn, that the original, long-standing concept of the occupation is not made obsolete by technology, but has other enduring supports.

Conclusion

In the landscape of journalism in the media of (mainly) western, developed democratic national systems and a more or less free press, it is still possible to identify something like a dominant model of professionalised journalism (in terms of skills and standards). The framework of analysis described and applied in this chapter still draws on a view of the occupation as having a primary location within a larger 'press institution' providing a number of services to individual citizens and other social institutions. The norms, standards and public expectations that apply to journalism are still largely shaped by this 'place' in the general scheme of things. It is a view that seems to invite a comparison with the characteristics of other established professions. This does not take us very far and may miss the direction of change. One version of ongoing changes, for instance, emphasises a process of 'de-professionalisation', certainly the rise of variants of journalism that do not seek the comparison and have alternative goals and possibilities. Nevertheless, it is easier to understand and track the significant changes if we take the status quo as a point of comparison. It does not have to be taken as an ideal standard for assessment and a new balance can be struck in what is thought desirable and useful, from a greater diversity of perspectives.

Further reading

Benson, R.D. and Neveu, E. (eds) (2005). *Bourdieu and the Journalistic Field*. Malden MA: Polity Press.

Hanitzsch, H. (2007). 'Deconstructing journalism culture: towards a universal theory', *Communication Theory*, 17: 367–85.

Janowitz, M. (1975) 'Professional models in journalism: the gatekeeper and advocate', *Journalism Quarterly*, 52, 4: 618–26.

Patterson, T.E. (2005). 'Political roles of the journalist', in D. Graber, D. McQuail and P. Norris (eds), *The Politics of News: News of Politics*, 2nd edition. Washington: CQ Press, pp. 23–39.

Singer, J.B. (2007). 'Contested autonomy: professional and popular claims on journalism norms', *Journalism Studies*, 8: 79–95.
Waisbord, S. (2000). *Watchdog Journalism in South America.* New York: Columbia.
Weaver, D. (ed.) (1999). *The Global Journalist.* New York: Hampton Press.

Online readings

Go to www.sagepub.co.uk/mcquailjournalism for free access to the online readings.

Brodasson, T. (1994). 'The sacred side of professional journalism', *European Journal of Communication*, 9, 3: 227–48.
Deuze, M. (2005). 'What is journalism? Professional ideals and ideology of journalists reconsidered', *Journalism,* 6: 442–64.
Fengler, S. and Russ-Mohl, S. (2008). 'Journalism and the information-attention markets', *Journalism,* 9, 6: 667–90.
Hanitzsch, H. et al. (2011). 'Populist disseminator, detached watchdog, critical change agent: professional milieus, the journalistic field and autonomy in 18 countries', *International Communication Gazette*, 73, 6: 477–94.
Laetila, T. (1995). 'Journalistic codes of ethics in Europe', *European Journal of Communication*, 10, 4: 527–46.
Marliére, P. (1998). 'Rules of the journalistic field', *European Journal of Communication,* 13, 2: 219–34.
McManus, J.H. (1992). 'What kind of commodity is news?' , *Communication Research,* 19, 6: 767–85.

5 The Central Role of Monitor and Messenger

Introduction

Early thinking about the media and society pointed to three main functions of communication for the social system, under the headings: 'surveillance of the environment', 'correlation of parts' and 'social and cultural continuity'. All three are relevant for journalism, although the first most directly – this refers to the provision of information needed for all essential activities of society. The second refers to the promotion of social cohesion, also necessary for a complex society and the third to the transmission of values, culture and identity across generations. This way of thinking provides a basis for a more specific version of the informative role of the press. In particular, there is need in a democracy for: some commentary on and interpretation of 'facts' of public relevance; a forum for the public expression of diverse views; a two-way channel between citizens and government; a critical or watchdog stance to hold governments to account to the people. These points have often been elaborated in the tradition of press social theory (e.g. Lichtenberg, 1991; Nerone, 1995; Siebert et al., 1956). The following questions arise.

Functions and roles of the press in society

- What are the main roles that have been identified?
- How are they best formulated?

The monitorial role

- Why single this out above others?
- What range of differences of practice is covered?
- What tensions are inherent in carrying out this role?

Objective news journalism as the central practice

- What is meant by this?
- Why is it so much preferred?
- What are its limitations?
- How does it relate to political power?

Mediatisation

- What is its nature and causes?
- What are its effects?
- How far is it compatible with the 'ideal' of objective journalism and other press roles?

The main roles or functions of the press

A recent approach to this topic (Christians et al., 2009) has proposed a basic structure of normative roles for the (news) media, as follows:

- *A monitorial role,* involving both collecting and publishing relevant information about current events and circumstances, and drawing on sources of all kinds, ranging from governments to private individuals. The role is open-ended in respect of purpose, guided only by potential interest and utility. This largely corresponds to the idea of 'surveillance'.
- *A facilitative role*, referring more specifically to the provision of information (and means of informing) that services many social processes and social institutions, especially in the field of politics, but also in relation to the economy, law, education, and other things.
- *A radical role* focusing on the warning, watchdog, and critical aspects of news reporting that are a necessary feature of open and democratic societies.
- *A collaborative role* describing a reverse relationship that may develop between the press and sources of authority (and information) in society. This applies especially in conditions of emergency or threat to the state, for instance, in time of public disorder, war or insurgency. We are reminded that journalism does not operate in a social vacuum, but in relation to other social actors in a wider context.

These four roles are overlapping as well as complementary, although there is an obvious tension between critical and collaborative purposes. Even so, both are consistent with the condition of press freedom.

The monitor and messenger role characterised

This is essentially an elaboration of the notion of surveillance mentioned above. The term 'surveillance' refers to the process of monitoring a wider environment in order to discover and report relevant information about current events, personalities, conditions, trends, risks and dangers. It conjures an image of a watching post, a look-out tower, or the 'crow's nest' of a ship, which gives a longer and wider view and early warning of developments at the horizon, whether natural or human. It not only implies 'looking out', but doing so in a systematic way, guided by criteria of relevance to a particular public and of reliability of the resulting reports. In its more general use, the term surveillance now includes the idea of reporting back to authorities or interested parties and also intelligence-gathering and keeping watch for purposes of covert control (as in the expression 'under police surveillance' or in contemporary references to the 'surveillance society').

Because of this somewhat sinister connotation (of espionage, control and invasion of privacy), the term is no longer really very suitable to describe the work of journalism. For the most part, the information-gathering activities involved have an open character and the results of surveillance are intended primarily to benefit the receiver of information and the wider public. Even so, journalism does also furnish governments with useful 'intelligence' about current conditions and popular opinion.

Despite the diversity of types of press and journalism, the first of these four roles seems best to represent the main tasks and aspirations of journalism. It is the one necessary condition for achieving other purposes. As we have seen (in Chapter 4), much research, world-wide, into the way journalists view their own roles consistently highlights a priority to the task of providing information quickly and reliably. Research findings in the United States and many other countries (e.g. Hanitzsch et al., 2011; Preston, 2009; Weaver and Wilhoit, 1986; Weaver, 1999, 2012) have given priority to this general journalistic purpose, although the way in which the role is interpreted varies greatly according to national context. A cross-national study of news journalistic milieus in 18 countries world-wide concluded that the role of 'populist disseminator' has the broadest appeal in quite disparate settings (Hanitzsch et al., 2011). It combines qualities of 'detachment, non-involvement, providing political information, as well as adherence to universal ethical principles', with elements of wide audience appeal. However, it takes second place in the USA and Western Europe to the role of 'detached watchdog' with which it generally has a negative correlation. It is also displaced by the role of 'critical change agent' in more developing society settings. It looks as if two quite different versions of objective journalism are being combined under the general heading of 'informing' the society.

The informational, or monitorial, role largely fits within a model of *mediation* in which news media are seen to 'intervene' between events and sources on the one hand and individual members of the public on the other. They act both as agents of communication for many sources and also as representatives of the public in the search for information. According to this, essentially liberal, model, news is selected from available sources by an intervening agency (the media) in line with the anticipated informational needs of an audience. Such intervening agencies extend to providing primary sources with 'feedback' about public interests and reactions, which is also a guide in future news selection. Although the public is supposed to be the primary beneficiary, considerations of ease and cost of supply give some advantage to news sources. The most basic meaning of the term 'monitorial' as used here is that of an organised 'scanning' of the real world of people, conditions and events. A subsidiary meaning is of evaluation and interpretation, guided by criteria of relevance, significance and reigning norms and values. This element (of planned discrimination) differentiates monitoring from the now familiar model of the omnivorous electronic 'search engine' that assembles information more or less blindly into a searchable database. It is also often missing from online news summaries that many internet portals now provide.

In respect of its contribution to the democratic political process, the underlying normative basis for the informational role is, on the one hand, the notion of the 'monitorial citizen' (Schudson, 1998) – one who (in an ideal conception) actively seeks information in order to participate in this process – and, on the other, the idea of a 'Fourth Estate' (see Chapter 2). The (self-appointed) task of the latter is to hold government and other power holders to account to the public for their actions and omissions.

Nevertheless, there are several acceptable variants and styles (e.g. about forms of presentation, selection of topics, degree of neutrality) as well as gaps in the relevant corpus of professional ethics. There are also failures and weaknesses that arise from the fact that journalists are not independent of their masters – the owners and managers of the press, who have other goals besides those of the journalist. Nor is the press independent of the power of those it seeks to monitor, who are in many cases also the sources of information with their own interests to promote.

The standards (as described in Chapter 2) proposed by social responsibility theory in various public inquiries, and also in the statements of purpose formulated to define the informational tasks of public broadcasting, usually go well beyond what is required by journalistic ethics. The American Commission on Freedom of the Press (1947) attributed specific social responsibilities to the press. The Commission spoke of several duties incumbent on a press in a democratic society and occupying a dominant and somewhat privileged social position. These duties included the provision of: a full and reliable account of daily events, separating fact from comment; a forum for the exchange of comment and criticism; and a representative picture of the society. The unwritten contract that gave the press its right to publish in the public interest (and protected it even beyond the freedom of an ordinary citizen) called for some services in return. Broadcasting, from its earliest days, primarily because of its quasi-monopoly position, largely ruled out the partisanship and the expression of editorial opinion that was open to newspapers (see Appendix §4). This mode of reporting entered into the culture of broadcasting and is still widely followed if not required.

The question as to whether this role represents a universal basis of principle for the practice of journalism must be answered in the negative, not only because of differences in the way it is carried out, but also because it is only one of several roles relevant to the social tasks of journalism. Nevertheless, the globalisation of news and the market for news seems to have led to a great similarity in the content of news and in the daily news agendas of countries around the world (Shoemaker and Cohen, 2006). Deuze (2007) comments also on the remarkable similarities of the actual newsrooms, in appearance and in organisation, world-wide. But national differences are always there and they still count for a great deal, especially at times of global crisis and tension.

Objectivity as a guiding principle

Performance of the 'monitorial' role is strongly associated with the principle of objectivity (see Chapter 3). Objective news, as widely understood, should meet the criteria listed in Box 5.1.

Box 5.1 Criteria of news objectivity

- Relevance
- Accuracy
- Reliability (trustworthy sources)
- Factuality (as style and form)
- Separation of fact from opinion and interpretation
- Balance and impartiality as between 'sides' in any dispute
- Neutrality in wording and presentation.

Objectivity is a particular form of media *practice* and embodies a neutral attitude to the task of collecting, processing and disseminating information. It presumes a lack of ulterior motive or concealed service to a third party. This means being rational, logical, undistorted by emotion or manipulative intention and dedicated only to uncovering and disseminating demonstrable truth. It invites the trust of those who accept the sincere intention of being truly objective.

This version of reporting practice has become the dominant ideal standard of quality within the belief system of journalism itself. It has a number of practical advantages both for journalists and sources of news as well as for objects of reporting. It has links with the principle of *freedom*, since independence is a necessary condition of detachment and truthfulness. Under some conditions (such as political oppression, crisis, war and police action), the ability to report at all can only be secured in return for a guarantee of formal objectivity. Although widely adopted as the standard for news, there is evidence of significant variations in the meanings attached to the term (and thus its requirements) both between national news cultures and (not surprisingly) between 'public' and private media (Patterson, 2005).

News media claiming to be objective have advantages as channels of communication to the public for agencies of state, advocates of various interests and commercial advertisers. They are likely to be perceived as more independent of their sources. News media can carry information from such sources without their own independence being compromised, while sources can still keep some control over their self-presentation. Because of the established conventions of objectivity, media channels can also separate their opinions from their factual reports and their editorial content from the advertising matter that they carry (which also generally suits advertisers).

In general, media audiences appear to understand and appreciate the principles of objectivity well enough, and it helps to increase credibility and trust in the information and opinions which the media offer and, therefore, the utility of information received. The media themselves find that objectivity gives their own news product a higher and wider market value, enabling the news 'product' to be marketed outside the immediate context for which it was originally produced. In the circumstances, it is not surprising that most news media set a lot of store by their claim to objectivity in its several meanings. Policies for broadcasting in many countries usually impose, by various means, a requirement of objectivity, on their public broadcasting systems, as a means towards securing a necessary degree of impartiality in contentious matters as well as independence from government (see UK example in Appendix §4).

Limitations to objectivity

Despite these important benefits, there are several major difficulties entailed in the practice of objectivity. It implies that a single uniquely true version of a particular reality is attainable and also that all perspectives on events are equally deserving of representation, even when other values and our common sense might tell us otherwise. Each of the component criteria of objectivity mentioned above presents difficulty. *Accuracy* is essentially a relative notion, depending on the availability of reliable records, witnesses and supporting evidence and not easy to determine in human affairs.

The criterion of *factuality* refers mainly to a form of reporting which deals in specific events and statements which can be checked against sources. This central idea is shaky, once one goes beyond the simple idea that a fact is a precise answer to a question about Who? What? When? and Where? In practice, 'dependable' sources often means officials, authorities and interested parties to events, plus certain accepted forms of record. The question concerning the 'Why?' of events can scarcely be answered at all by this route, since true causes are rarely simple or observable. A good deal of potentially relevant information cannot be reduced to the form of facts, or is distorted in the attempt to do so.

Relevance requires that selection take place according to clear and coherent principles of what is significant for the intended receiver and/or the society. In general, what affects most people most immediately and most strongly is likely to be considered most relevant. However, there is often a gap between what the public perceives as of interest and what experts think is significant. There is often a contradiction between what is fundamentally significant and what is interesting, novel or attention-catching (matters closer to the heart of the journalist). News selection is strongly influenced by attention to celebrities in all fields and differential attention to sensational, dramatic or negative events. The factors of 'novelty' and 'actuality' carry more weight than long-term significance as judged by experts. 'Scoops' and 'exclusive' reports are also more valued than depth or intrinsic importance.

Impartiality presumes that relevant perspectives on events can be recognised and treated with equal respect while the requirement of *balance* puts a barrier in the way of introducing any value judgement, even when dealing with matters of great apparent evil or great good. A permanent stance of *neutrality* is not natural, convincing or necessarily helpful for understanding, leaving aside the need to engage the interest and attention of an audience. In societies, or conditions where freedom is limited, where there are sharp internal conflicts or threats to social order, it may simply not be possible to practise objective journalism as envisaged in the 'dominant model'.

Largely because of these and related objections and difficulties, critical communication theory has generally rejected the very notion of objectivity as neither attainable nor even especially desirable. This critique has been applied to the monitorial role as typically practised by 'mainstream' news media. The provision of news information is perceived to reinforce, by way of reproduction, the dominant (and basically ideological), interpretation of the world circulated by power-holders and elites. The neutrality enjoined on the news protects the essentials of the established social order from fundamental questioning. Deliberate propaganda does in fact often make use of rules of objectivity so as to obscure true purpose and increase credibility (Norstedt et al., 2000).

Not all critics of media condemn the whole enterprise of objective journalism, calling instead for more awareness of its limitations, more moves to secure more freedom for journalism and greater diversity of news channels and perspectives. To abandon objectivity would also be to abandon the presumption that we can have any certain knowledge of the world. As Lichtenberg (1991:230) observed 'insofar as we seek to understand the world we cannot get along without assuming both the possibility and value of objectivity'.

Degrees of purpose and activity in objective news journalism

The monitorial role can involve a number of distinct journalistic tasks that are all in some way informed by the principle of objectivity but not equally or necessarily open to objection on the grounds that have just been outlined. The main components in journalistic practice are summarised below in a sequence that implies a *continuum of initiative and activity* according to which they can be ranked in ascending order of activity, as shown in Figure 5.1. As recorded in the previous chapter, there are recurring and often deep differences in the interpretation of the role of journalism and they often relate to the question of activity and engagement. This figure probably stretches to its maximum the range of different views that might just be encountered in journalism that is not openly partisan or 'alternative', or subversive in purpose.

LEAST ACTIVE

1 **Receiving and transmitting notices of events (a transmission function only)**
- Keeping and publishing an agenda of forthcoming public events, plus keeping a record.
- Receiving and screening notices and messages intended for further public dissemination.
- Maintaining a reportorial presence at the main public *fora* (parliaments, assemblies, law courts, press conferences, public demonstrations, etc.) where news events are announced, set in motion or decided.

2 **Selectively observing, reporting, publishing**
- Signalling to the public a certain view of what are the most significant current events, problems and issues.
- Publishing reports of significant current events and reproducing key factual data on a continuous basis (ranging from social and economic facts to sports results).
- Providing a platform for the expression of opinion by participants in the public sphere.

3 **Giving warnings and advice**
- Selective provision of warnings of risks, threats and dangers facing the public on a wide range of issues.
- Providing analysis and interpretation of events and opinions.

4 **Participating in public affairs**
- Acting as a 'Fourth Estate' in political matters, by mediating the communication links between government and citizens, and providing a means for holding government accountable at the bar of public opinion.
- Adopting an active role as source and channel in public sphere activities.

5 **Actively investigating, exposing and advocating**
- Adopting an active stance of watchdog of the public interest, by 'barking' when some major social actor is perceived to be acting against the public interest, especially in a covert way.
- Initiating and pursuing inquiries on self-chosen topics, when information obtained suggests major deviance from the moral or social order.
- Campaigning by information and persuasion for a chosen cause.

MOST ACTIVE

FIGURE 5.1 Main tasks of the press in ascending degree of activity

The entries in Figure 5.1 range from a purely observational and transmission role, to a stance of readiness to take pre-emptive warning action, and finally to active investigation and actual pursuit of alleged public wrong-doing or failings. All these activities, including partisan and committed journalism, can just about be carried out within the flexible boundaries of the 'monitorial/informational/role', but beyond a certain point, the informational role gives way to the critical and dialectical mode, which is essentially different.

The continuum is reflected in conventional styles of radio or television documentary reportage. For instance, there is a clear difference between: the descriptive mode, where the audience is a spectator guided by a reporter; the mode of analysis and interpretation of what is being observed; the mode in which the journalist plays the part of detective, looking for causes and agents of social and economic problems especially; and lastly, there is a mode in which judgements are made and wrong-doing exposed (investigative journalism). Usually, such variations are distributed across different publications and formats, designed for different kinds of audience and with other differences of topic and time-scale of events.

Tensions internal to the monitorial role

The main division is that between neutral reporting and critical or investigative reporting. This was first described as a choice between the 'gatekeeper' and the 'advocacy' model (see Chapter 4). In the former case, news media have no policy or criteria for selection of objects for attention, but are guided by customary 'news factors' or values. These relate mainly to: the scale of events and of potential effects; their immediacy and dramatic quality; their established familiarity as the 'stuff of news'; the prominence of the persons involved; the definitions of what is significant deployed by actors and agencies with power and legitimacy. On the other hand, Ettema and Glasser (1998) speak of journalists as acting as 'custodians of the public conscience'. However, they do not usually have a mandate for this task and there is a paradox in journalists claiming to be able to do this without also applying their own personal moral sense, which seems inconsistent with principles of objectivity. However, investigative journalists claim to be applying *news* judgements rather than value judgements when they identify victims and wrong-doing, and they ostensibly pursue the culprits on behalf of victims and society at large.

There are reasons aside from the claims of conscience for finding strict objectivity too restrictive. Probably even more common is an aspiration to participate and engage in public life, in accordance with an often proclaimed role of the press as a whole. This does not necessarily involve advocacy of a particular view or value. The 'Fourth Estate' theory of the press (see Chapter 2) presumes, for instance, that political journalists will consciously play an active role in facilitating the political process, but without necessarily having any personal commitment.

The problem of separating facts from values lies at the heart of the critique of objectivity and threatens to undermine the integrity of the media monitorial role. When values and opinions guide the selection of facts for attention, even when the choice is based on some clearly expressed public concern and has some demonstrable basis in fact, the basic understanding of the role as described above is violated at least to some degree. There is no general solution to this dilemma, but it looks as if the informational role can only extend as far as truly active investigation where there is a high degree of value consensus on the matter at issue and either some major violation of the moral order, or some compelling source of danger for the society as a whole. Beyond this point or without these conditions, journalism shades into advocacy or even propaganda. It does seem that objective neutrality is a *means* to an end of uncovering truth and not an absolute end in itself. It cannot be relied on to determine the ends for which information is pursued and made public. These require the exercise of value judgements.

The 'dilemma' outlined need not be too troubling most of the time for journalists, since it is often taken care of by the differentiation within and between news channels and sources. This was clear enough in the traditional print newspaper where news is separated spatially from editorial opinion, columnists, letters, etc., or where publications aligned themselves openly according to political or other value positions. These traditional solutions are less easy to adopt in broadcast and online media, where there is no longer any clear rule-book. Perhaps more immediately and fundamentally they are challenged by the growth of media monopolies, the decline of news diversity, and the ostensible 'depoliticisation' of news discourse, for commercial reasons. Our attention is thus drawn before long to issues of media structure.

The monitorial role and state power

Theory about press and society often refers back to the comment of F.R. Siebert in *Four Theories of the Press* to the effect that 'the press always takes on the form of the social and political structures within which it operates' (Siebert et al., 1956:1). This applies especially to relations with the formal authority structures of society. The question at issue here is how journalism itself deals with the conflict that is always latent in relations with authorities and powerful sources. One obvious explanation for the widespread attachment to the monitor role is that it provides a viable way for journalists to avoid serious trouble from authorities, even in countries where freedom of the press is not really tolerated. While the state can afford to be relaxed about what it regards as a neutral flow of information, at a certain point in the 'continuum of activity' described above, less tolerance will be shown, especially where authoritarian tendencies are alive and well. As a result, the press may decide that their role does not oblige, or maybe not even legitimate them to cross some limit of disclosure or criticism. Experience of this as a problem varies a great deal, but it arises in some fairly predictable circumstances and is never completely absent.

There are different ways of accommodating to the situation of power imbalance between press and state, depending on the nature of the regime and degree of freedom available. The theory of 'indexation' outlined by Bennett (1990), applies in the US, but often covers the situation elsewhere in one form or another, as long as norms of democracy and journalistic neutrality are well established. The essence of it is that the press recognises a range of voices in the public arena as having a legitimate claim as sources of information and opinion and as objects of reporting. The government itself and related agencies figure prominently in the recognised spectrum of voices and sources as well as actors in events. Recognition is based pragmatically on the existing balance of power in society, the distribution of voting and public opinion, the pattern of events and flow of communications in the society. The news media themselves play a major role in constructing the base from which to 'read off' an appropriate indexation.

This conforms to the norm of neutral (and useful) monitoring. It is reasonably pluralistic as a practice, but has some limitations, especially the power it gives to the press to decide for itself whom to give access to, and it has a self-fulfilling tendency to exclude marginal voices, who continue to be excluded from the political mainstream. The notional 'middle way' in a judgement of neutrality tends to lie in the direction of established institutions and power structures. The self-confessed failure of some leading US newspapers to adequately report the stages leading up to the invasion of Iraq in 2003 have been partly attributed to an inbuilt bias that favoured official sources (or the 'loyal opposition' – Bennett et al., 2007). Even if 'indexation' is accepted as a reasonable way to deal with sensitive problems of selection, it has the drawback of legitimating the claim by governments and powerful elites to relatively greater access to the news media on their own terms. In the particular case of the United States, where the theory originates, politics is largely monopolised by only two large (centrist) political parties, thus potentially marginalising a wide spectrum of alternative views.

The alternatives to 'indexation' are mixed and depend also on social and political circumstances. The options range from total conformity to information policies of authorities, with varied motivations, including patriotism and service to a 'public interest' at one end and rejection of all constraint at the other. This last is hardly possible for established news media. Another alternative lies in the rejection of the overriding claims of objectivity and the practice of a different kind of pluralistic journalism, following political or ideological grounds. This was institutionalised in some countries in the past but is not usually regarded with much favour by today's profession of journalism. In some libertarian concepts of press purpose, a consistently adversarial stance to authority may be preferred and tolerated for some channels, but hardly for a whole news sector. The larger question of the relation between the news media and the political system is dealt with in the following chapter.

Box 5.2 The monitorial role: options in response to state pressure

- Indexing attention and access by degree of current visibility and significance of sources in the public arena
- Abstention from active 'gate-keeping', with consensus as the main value
- Cooperation with information policy of authorities, ostensibly for the public good
- Active and transparent politicisation of access and attention-giving
- 'Clientilism' and symbiosis in relations with power sources
- Adversarial and critical stance across the board.

The monitorial role and democracy

In its fullest expression, the monitorial role appears well-suited to the needs of a democratic political system, provided the conditions of independence of 'monitors' from power holders are met and there is freedom to express unwelcome ideas and transmit uncomfortable information.

Democracy implies a view of society as one in which there are many competing voices and interests, although news media do not have to take sides or to advance a vested interest of their own. Society is also presumed to be fundamentally united, sharing the same basic values and a common interest in survival and prosperity. Theories of pluralistic democracy of the kind formulated during the twentieth century (especially in the United States) are also based on this view, even if some of its assumptions may be illusory, especially the notion of a basic shared interest between social classes. The media monitorial role is most compatible with a liberal-individualistic view of society, in which there are self-righting forces at work to solve problems and relieve tensions, given sufficient freedom of information and action. This more optimistic presumption is open to question and the more it is questioned, the less adequate the media monitorial role will seem on its own, except perhaps in its most active variants.

The availability of the 'watchdog' role is usually cited as a principal benefit of the liberal model of media freedom, on the assumption that the main enemy of freedom and democracy is likely to be the state or government, as it was in the beginning. However, under modern mass media conditions, direct power over news media is mainly exercised by private corporations, even if they lack legal means to silence journalists directly. They do have economic interests that might be harmed by political or other change and there are plenty of examples of indirect steering of news content and sometimes of transparent intervention to subvert democracy. Latin America has provided the most egregious examples in recent times (Waisbord, 2000).

According to contemporary theory of the public sphere, the monitorial role of the press is a dual one. First it serves to mark the boundaries of the public space by signalling the actors, issues and events that lie within these boundaries and on which public opinion forms and collective decisions are taken. The press is continually constructing and re-affirming the shape and contents of a public sphere. What is not noticed or not published is essentially invisible and cannot easily be made the stuff of politics or even opinion and debate. The second aspect of the public information role is the detailed work of filling in the foreground and background of the social world as sketched and identifying the figures within it. The boundary between what is private and what is public has to be maintained and policed. The press does this job by way of routine news without specifically choosing the task.

Liberal democracy presupposes that citizens as voters only need to know enough to make informed and rational choices and decisions (according to their own self-interest) when called upon, especially at periodic elections. The press has to be a major source of such information, since no other institution is able to offer enough ostensibly disinterested knowledge on such a scale and in so timely a manner. Nevertheless, this model of journalism largely ignores the issue of values, beliefs and emotions that cannot be excluded from journalism. Objectivity is not enough.

It has been argued (e.g. by Zaller, 2003) that, for healthy democracy, news only has to serve a 'burglar-alarm' function and does not always need to meet the criteria of news set by social responsibility theory, what he terms the 'full news standard'. In his view, news should be *feasible* (to cover and consume) as well as intrinsically useful. It should reach enough people in a form that is likely to be noticed and understood. According to the burglar (or fire) alarm standard, the essential value of news in a democracy is to enable a concerned citizen to maintain a routine vigilance in respect of emerging political issues and problems, without paying continuous attention or needing deep knowledge. On occasions, the citizen needs to know more and be more active, but not all citizens and not continuously.

This view is consistent with the notion of the 'monitorial citizen' mentioned earlier, although in a weak form. It is also in line with principles of liberal pluralism and economic theory of democracy that sees the consumption of political information as guided by the personal need of the individual and the cost in time or money he or she is prepared to pay. There is also empirical evidence from the long tradition of news learning research that shows that the general news public appears to learn rather little from even extensive and good quality news, when it is routinely received by way of television or other mass media (e.g. Robinson and Levy, 1986). At the same time, Graber (2003) has made a strong empirical case for the view that the general public can understand and learn the essentials on important matters without needing a great volume of information. Most news consumers most of the time would seem to be both sufficiently served as citizens by a minimal, but well-chosen and presented news provision. Providing such an effective service can be considered in itself a challenging professional task.

This line of argument has been challenged on the ground that it implicitly endorses current media trends of 'soft news' – sound-bite news as well as personalisation, sensationalism and scandal – which are said to divert citizens from participation in politics and to devalue the currency of news. In particular, Bennett (2003) points to the fact that if the news is indeed supposed to be a burglar alarm then it is one that often sounds false alarms or fails to sound an alarm when there is a real problem. He also notes that the two standards of news are not, and should not be, alternatives. In practice, they do tend to be in tension in newsrooms and the burglar alarm tends to be preferred to the full news standard, for reasons of journalism culture as well as market thinking. Recent cross-country comparisons (e.g. Curran et al., 2009) of average levels of public information suggest that quite large differences exist, especially between the US and some European countries. It is plausible to suppose that one main cause is the high standard of news quantity and quality that public broadcasters are obliged (and choose) to attain, coupled with continuing high levels of audience ratings received. The 'full standard' of news can be attained and it has potential benefits well beyond that of the 'burglar alarm' that seems more characteristic of a fully commercialised system of provision.

Despite the apparent affinity between democracy and a neutral and objective system of public information, there is no necessary conflict between other press roles and democratic politics, and they may even be required in order to fill some of the needs that monitorial journalism neglects. These relate in particular to matters of value, belief and principle. Having the facts relating to social and political issues is not enough without interpretation, advocacy and impulse to citizen action. The formation and expression of public opinion requires encouragement, engagement and commitment by some journalists at least. The existence of competing political parties and ideologies is part of the reality of society that should not be ignored. This is not necessarily an alternative form of journalism but an extension – an application of public knowledge to problems of the moment. In the past this was often taken care of by an openly partisan press. It is now more likely to occur as a result of the work of editors and journalists working via media channels that have no formal commitment to one party or set of beliefs. Whether or not taken care of, a dynamic, changing society needs more than access to 'factual' accounts of what happens to be going on.

A departure from strict neutrality also often occurs on a wide scale in respect of patriotism and national self-interest. The evidence from cross-national comparisons of news content consistently shows up strong attachments to national interests. Within countries, sectional, class and regional loyalties also shape reporting in predictable ways. There is often consensus on 'foreign' news topics, even when much conflict exists on domestic issues. This is a reminder that news and public information generally has other social roles to perform, namely those relating to cohesion, identity and continuity.

Box 5.3 The monitorial role and democracy: main features

- Follows liberal-pluralist theory of democracy – shared needs of society, alternative solutions
- Marks out the boundaries of a public space
- Fills in this space in terms of actors, issues, events, etc.
- Serves, as a minimum, as a 'burglar alarm' to alert citizens to crisis and danger
- A 'full standard' of news is also possible and beneficial
- A monitorial role does not exclude other democratically essential roles – of watchdog, advocate, critic, opinion-formation, agent of both change and social cohesion, etc.

Sources of bias in the monitoring role

Communication research has exposed systematic tendencies for news reporting to deviate from the ideal requirements of the neutral informant role even when it is aspired to. Some of the limitations of objective news reporting have already been mentioned (see above). While journalism strives hard to achieve objectivity in respect of attitude to the task and the form of reports, decisions about what to monitor are more subjective and open to other influences. The world of potential news topics is simply too vast to escape systematic distortion of selection patterns, given the organised purposes of many original news sources and the limited needs and capacities of the news system. The main forms and sources of bias that can (and often do) emerge in the process of selection have been uncovered in the systematic study of content. The most typical of recurrent results can only be described in a few brief paragraphs as follows.

- Geographic and cultural (including linguistic) factors limit the range of attention of journalists (and their audiences), as does the technical and organisational capacity of any medium. The nearer to home, to existing reporting resources and to current concerns of the public, the more chance of coverage.
- The periphery of a given country is typically viewed from a metropolitan centre; similarly, more powerful nations receive much more attention than weaker, poorer and more peripheral states. The news gaze is inevitably ethnocentric.

- Other things being equal, news attention to objects, persons and events will be guided by factors of scale and status.
- What is believed to be of consuming interest to an audience (e.g. sport, popular culture, celebrities, war, etc.) will also attract most news attention.
- Other things being equal, more attention is paid to objects that seek publicity for themselves and less to those that wish to avoid it (somewhat contrary to the theory of the critical, watchdog role of accountability). The environment is simply not evenly or neutrally open to observation.
- Officials and authorities and other well organised and funded suppliers of 'news' have a large inbuilt advantage in gaining, or being given, access for their version of events.
- For factual information to make sense to non-experts it has to be placed in some context or frame of reference, or labelled in some way. This process of 'framing' inevitably opens the way to familiar stereotypes and less than neutral interpretation.
- A well-attested element of the dominant news culture, partly a result of its competitiveness, is the enormous regard for the 'scoop' that gives, relatively, much greater value to early and unique ownership of some information (the exclusive) than to its deeper significance. The monitorial role is not usually well-served by this.
- Competitive pressures can lead to an exaggeration and prolongation of certain very 'newsworthy' stories, especially where negative events are involved (crime, scandal, dangers, etc.). The process has been called 'media hype', by definition a departure from objectivity (Vasterman, 2005). This is related to 'pack journalism', where resources and attention are concentrated on a narrow range of the spectrum and often a uniform version of reality.
- Lastly, and far from least, is the impossibility of removing values and 'ideology' from factual accounts. One study of news values in foreign news concluded that ideology is 'the main source of deviation in news reporting from a more or less standardized base' (Westerstahl and Johansson, 1994). The ideologies vary, but the prominent ones are or have been: patriotism, nationalism, anti-communism, pro-freedom, and anti-Americanism.

There is more to be said on all these matters, but this is sufficient to indicate the many constraints within which the monitoring role is typically performed.

'Media logic' and 'mediatisation' effects on monitoring

Other limitations arise from the process of 'mediatisation': essentially the adaptation of information to the modes of presentation that are favoured by news media and have often become firmly embedded in the culture of journalism. Professional communicators, on behalf of their clients, also seek to adapt the message and image to media requirements. Although the latter often deviate from the ideal of objectivity, they are valued for their contribution to gaining and keeping public attention and to actually communicating effectively. We could also say that mediatisation is also favoured by the news public, since it refers to features that make news more accessible, interesting and even entertaining. Mediatisation is different from 'mediation', in that it refers not to the act of communication, but to changes of meaning and the likely effects that follow from mediation (Meyer, 2002; Schulz, 2004; Hjarvard, 2008). It may be described as follows: a process by which both the representation of social reality in news and advocacy is increasingly influenced by the principles of a so-called 'media logic'. This refers to a set of principles or 'rules', originating with the culture of the media that are believed to maximise public impact and appeal. The main elements include any or all of the following: visualisation, personalisation; dramatisation, popularisation, spectacularisation, narrativisation.

In short, image or appearance takes precedence over reality and presentation is not constrained by unwanted truths, a clear challenge to the standard of 'objectivity'. There is bound to be a tension at the heart of journalism between the bare factuality of the basic version of the news genre and the embellished narrative versions that often emerge. The attraction of the story-telling form in the writing of news is not new or hard to understand. The most interesting items of news in every sphere are likely to be those in which familiar components of the fictional story can be recognised: a cast of characters – some good, others villains or victims; a progression from start to denouement; an element of drama or surprise; some lessons or morals to be learnt, etc. This basic formula makes for easier exposition and greater motivation to pay attention. Problems only arise when it leads to unwitting distortion and invention that is less than 'objective'.

Central to media logic is the premium on action, surprise, excitement and emotional involvement, as well as on what can be captured or visualised in the most compelling way. The effects on the reporting of war provide a particularly clear warning of the consequences for truth, very vulnerable in any case. The mediatisation of war coverage encourages and protects the propaganda efforts of whoever has most control over access to the battle zone and to communication facilities (Kim, 2012). Pursuit of the monitorial vision gives way before the allure of privileged access to scenes of live action and first-hand accounts of events (McQuail, 2006). There is also a bias in media logic against length, words, complex, abstract or unfamiliar ideas, memory and explanation. Media logic in turn affects those who seek access to, or 'make', news, transferring the same kind of criteria for successful news communication to the sources and shapers of information for public consumption. There is a case to be made for the merits of 'media logic' as a way of securing audience attention and interest and in theory it need not interfere with other selection criteria.

The net effect on the news of the factors outlined risks transforming 'reality' into a new form (often called 'infotainment') that is not primarily designed to meet the informational needs of audience or society. Virtually all significant actors in the public sphere, especially those with most economic and political muscle, invest heavily in their efforts to influence the supply of information on which modern news media are heavily reliant. The mediatising process begins at this stage.

In the case of politics, mediatisation goes to the heart of the process of influencing voters. The personal qualities of candidates and leaders, especially their perceived 'charisma' and their media performance and appeal counts for more than more mundane qualities or the substance of policy debates. The choice and presentation of policies is affected and relations of cooperation tend to develop between politicians and media, subverting the goal of public accountability. Incumbent governments have the advantage of being able to make events happen and to reward the press with much prized scoops and disclosures. The trend towards personification in European politics has been remarked on, especially with reference to figures such as Berlusconi and Sarkozy (Campus, 2010). Demonstrations and manifestations of public action are encouraged and more likely to gain media attention than reasoned argument and other forms of publicity.

Box 5.4 Main effects of mediatisation

- Gives advantage to the sources with best media resources
- Encourages populism in appeal and sensationalism in form
- Promotes the personal in image and performance

(Continued)

(Continued)

- Media presence and presentation skills are more important than other qualities or beliefs
- Gives advantage to incumbents, who have more power to manage news
- Encourages the 'making' and 'manipulation', as well as the presentation of news 'events'
- Distorts the selection and objectivity of content.

Conclusion

As described, the media role of monitoring and informing in its more ideal form is now well established and even protected in many countries by constitutional and other legal provisions. The press often has certain customary or even legal privileges (e.g. in respect of criticism of public figures, protection of sources, access to sites of news events). However, even in well ordered and relatively open societies, there are barriers to fulfilling the role, aside from the limitations inherent in objectivity and in the culture of journalism. Some of these arise from the circumstances in which news collection and dissemination have to operate, but others have deeper roots in the structure of society, the structure of the media system and the needs of media firms as organisations competing in a highly competitive market.

In societies with a genuinely free press, the quality of performance of the monitoring role is inevitably vulnerable to numerous sources of failure. Media quality is determined by the general vitality of society, especially in relation to citizenship and civil society and the degree of freedom enjoyed. It also depends on journalists living up to the ideals of their profession. There is no special or certain remedy for apparent failures, although there are safeguards in the openness of a media system to new entrants and alternative services. In general, a media structure marked by diversity will make up for some of the limitations described.

There are strong 'natural' supports for the monitorial role both in the information needs of the public and society that are continuously and widely experienced and also in the traditions of the press itself. Many elements of the 'culture of journalism', criticised above, also have positive aspects. They may sometimes be deliberately manipulated but they also contribute to the ultimate independence of the press (if only by giving them some power of their own). The role of critic and watchdog may be more encouraged by media logic than it is by the logic of objective factual reporting.

The informational role is still at the heart of journalistic activity and it is what the profession (or craft) has learned to do best. It is unlikely to fail completely or to lack self-provided remedies, given the necessary conditions (especially freedom and diversity). On the balance of the evidence, we might conclude that, in one or other version, this role is universally recognised as a standard to be sought. This universality is reflected in the aspirations and opinions of journalists and often of the wider audience for news. It is confirmed by the apparent similarity of the news genre across widely differing political and media systems.

Further reading

Bennett, W.L. (1990). 'Towards a theory of press–state relations in the US', *Journal of Communication*, 40, 2: 103–25.

Bennett, W.L., Lawrence, R.G. and Livingston, S. (2007). *When the Press Fails*. Chicago: Chicago University Press.

Christians, C., Glasser, T., McQuail, D., Nordenstreng, K. and White, R. (2009). *Normative Theories of the Press,* Chapters 5 and 6. Champaign, IL: University of Illinois Press.

Deuze, M. (2007). *Media Work*. Cambridge: Polity Press.

Meyer, T. (2002). *Mediated Politics*. Cambridge: Polity Press.

Preston, P. (ed.) (2009). *Making the News: Journalism and News Cultures in Contemporary Europe*. London: Routledge.

Weaver, D. (2012). *The Global Journalist*. Creskill, NJ: Hampton Press (new edition).

Online readings

Go to www.sagepub.co.uk/mcquailjournalism for free access to the online readings.

Brants, K. (1998). 'Who's afraid of infotainment?', *European Journal of Communication,* 13, 3: 315–35.

Campus, D. (2010). 'Mediatization and personification of politicians in France and Italy: the case of Berlusconi and Sarkozy', *International Journal of Press/Politics,* 16, 1: 215–35.

McQuail, D. (2006). 'The mediatization of war', *International Communication Gazette*, 68, 2: 107–18.

Pasti, S. (2005). 'Two generations of Russian journalists', *European Journal of Communication*, 20, 1: 89–116.

Schulz, W. (2004). 'Reconstructing mediatization as an analytic concept', *European Journal of Communication*, 19, 1: 87–102.

Strömbäck, J. and Danilova, D.L. (2011). 'Mediatization and media interventionism', *International Journal of Press/Politics*, 16, 1: 30–49.

Westerstahl, J. and Johansson, F. (1994). 'Foreign news: values and ideologies', *European Journal of Communication*, 9, 1: 71–89.

Media Structure, Performance and the 'Power of the Press'

Introduction

The character of journalism and its relation to society have roots that go far deeper than the role choices of an occupational group and the factors discussed until this point. In brief, they are strongly influenced by conditions of the particular society in which they are found, most fundamentally by the social structure of the society that cannot easily be altered. These conditions help to shape the form taken by a media system, which in turn affects the circumstances of operation of media firms and organisations and ultimately the work of journalists themselves. In brief, the structure of society (itself an outcome of historic forces) influences the shape of a media system, which in turn governs the choices open to, and made by, journalists.

These different levels are interrelated in a hierarchical as well as sequential way, but relations are not determined. There is scope for variation and resistance, especially as a result of cultural differences or simply human choice. Moreover, conditions in society change and media systems adapt to changes in media technology. The political and ideological climate can also change, even quite dramatically in the short term. It remains the case that many underlying conditions of social structure and media system cast a long shadow on the conduct and performance of journalists and thus on the production of news. All national media systems are in some respects unique and the purpose here is not to describe all the variants or propose one modal type, but to focus on a few key system factors that are known to affect standards of journalistic performance and eventually the 'effects' of journalism on society. The following are the main questions arising.

Media systems and social structure

- What do these terms refer to?
- How does social structure in general influence the shape of the media system?

Lines of influence

- In what ways do political factors affect media systems?
- How do economic factors operate?
- What are the main social-cultural influences?

Media systems and journalism

- What are the lines of influence from system to performance?
- At what level in media organisations do the main effects take place?
- What accounts for effects and variations?

Press–society effects

- What is the basis for a belief in 'media power'?
- What kinds of effect are involved?
- How are cognitive (informational) effects connected to changes of opinion or attitude?
- What are the main variable conditions of effect from the press?
- Has journalism any unique power of its own?

What is a media system?

The term 'media system' is used here to denote all media (but especially those of news and information) in a given national setting, or with some kind of international presence and purpose. It does not imply any planned or organised set of activities and, in reality, there are few if any organised media systems, in any strict sense of the term. However, different news media in a system are related to each other at the very least by dealing with much the same corpus of news events, serving the same overall national public/audience and sometimes by sharing ties of ownership. Further unifying system influences are the subjection to a set of laws and regulations held in common or logically inter-related. The component elements of the 'system' also often share the same journalistic culture, with distinctive features, rooted in historical experience.

Media systems are typically composed of multiple separate firms or organisations, each with a measure of freedom of choice about purpose and conduct. The main elements in a typical modern media system can be sketched as follows. Given the path of technological development, an obvious differentiation within a system is between different media types, notwithstanding convergence. Different media *sectors* still, by and large, have separate forms of governance, business models, and sometimes ownership. The main division is between print media, audio-visual (radio and TV broadcasting and cable) and online forms. The form and means of dissemination are the primary factors. A second differentiation is according to the many separate organsations, of various kinds, that supply news. Not unimportant are the organisations that supply news to the news disseminators, especially the news agencies, but also many that are active on their own behalf in entering the flow of information. Third we can differentiate by the audience served, on more than one dimension, but especially location (national, local, global, etc.), by socio-economic position and by a range of social-cultural factors. A media system has several other relevant features, but especially a certain system of control and a rationale of operation. It begins to seem quite a firm concept, but the internal boundaries of systems are increasingly being blurred by the open and undetermined nature of online media as well as more general convergence.

The uniqueness of all media systems, as noted above, makes it impossible to summarise the types of system to be encountered world-wide. Aside from infrastructural features and level of development in range and in production, the main variable factors of media systems have to do with: the sources of finance; the degree and methods of political and social control applied; the range of content in terms of social and cultural goals served; and the degree of monopoly or plurality (and its basis) to be found.

Influences from social structure on media systems

As we have seen, the roots of modern media are found in countries and regions that were first to develop economically and politically, with features of urbanisation, industrialisation and centralisation that in turn encouraged forms of 'mass communication'. These forms are especially evident in the traditional media of press and broadcasting. Within societies, the very uneven distribution of wealth shaped the markets for the mass distribution of news, in respect of amount, variety and information quality. This is reflected in a categorisation of news outlets into 'elite' (or 'quality') and 'mass' (or 'popular') types, that is widely current, although very imprecise.

The idealised model of the 'elite' or 'prestige' newspaper, often likely to be regarded as the voice of the establishment if not the nation, has its origin in provision for an educated, 'bourgeois', class who needed much reliable information for business and administration. The readership of this type of paper spread 'down' the social hierarchy to a larger middle class. According to Gans' (1979) study of leading American papers and news magazines, the journalists involved largely shared the same class position, values and outlook as the class for whom they were writing. The mass popular news paper was produced largely by the same class for its social 'inferiors', but with a convenient adaptation of values as well as of style and content. Commercialisation, according to Pierre Bourdieu, has led to the 'further isolation of the journalistic field from the everyday concerns of working class and poor citizens' (Benson, 2006).

The successive technologies for news transmission of print, radio, television and online have all left their distinctive footprint on the pattern of distribution of news, as have social structural and other differences. The newspaper offers the clearest evidence of such influence. There are still very large variations in the degree of newspaper reading, once simply a reflection of distinctions of class and education found everywhere, with little sign of its reduction, even within the boundaries of Europe (Elvestad and Blekesaune, 2008). Television encouraged a new, more equal distribution of the news audience across social classes, leaving the older (press) pattern intact. Access to online news has been shaped by much the same factors as its predecessors, but it is also not really helpful to restore the role of 'news in print form', although, strictly speaking, that is what it is.

The distribution of news had been initially shaped more by geography than anything else, due to difficulties of physical transportation, for example, between town and country and between cities. Gradually, cities and regions acquired their own print news media, a development accelerated by the coming of the railway. Print news media serving a whole nation were more the exception than the rule and so it largely remains.

While demographic factors have also played an obvious part in shaping domestic media systems, geo-political forces have had comparable effects on the global flow of news. The channels for the distribution of news between, rather than within, countries initially followed the lines laid down by international trade routes and the colonial and imperial structures that were already emerging at the time of the invention of the book. The 'industrial' media came to rely on cable, telegraph and wireless networks, but these still reflected the strategic needs of empires built on trade or conquest and often in global competition. These various strands of influence were consolidated in the 'system' of international news agencies during the later nineteenth and early twentieth centuries, with their nation-state basis and their own spheres of influence. We were left with a heritage of a 'world system' of dominance and subordination in media matters, only recently disintegrating in the face of the 'communications revolution' and changes in global geo-politics (Gunaratne, 2002).

Although international news flow is shaped in detail by a set of news values, the most fundamental explanatory factors, in overall volume terms, seem to be patterns of trade and diplomacy between countries and world regions (Wu, 2003). The pattern shown by online news does not appear to be greatly different (Chang et al., 2009; Arcetti, 2008).

Aside from the physical factors affecting news distribution, social structure has had its main effects by way of the needs and interests of potential audiences. The non-economic demographic variations are mainly accountable in terms of differences of age, sex and life-cycle position. These differences, along with many refinements, still provide a basis for attempts to recruit and keep varied news audiences. The topic returns shortly under the heading of 'social-cultural' factors.

Box 6.1 Social-structural factors affecting media systems

- Geographical circumstances
- Social class differences
- Life-cycle position
- Basic demographics: population size, age, sex, etc.
- Global communication networks.

Political factors

Political system differences are also reflected in the structure and operation of media systems. These differences show up most clearly in the formal legal and regulatory arrangements that apply, but also in customary and informal linkages between political actors and journalists. Even amongst countries that claim to be democratic and free, there are system variations with historical and cultural roots. Relations between political and media systems under these conditions differ according to the medium involved, but in other ways as well. Three main types of relationship have been identified by Hallin and Mancini (2004) that capture empirical variations of relationship in a number of established 'western' democracies (see Box 6.2). These countries were classified as belonging predominantly to one or other of the three variants.

Box 6.2 Three models of political and media system relations (derived from Hallin and Mancini, 2004)

- A liberal model: the media market (owners, audience, and advertising) determines the degree and type of political influence on journalism. Government keeps its distance.
- A 'democratic corporatist' model: government can legitimately intervene in the media market to secure diversity and fairness of access and quality of political journalism.
- *A model of* 'competitive parallelism' *between media and politics:* competing political parties have close and transparent ties with certain media and journalists (contrary to the norm of impartiality) and play a role in shaping the direction and diversity of political journalism.

These types have never had an exclusive hold on any single media system (except perhaps the first) but the two non-market variants are in decline (especially the latter) and barely recognisable in some countries (notably the USA). However, the principles underlying both of them concerning the relation of politics to journalism are still relevant and they contribute to the performance of journalism and attempts at reform. The three models represent attempts to uncover the main mechanisms by which societal power establishes its hold on media systems. At the same time they identify acceptable rationales for the exercise of such power and also where the limits to its exercise might lie. These are not meant to be 'models' in any normative or ideal sense, although it is hard to ignore the normative implications. The typology is useful as a guide to alternatives, but it is based on a limited range of cases.

Many other national media systems present arrangements that differ in substance or detail, even where news journalism, according to the same 'dominant' professional model, seems to be fairly well established. This comment relates to large areas of the world, including countries of the former Soviet Union, Latin America, large parts of Africa and Asia, and a number of Asian democracies. Most of them are places where some former authoritarian tendencies have survived, or where under-development still makes a large impact, but these are not the only reasons for variation.

Systematic attempts to test the threefold typology against other national cases (especially as brought together in Hallin and Mancini, 2012) have generally led to its rejection as a solution, although it is useful for identifying essential issues. Comparative research suggests that substantial diversity results from quite different historical experiences and national cultures. Truly liberal systems are uncommon and 'democratic corporatism' is largely a matter of North European exceptionalism. World media systems are all likely to exhibit some forms and degree of political parallelism, often with vestiges both of authoritarian control and of elements of unbridled commercialism. Neither feature is likely to be very supportive of professional values. For instance, in her assessment of the important case of post-communist Russia, Vartanova identifies two intermingled strands of statism (or paternalism) and commercialism (2012:139–42). She suggests that Russian citizens still accept their subordination to the social power (p. 131). This does not prevent adherence by journalists to certain more or less universal professional values, with inter-generational differences showing up (Pasti et al., 2012).

Despite the empirical rejection of the 'three model typology' it does not seem as if any truly new 'type' has been identified elsewhere or that neglected dimensions have been brought to light (aside from authoritarianism and illegitimate/undemocratic means of control).

Economic factors

Since the early days of mass communication it has been widely believed that the power to influence news conferred by the ownership of media firms has set fundamental limits to the autonomy of journalism, especially where very large, sometimes multi-media, corporations are involved. There is no reason to doubt the general proposition and no shortage of particular examples of such power being exercised. However, there are counter-tendencies that are supported by an economic logic as well as by professional resistance. A well-functioning competitive market between diverse news providers is seen by supporters of the liberal model as the best safeguard.

Aside from influence of intrinsic features of each technology, it looks as if some other economic factors also play a determining role in the way media systems operate, with direct consequences for journalistic work. Foremost would seem to be the *source* (or type) of finance or income. This was succinctly put in Robert Altschull's (1984) 'Second Law of Journalism' as 'the contents of the media always reflect the interests of those who finance them'. In particular, there is a difference between income that is directly self-earned from an audience by publication and income that is effectively received to fund publication (especially advertising and sponsorship). Crudely, this affects the probable degree of independence of editors and journalists, and also relations with an audience. Money paid directly for news by audiences/readers is the least constraining, most liberating, with no third party interest likely to be involved.

Payment received from commercial advertisers (at least where large sums from major firms are involved) potentially ties the hand of journalists in some ways (or at least that of media management), despite the norm of separation between advertising and editorial content or the theory that advertising follows success in appealing to audiences, rather than leads in shaping content and taste (Baker, 2002). Other kinds of income can also have consequences for the media concerned. Leaving aside bribery and covert payments for access, two main forms of income are involved. One variant is that of direct public subvention on grounds of policy (as with public broadcasting or press subsidies). This is fully transparent and always comes with clear rules about purpose and standards, but it does tend to limit journalistic freedom and increase the ultimate influence of governments, even if democratically channelled, and with guarantees of independence. Second, there is financial support for publications that, also transparently, support a political party, ideology, religion or cause. There are other forms of income less easy to classify, for instance, payments to publish petitions, notices or propaganda, public advertising that is a hidden subsidy, etc. The potential effects are rather unpredictable.

A second economic factor relates to the degree of *competition* in a given news market. The more intense the competition for the same (mass) audience, the more pressure on organisations and newsrooms to supply news that puts the maximisation of popular interest and attention above other news criteria. This can lead to much duplication of news coverage (between channels) and less choice for audiences. Much the same effects flow from a high degree of *concentration of ownership*, sometimes across different media. The fewer owners, the fewer alternative publications and the fewer alternative editorial policies, the less opportunity there is for journalists to deviate from policy or find alternative employment. At one time, large public broadcasting monopolies in many European countries were also controversial on similar grounds, despite benevolent intentions and forms of democratic supervision and regulation.

A third factor comes from the economics of news information. Information comes at a *price* and unique or new information costs more than 'old news'. All decisions about news coverage are decisions about allocating limited resources of time and money. According to McManus (2009), the logic of commercial news-making requires competition to provide the least expensive mix of content that will protect the interests of sponsors and advertisers and gain the largest audiences that the latter are willing to pay to reach. The outcome of economic decisions has a bearing on the originality, speed and depth of reporting as well as on independence from would-be suppliers of ready-made information (PR in one form or another) and from news agencies. Such decisions are also related to the social-economic profile of the intended audience for news and information (income, occupation, education, residence, life-style, etc.) in several ways.

Most significant perhaps is the effect of finance on the socio-economic profile of the audience. The advertising market requires (aside from size) a differentiation of audience in terms of class and taste terms as well as income level in order to target consumers accurately. At risk of exclusion from attention are 'low-value' and certain minority sectors of the public. The internet has revived the model of direct sale to the news consumer, and the potential of profitably aiming at almost all definable groups. However, in so doing it undermines the goal of a more or less equal distribution of high quality information throughout a society and there is rarely much economic incentive to aim for the poorest consumers. The generally fragmenting effect of online media is not necessarily 'democratic' in its consequences.

Box 6.3 Main effects of economic factors on media systems

Factor

- Ownership:
  - governs degree of diversity;
  - possible owner intervention in editorial policy;
  - leads to market vulnerability.

- Source of finance:
  - advertising income's influence on content and audiences, and vice versa;
  - audience income liberates media, empowers audience;
  - public funding restricts and directs editorial policy.
- Competition:
  - Can raise quality, but also lead to less diversity and may lower average standards, due to cost-cutting.

Social-cultural influences

Cultural dimensions of social structure have also had a surprisingly durable influence, in the face of homogenising trends of technology, secularisation and globalisation. Social-cultural factors still act to drive and shape demand for different kinds of news and information (including advertising). The supply should be relevant to varying local circumstances, responsive to different interests relating to life-cycle, cultural tastes, norms and values, ethnic or other identities. This requirement is a strong stimulus to diversification of supply, where there is scope for this. It provides a basis for innovation and expansion and it looks as if online media are developing most rapidly by being able to respond to (and cultivate) such varying audiences, less hindered than old mass media by the absolute size of audiences sought and limited channel capacity. Initially, at least, there is a broad trend to diversification and fragmentation. It is also much harder to gain a complete view of the main features of any given 'media system' than was the case a generation or two ago.

Despite changes under way, there is still a striking continuity in patterns of media use in terms of time spent and media or content types chosen. Across the 27 states of the EU, for example, in late 2010, the main source of news was still television, out-performing the press and over-shadowing the internet that was a medium of choice for news only with the youngest age group, especially the longer educated (Eurobarometer, 2010). The dramatic advance of the internet as news medium, as is occurring in the US, does not yet seem to be a global phenomenon.

Language stands out as the most potent cultural influence, still governing the structure of media consumption, although with much less effect on systems and content. It reinforces national boundaries and it even helps to nurture the media systems of small countries, especially if they have their own language and they are also rich enough to have some self-sufficiency of provision. At the same time it preserves diversity of media forms and themes. Within larger nation-states, minority languages with regional roots create pressures for national media systems to accommodate them. Ethnic differences, sometimes following migration, also often follow lines of language and with similar effects. The rise of audio-visual media has somewhat diminished the isolating or protective influence of language, but has not done away with it. Nor has the internet done so in any notable way, after early beginnings of extreme English language dominance.

Any cultural factor that leads to the identification of a separate audience with alternative needs can be relevant and the situation varies from place to place. Even religion is still important in structuring media supply and demand, sometimes in association with ethnicity. Although the cultural factors mentioned affect the distribution of, and demand for, news of certain kinds, there is not much sign that journalism itself, in its professional goals and values or typical news output, varies accordingly. Minority groups and linguistic or ethnic minorities expect essentially the same quality of news provision as 'majority' audiences, although with different criteria of relevance and policies for access.

Box 6.4 Social-cultural influences on media systems

- Language as a shaper of content and setting boundaries to audiences
- Taste and taste cultures, often reflecting age and social status
- Ethnicity, religion and other sub-cultural divisions
- Locality and regionalism
- Class and status differences
- Reigning social norms and values.

Media system influences on journalism

The media systems of the mid-twentieth century could be readily characterised in spatial terms, with a predominant centre–peripheral layout, within national frontiers. Most newspaper production and distribution emanated from metropolitan centres, with a subsidiary system for regions and localities. The 'central' and large city press was more influential, prestigious, frequent in appearance as well as more profitable. Radio and television initially followed this basic geographic pattern, due in part to limited transmission ranges, as well as limited content. Technological advance has removed many constraints on range of distribution and capacity while online media escape these altogether. However, media systems are still anchored in a spatial sense by other factors, especially relating to the audience, which is still rather fixed in its location, despite mobility of reception.

During the twentieth century, new forms of international media developed, sometimes as elements of national systems (e.g. world radio networks). These supplemented a major feature of news supply that originated during the nineteenth century, following the invention of the electric telegraph and cable. This was the system of international news agencies that collected and sold news world-wide in competition with each other, although each major agency had its basis in a national media system, initially those of Britain, the US, Spain and France (Boyd-Barrett and Rantanen, 1998). The 'system' expanded to include powerful new players, notably the USSR, Japan and China. News agencies strongly encouraged the practice of factual, 'objective' news that could be supplied to the maximum number of clients and markets beyond that of the home country. Even so, there was an inevitable national bias, affecting choice of topics and events and also news values.

The arrival of cable and then satellite broadcasting towards the end of the twentieth century established a more or less genuine set of transnational news media, without any clear location in any single national media system, although, despite claims and aspirations, they have never lost their national-cultural identity, derived from their origins. For instance, research into the news performance of CNN has shown that its underlying tendency has been to follow an agenda in line with US audience interests, news sources and often US national policy aims (e.g. Thussu, 2000). The latest internet developments have added significantly to this international 'media system', although so far without much evidence of any adaptation of practice by the major news providers. The requirements of such new media forms in terms of journalism are still very much undetermined.

It is not easy to estimate how much pressure is actually experienced in the daily practice of journalism from the various factors that have been looked at, either working through the media system or more directly. Some evidence is available from studies of journalists, for instance, by way of the international 'Worlds of Journalism' comparative project. It seems that political and economic influences, that receive most attention from theorists, are not experienced in the self-perception of journalists as pressure as much as are procedural, professional and organisational influences. Also, journalists do not seem to be very sensitive to the political pressures that exist and the same applies to economic factors, although awareness of both is higher where democratic norms are less well established, for instance, in Turkey, China, Uganda, Chile, Egypt and Russia (Hanitzsch and Mellado, 2011). Government-owned media are also recognised as more likely to exert political pressure. The authors comment that journalists' sense of freedom from such pressures may in part be due to a 'professional illusion'. The same could apply to western countries, where a rather high level of autonomy is often claimed.

In assessing the potential influence of media system factors on journalistic performance, the following pathways of effect are most salient (Box 6.5).

Box 6.5 Main sources and pathways of media system effects on journalism

- The degree of editorial and journalist independence from political or economic power, sources of news, media owners, sponsors and advertisers
- The type (source) of income received
- The diversity of component elements (media types, firms, organisations) in a system
- The degree of concentration and competitiveness of the media sector or whole system
- Linguistic, ethnic and national/regional diversity
- Extent and range of a media system: the larger it is the more opportunities and choices for journalists as well as more variety of quality for audiences
- The type and effectiveness of (public) forms of regulation, governance and accountability designed to maintain and improve standards of quality and broad availability.

In one way or another, all the factors listed in Box 6.5 can affect any or all of the following: levels of skill and training; strength of professionalisation in all its aspects; relationships to the public/audience; resistance to unwanted interference from political or economic power. The pathways by which these and other effects occur can best be understood after looking at organisational factors.

Influences at the level of the organisation

Journalism has always been practised within formal organisations, of different kinds and with varied goals. News organisations have themselves been changing in various ways. In general, they are now bigger and more complex, often within a much larger media business, with varied sectors and audiences, and aiming for large profits. There is a greater division of tasks, and a tighter managerial control. Technology of production and transmission plays a greater role in decisions about content and coverage. Studies of journalistic work and output have exposed some systematic tendencies in such decisions which have implications for journalism practice and for the direction of effects on society. The purpose here is to call attention to some basic features of the organisational setting that can affect journalistic output. These are discussed in their approximate sequence in a process of production.

1. Phase of 'news discovery'

All news media need a constant and reliable supply of new information, either by way of their own reporting resources, which are always limited; or from news agencies and other media; or from information supplied by interested third parties. The last category includes large volumes of PR material plus reports, statements and announcements intended for public dissemination, but not paid for as advertising. Such sources have been shown to account for large, sometimes major, portions of news content. There is nothing inherently inappropriate about this, but it has some potentially systematic consequences for the role and effects of the press and much is not itself authored by journalists. It gives advantages to sources with most resources to supply possible news content in ways that are easy to incorporate, often the same sources that in one way or another tend to 'make' news anyway – governments, political parties, large firms, big institutions, etc. In more extreme cases, the term 'pseudo-event' is applied to describe such artificially staged happenings. Anti-authority movements have also made use of opportunities to gain publicity by various actions and initiatives. It is often left to journalists to settle the difficult question of which 'events' they should be expected to report.

The dependence on supply leads news media to concentrate resources or attention on those places where information of potential audience interest can be expected to surface, e.g. in courts, with the police, parliament, etc. This applies also to demonstrations, scenes of disaster, accidents, etc. The results include a reinforcement of certain news values and a predictability of content, as well as giving more privileged access to voices of authority in the society. The combination of these two features of news 'sourcing' can encourage the forging of relations of mutual advantage between journalists and potential sources. This too is not inherently contrary to public purpose, but it does systematically skew attention and it can lead to loss of impartiality and of autonomy.

A feature of recent war reporting, for instance, has been the widespread system of 'embedding' accredited reporters with (allied) military units. At one stage in the 2003 Iraq war, over 600 journalists were said to be engaged in this way. This satisfies needs for fresh and vivid 'news', but strengthens the hand of military information management, without arousing antagonism at secrecy and censorship, once the primary tools of news control. Inevitably, embedded reporters are not inclined to be critical of the aims or methods of the forces they are with, and reporting tends to be 'sanitised' for domestic consumption (McQuail, 2006).

Another factor at work at this stage is the operation of selection processes that have to be carried out very quickly and according to a certain routine. This applies especially to news agency material which is available in very large amounts. Such material itself is the result of an earlier, less specific or guided selection process but, taken together, there is a tendency to reinforce conventional ideas about 'news' and audiences and screen out content judged as marginal, too complex, unconfirmed, too remote from the potential audience, etc. The selection process cannot be random and inevitably requires subjective judgements by editors that may reflect certain personal values and interests or editorial policies. Finally, discovery and selection of all sorts are influenced by practical considerations. Own reporters aside, the most accessible, best validated and readily available news comes from agencies. New and breaking events in distant places require more time and expense to cover and therefore need to exceed a higher newsworthiness threshold to be considered. This may lead to neglect of more fundamental, but remote, information.

At the stage of 'discovery', the pressure for exclusive news, especially in relation to scandal, celebrities and crime, can lead to dubious or unethical practices of information collection, with potential harm to those involved. Typically, media organisations adopt their own style and culture, which exerts pressures on their journalists to conform to expectations.

Box 6.6 Influences on news content at the stage of selection

- Flow of external source material (agency, PR, public information)
- More attention to locations of familiar news events
- Privileged access to voices of authority that validate 'facts'
- Close cooperation with news-making actors (e.g. government, military, police)
- Subjective influences on editors
- Preference for scoops, exclusives, celebrity news, etc.

2. News processing and presentation

At this stage, organisational pressures have three main kinds of effect. News is processed with the aim of indicating to the audience the relative importance attached to different news 'stories'. Second, the form to be taken by the 'news story' and the 'frame of reference' in which reports or events is placed, are chosen, mainly for purposes of audience recognition and comprehension. Third, there are features designed to involve and animate audiences, catching attention, arousing emotions, etc.

In respect of the first, there are conventional cues as to the implied significance of events and 'stories' – order of appearance in bulletins, length of story or item plus other marks of prominence. The judgements made in such matters are likely to be interpreted as implying some opinions or values/beliefs. The form taken by a 'story' also implicitly assigns roles to the various actors involved, with some as 'perpetrators', others as victims, etc. Whether an event is treated as 'good news' or 'bad news' is a routine feature of story-telling and also underscores certain attitudes and values, usually of a conventional kind, for instance, the values of patriotism, justice, freedom, ethnicity or national interest.

The 'framing' of news items by the media has received much attention in the study of underlying 'ideology' in news, whether intended or not, or simply the result of routine processing to make sense of otherwise isolated facts (Entman, 1993). Framing has two aspects. On the one hand, it refers to the way in which news content is put together so that it fits with a familiar frame of reference derived from past accounts. On the other hand, framing refers to effects on the audience, who are inclined to adopt the frame offered and see the world in the same way. Journalists can hardly avoid drawing on certain familiar themes and topics to provide the context and point for news reports. However, the result can also be to narrow down interpretation and understanding, leading to accepting the definition of events by powerful sources and interested parties, and limiting original or alternative perspectives.

There are many documented examples of such outcomes, especially in respect of war or crime, insurgency and conflict. Authorities can sometimes pre-empt the news process and continue to manage overall presentation. The evidence shows that the 'biasing' effects of framing are most apparent in situations of conflict and divergent national perspectives and values. For instance, most of the major military engagements of the last two decades have been framed quite differently in the various national media systems of the world, with particular differences showing up between the US, Europe, the former Soviet Union, the Islamic world and the Far East. There is no longer a united world media gaze matching western eyes. There is a good deal of agreement that 'framing' of news begins with sources and cannot be avoided by journalists following normal routines.

In this context it is also relevant to recall that it has always been quite normal practise for established news services (especially newspapers) to establish their own individual 'persona' and style, leaving ideology aside. An in-house culture develops which is inevitably somewhat personal and idiosyncratic. The continuing process of recruitment and socialisation of journalists tends to confirm the original social-cultural profiling. There is a rational basis for this in the differentiation of audiences.

Factors of news presentation relate primarily to the devices used for attracting attention. Presentation of television news and documentary has favoured the enrolment of personable and skilled presenters and anchors to help attract and keep audiences. The conventional assumption within and outside journalism has long been that audiences are more attracted by pictures and film, extreme language, personification, dramatic events, often with violence involved, scandal and sex. The terms most used to cover all this are 'sensationalism', 'tabloidisation' or 'infotainment'. Although 'tabloidisation' initially referred only to the format of mass market newspapers, it became a shorthand for all forms of popular press, with different descriptions elsewhere, e.g. 'yellow press', 'boulevard press', etc. It is always derogatory in meaning reflecting an entrenched class bias in the way the press has traditionally been viewed.

Box 6.7 Influences stemming from news processing

- Facts are fitted to the requirements of an ongoing narrative
- Variations in relative prominence provide a guide to significance
- The 'framing' of news by theme and relevance guides audience interpretation
- News outlets develop their own style and persona, often involving their own 'celebrity' presenters
- Presentational devices of sound, pictures, choice of words also guide meaning.

3. Competition effects on performance

Observers have often commented on the intense competition that has developed in the media market place between providers of news, accentuated by the entry of successive new forms of media, most recently online. Essentially, more and more media are pursuing much the same (or even diminishing) audiences for much the same news content that fits dominant news values and the current agenda.

The clearest effect is a tendency for journalists to focus on the same events of most immediacy and highest profile. This has been referred to as 'pack journalism' and results in a reduction of diversity of news attention and over-emphasis on a few events. A related tendency for a single basic story to be reported exhaustively and in a self-generating spiral of attention and emphasis has been labelled as 'media hype' (Vasterman, 2005). The term 'moral panic' has also been applied to concentrated and growing attention to some allegedly alarming event or trend, usually relating to crime or disorder. Such stories dominate the news until they peak, decline and eventually disappear, sooner or later followed by a replacement. In some cases, after the event, it seems as if the coverage was disproportionate to, even deviant from, the reality.

In summary, if we take account of these different features of the context in which journalism is practised, it looks as if many features of content, except the most specific and transient, can be accounted for by pressures and limits that are built into basic structures and then further shaped by organisational needs, especially to meet audience demand for a regular and familiar supply of information and much besides. A number of the (albeit unplanned) effects of media structure and organisation have further consequences on society. The whole complex is another way of describing relations between press and society.

Some of the influences on performance indicated do clearly limit the ideal practice of journalism as it can be found in normative theory and professional aspirations. However, it is impossible to escape from constraints of this kind. At the same time as limiting what journalists do, they also provide security and continuity for the institution of the press and the work of individuals.

Box 6.8 Competition effects on news content

- Media competing in the same market concentrate on the same leading news stories
- The process of 'media hype' keeps some stories alive and prominent beyond a reasonable span of time
- Existence of a 'moral panic' strongly skews reporting of news facts
- The pressure for scoops and exclusives becomes intense.

The question of press effects on society

The comments that follow are relevant only to circumstances where journalism is at least relatively independent from the state and has some freedom to report. Under authoritarian or arbitrary conditions of power, another set of possibilities arises, ranging from large effects due to monopoly position of the source to no effects due to lack of trust. Elsewhere, the steady rise of news media to the position of a social and political institution that cannot be ignored depends on the belief that journalism can and does have significant consequences, not only for individuals, but also for other institutions and society as a whole. These are mostly of an intended and beneficial kind (informative, cohesive, etc.) but also include possible harm, whether or not intended. The possibilities are so diverse they defy brief assessment and, in fact, much about press effects depends on circumstances of time and place. It is plausible to suppose that an intensive media campaign, under the right conditions, will have intended effects in some degree, whether to influence public opinion or the agenda of government. There are plenty of examples in different national histories of such cases, ranging from matters of war and peace to consumer habits, although there are many more unproven cases. The reputation and electoral chances of politicians may also be at stake and the process of 'mediatisation' described earlier seems only to increase the potential for news influence by promoting the interests of the media over those of social actors.

It remains true that journalists are not the main originators of news, but are generally still only messengers about the doings and views of prominent actors and institutions, indeed, sometimes they are merely a channel used to communicate to the public. Looked at in this way, the news process can be seen as starting in society and ending up there – a matter of 'society talking to itself', with the news media simply facilitating the flow and acting as an intermediary. This notion of journalism as impartial messenger is consistent with the 'dominant model' outlined in Chapter 5, although it implicitly downgrades its independent influence.

The belief in the power of news to influence is in some respects self-fulfilling, since most participants in public events feel obliged to act as if the press has some power of its own and might even be decisive for success or failure of certain projects of information and influence. It would seem rash to do otherwise but this way of thinking is quite speculative, despite being the basis for a large advertising, PR and marketing industry as well as for political campaigning. Despite the plausibility and durability of the belief system, the extent of any influence has proved very difficult to quantify and is sometimes even hard to demonstrate at all.

A fundamental reason for this persistent uncertainty lies in the intrinsic difficulty of finding proof of any media effects. There are usually too many factors at work besides the news itself, for an estimation of independent news effect to be made. There are also potential effects beyond those of transmitting information, for instance, on immediate actions and emotions. More significant, perhaps, is the fact that news is primarily a reflection of what is going on in the real world, and is meant to be so. It is hard to separate a person's experience of reality from the news about that reality, and one source of influence from another. News (in free and open societies) usually has no organised purpose, so that possible effects are likely to be very mixed, often contradictory, rarely planned or even predicted.

Nevertheless, even if we accept this and take the position that news is neither predominantly a 'mirror' nor a 'moulder' of society, then we can form some idea of the likely nature and extent of news influence. The perspective adopted here is to see journalism primarily as a 'mediator' of our knowledge and understanding of the world around us, material as well as social. It provides approximate guidance for focusing on events around us and helping to understand them in a certain way. It is a substitute for the specialist knowledge that we do not have the education, capacity or time to acquire. From this point of view we are inevitably very dependent on 'the news' in public matters, with consequences for the way we perceive our relation to events and society around us.

Box 6.9 The basis for a belief in press 'power'

- There is a belief system based on the presumed rationality of all who participate in the flow and reception of news
- A typical modern society is permeated by a continually updated and extensive background knowledge of events and circumstances that facilitates everyday life in all public contexts
- It is unsafe for actors in the public arena to make any other assumption besides that of potential influence
- Several sectors of the information economy are very dependent on the 'belief system' referred to
- Uncertainty about the amount and direction of news effects can be explained by the complexity of the measurement task and the open-ended nature of many effects.

To take the question further in detail requires a close look at different types of potential effect, about which we do have some evidence. A basic distinction can be made between: effects on knowledge and understanding; persuasive and attitudinal effects; and effects on actions, whether by individuals or collectively.

Informational effects of news

To start with, we have enough research evidence to be sure that *some* learning by the news audience does normally take place, as measured by recall or recognition of news items (e.g. Robinson and Levy, 1986). The amount, on average, is not likely to be large, nor is understanding likely to be deep, and it probably decays quite quickly. However, learnt information accumulates gradually over time and provides a shared background of knowledge for a 'mass public'.

This kind of incidental learning is not planned or sought out by most in the audience (in search of varied satisfactions), but it does seem to follow criteria of relevance built into the selection process. Several known and thus predictable factors of audience competence and interest affect how much is learnt. Learning from news, by whatever medium, has been shown to depend on the type and strength of motivation. Furthermore, by other measures, we learn that awareness of events is diffused in varying degrees through a population by way of news media (Rosengren, 1987). The extent of awareness achieved, and the speed of diffusion, depend firstly on the nature of the event (salience, dramatic nature, potential impact) and secondly on the capacity of the medium (range and reach). The most dramatic and striking of events (such as the 9/11 attacks on the US) are likely to be diffused by a combination of major media and word of mouth, very rapidly and very widely. Thirdly, all societies show inequalities in the distribution of knowledge that are related to social structure and also to media structure (Tichenor et al., 1970).

The gradual development of mass media initially helped to narrow such gaps over a period of time, but persistent inequalities of education, income and social position still act as barriers. Different media have a varying capacity to close or widen such gaps. Historically, radio and television generally helped to raise average levels and reduce 'gaps' between social strata, but print media give differential benefit to the socially advantaged and online news media now probably even more so. Structural intervention in media (e.g. by way of press subsidies or public broadcasting with an informational mandate) can make a difference in addition to the effects of social and educational improvements (Curran et al., 2009). There is no real evidence to show that the internet has in itself any capacity to narrow 'gaps' of this kind, even if the so-called 'digital divide' were to be overcome.

Not surprisingly, given the nature of news, the most reliably demonstrated effects are on 'cognitions' rather than beliefs, attitudes or actions. Three examples of types of cognitive effect can be given that are consistent with what has been said earlier about the structuring effects of news. Firstly, there appears to be a so-called 'agenda-setting' effect, according to which the public tends to take over, as a guide to what is most relevant for attention, the order of importance assigned by the news media to issues and events, and built into decisions about selection and relative prominence (McCombs and Shaw, 1993). In this case, however, it can also be recalled that the 'media agenda' often originates with the agendas of other social institutions, especially those of politics and the economy, that are then channelled to the public by way of news.

Secondly, the journalistic process of 'framing' of news information by topics and themes (see above, Processing effects), as a means of handling diverse facts, tends also to be taken over by the public as a convenient way of organising and making sense of incoming information. While basically an unplanned learning process, this does open the way for directing attention and for some kinds of interpretation to be transmitted. Several studies have confirmed that consistent 'framing' of news events is causally linked to public opinion. For instance, Iyengar (1991) showed that the way in which news presented social problems affected whether the audience were likely or not to 'blame the victim'. However, in such cases, the direction of influence is never easy to prove.

Thirdly, a feature of news in certain circumstances is a tendency to amplify some issues, events, attitudes and opinions in a way that signals (sometimes in reverse) what is currently significant and most normal or consensual in a society, especially in relation to matters of controversy. This amplification is accompanied by a corresponding neglect of alternative or deviant perspectives and information, possibly leading to a reluctance to speak out against the supposedly dominant view. The latter process has been called a 'spiral of silence', a trend towards social conformity that is not deliberate, but becomes self-fulfilling (Noelle-Neumann, 1984). It may be driven by a very vocal or influential minority, as well as by an over-bearing majority. It can be that it results in a very misleading impression from news of the true underlying climate of opinion at a given moment. The less diverse a news structure is, the more likely that we will see this particular effect.

Box 6.10 Informational effects from news

- General information about current events is routinely acquired and accumulated
- The speed and extent of diffusion of information varies in predictable ways
- This results in a broadly shared body of similar background information
- Individual differences account for most variance in learning
- Different types of media (and of media structures) have some variable effects overall
- As a result, we find structured differences (gaps in knowledge) between social strata
- News sets the public agenda of issues requiring attention and thus also 'public opinion'
- News events are 'framed' in certain consistent ways that guide audience interpretation
- Systematic omission from news has consequences of selective public ignorance.

Persuasion and influence via news

There is much more uncertainty about the influence of the press on opinions, attitudes, values and beliefs, despite a widespread assumption that such effects do occur, even if not intended by journalists. The line between informative and evaluative effects is not all that clear. The assumption about possible effects lies behind concerns about 'bias' in news and the dangers of concentration of media ownership and control (especially of audience reach). It drives the conviction, itself rooted in the world of advertising, that the acceptability and popularity of political and other public figures (their 'image') can be shaped by the mass media. The belief that publicity can have the capacity to influence one's public reputation is well founded and in accord with experience. The further conclusion that those who control agencies of publicity might use their power to harm or benefit their political enemies or friends is also justified. The more power of publicity that is concentrated in one set of hands, the more dangerous it can seem.

Concern about unintended or hidden 'bias' in the news often depends on the political or ideological perspective of the observer. Aside from the direction given by media owners to news editorial policy, suspicions have often been voiced about the general political tendency of the journalist corps and the society, either as left-leaning or liberal, or as too close to political or economic power to be independent or critical. In recent history, both types of bias have been alleged in different media systems. A pervasive concern of interested parties is usually to ensure that their own interests, or organisation or cause is not damaged by association with 'bad news' of one kind or another. This is a question of the predominant formation of images (of politicians, policies, firms, industries, etc.) that is not ruled out by the practice of essentially objective and impartial journalism. The very prevalence of (competitive) efforts to manage news in a favourable way adds strength to the belief system that attributes power to the press on key issues of societal concern.

Box 6.11 Persuasion and influence from news

- Journalism does not normally set out to influence opinion or belief in any particular direction
- Influence may, however, result from some form of unintended 'bias', for instance, by framing or by association with objectively negative news happenings

(Continued)

(Continued)

- Deliberate attempts to influence may enter into news by way of: manipulation of events; effective PR and news management; owner intervention; ideological leaning of journalists
- A number of the 'cognitive' processes described can also lead to opinion and evaluative effects
- Over-concentration of power of ownership and control of news media in the same hands in the same system increases danger of intentional and one-sided influence.

Effects on behaviour in society – individual and collective

In the realm of politics and elections, the news media are typically subjected to intensive and minute scrutiny concerning their possible effects on voting behaviour, often as an adjunct to political campaigning. The results confirm that effects do occur, sometimes as intended, but usually refer us in the end to the many contextual factors of time, place and the event itself. A more general kind of effect is on participation in the democratic process, especially in an era of seeming decline in voting and interest in politics. This has been blamed on journalistic neglect and negativity towards politics and politicians (a typical example of 'tabloidisation').

The charge against journalism, perhaps especially in the US and the UK, for some time has been that it has persistently concentrated on aspects of politics that are likely to interest the politically uninvolved, for example, focusing on personality, the 'horse race' aspects of elections, and on the most negative and unappealing features of politics. The result is to neglect to inform the public about the substance and issues of politics (cf. Blumler and Gurevitch, 1995; Capella and Jamieson, 1997). Although a plausible case has been made, with some correlative evidence in support, there are too many variables in the complex thesis to reach any certainty. The complaint touches on a deeper issue concerning who should control the 'gates' – journalists or politicians.

Beyond the matters discussed lies another long-standing concern about effects that originate less with news than with other elements of mass-mediated culture. Normal journalism certainly does not set out to promote crime, violence or disorder in society, even the reverse. But unintended consequences may occur from reporting, especially when there is a high concentration on such news. This can at least be hypothesised and is sometimes advanced as an argument for control of the press. Theoretically, criminal tendencies might be encouraged by publicity and details of crime, making it seem glamorous or even just normal. Desensitisation to the consequences of crime might occur, reducing normal constraints.

Another, and more plausible, kind of effect is the potential for news to identify and stigmatise likely objects of popular dislike and possible violence, especially out-groups such as gypsies, immigrants, sexual deviants, the mentally ill, past offenders, and so on. Periodically, much attention is given to activation effects on civil unrest, demonstration and protest. Events of this kind are often treated by news in a sensational way, emphasising their violent nature and resulting danger to the public, but also excitement and popular participation. This may sometimes seem to harm the cause at issue or people involved. Or, as often charged, it may just stimulate and help to spread the behaviour in question. Moreover, it offers a strong motive to protestors to frame their own actions in a way that attracts news attention. However, the news does not *cause* the collective 'violence' but it gives it amplification and may lead to 'contagion'. Some such effects may even be welcomed by event organisers, but more often the news media are thought to have repressive effects on the side of 'forces of law and order'.

Box 6.12 Effects on behaviour

- News can stimulate social-political interest and participation or demotivate through diversion and negativity
- Some limited effects usually do occur on the direction and degree of voting turnout in elections
- Media reports can act as a stimulus to collective protest and civil unrest, if only by acting as publicist, amplifier, agent of contagion or shaping strategies of protest in a more violent direction
- In times of emergency or crisis, 'pro-social' effects are also possible.

In overview: primary determinants of the 'power of the press'

Both the expected beneficial and problematic effects often stem from known conditions of social structure, media system and journalistic conduct that we can identify. The audience reach of a national media system is one precondition for learning and opinion effects on a broad scale. The degree of concentration of ownership and lack of diversity in the supply of news is another primary condition. The more concentrated, consistent and cumulative the main body of news supplied by the media, the greater the likelihood there is of a corresponding outlook on the world developing over time. Lack of diversity of ownership and media system also increases the risk that systematic biases, distortions and omissions will develop and go unchallenged by any alternative, in the absence of an effective 'free market place of ideas'.

Secondly, it looks, not too surprisingly, that a well educated and engaged citizenry in an active democracy provides a corrective to manipulative or propagandist uses of news media for sectional or ideological ends. They express the demand that ensures quality and their requirements as news consumers help to channel the 'power of the press' to purposes other than those of political and economic power holders. It is the presence of such audiences that answers the question just posed about the limits set to 'press power'.

Thirdly, we can name several inter-related conditions that contribute to *trust and credibility*, both of which make news likely to be more effective because it is more likely to be believed (in this case usually for beneficial ends). Contributing to public trust in the media are various perceptions of the press that have to be earned: of honesty and authority as a witness of events; of professionalism and skill; of fairness and impartiality. In addition, trust is fostered by there being known and effective arrangements for accountability and redress of complaints.

There are other supports for forms of trust that also foster effects amongst some sectors of the public, for different reasons. For instance, partisan news sources can be effective with a relevant self-selected public precisely because they are transparent and altruistic in purpose as well as rousing. Links to celebrities and sensational presentation can help to increase impact on an uncommitted and ill-informed audience sector.

This overall assessment of the conditions that contribute to journalistic influence on society has not paid much attention to the beliefs that journalists sometimes hold about their own distinctive capacity to influence or to the belief that many people have that they, or others, are so influenced. The so-called 'power of the press' is not the same as the 'power of journalism'. This has never been evaluated, partly perhaps because it does not lend itself to either social scientific or literary methods of research and is, of its nature, very hard to pin down and test.

However, it is evident that journalism acts as a vital witness and a record on a routine and continuous basis. At exceptional moments, the chances of an impact are much greater and journalists are likely to value such occasions. Journalism can involve, reveal, inspire, move and motivate and often does so at key moments. There are well known examples of photo or film images capturing public attention and imagination with a potential for any of the effects mentioned. Sometimes a journalistic voice (individually or as a unit) will speak truth eloquently and bravely. The creativity and rhetorical skills developed and deployed on critical occasions can have significant particular effects that are lost in the averaging of influence (Eide, 2007).

Belief in the 'power of journalism' is sustained by the fact that certain known harmful effects are often experienced by particular individuals, groups and organisations. The main essence of such power is that of publicity, since it is the press itself that largely decides how much or little attention to give and on what terms. The allocation of publicity is often not guided by norms of objectivity, fairness or even ethics, but determined by the self-chosen policy and culture of each news organisation, sometimes by the personal preferences of individual editors and journalists.

The general validation of the 'power of the press' and our knowledge of the conditions of greater effect, leaves us with limited ability to predict what might happen in the future under different conditions of journalism. Nevertheless, we know enough to justify some forms of public control, supervision and accountability, alongside the protection of press freedoms. However, the distinction between 'good' and 'bad' effects is an uncertain one and there is a risk of inhibiting publication in areas of controversy where the news may perform a vital task for democracy. This refers to: the exposure of scandal and abuse; revealing confidential or secret information 'in the public interest' that may offend private interests or public authority; plus giving access to minorities and unpopular causes. Because of the extent to which the degree and 'quality' of effects depends on structural and system factors, a path is open for forms of regulation that can respect freedom of content, while still looking out for the public interest.

Box 6.13 Main variable conditions relating to the 'power of the press'

- Extensive penetration of a society by a system of major media
- Concentration of news media ownership in a few hands instead of a diversity of sources, channels, firms and organisations
- Consonance and consensus in news content: topics, themes, values

(Continued)

(Continued)

- A capacity to reach the least interested and attentive sector of the mass public, thereby susceptible to influence
- Degree of civic activity and level of education of media audience
- News media serving political or other causes
- Existence of well-funded and enlightened public service media
- A general condition of public trust/confidence and respect in relation to the press
- Certain events offer exceptional opportunities for powerful and immediate journalistic impact, as well as long-term contributions to collective awareness and memory.

Conclusion

This summary account of what is known or believed about the effects of journalism does, on the whole, confirm the view that journalism has potentially significant consequences for society. At the core of several different kinds of effect process is the simple fact that in modern societies we are, as individuals, almost entirely dependent on remote others and intermediaries for the very large amount of information needed to carry out several essential social roles – of parent, citizen, employee, etc. The situation of organisations and institutions is a parallel one, just much more complex and dependent in different ways. It needs to be kept in mind that the 'power' at issue (not one of coercion) is in some respects self-fulfilling by its very exercise. Moreover, it is in many respects just an expression of more direct and real power that is already in the hands of those with most access as sources and originators of mediated information.

The more interesting questions may now relate to the journalism of the 'new media', which seem favourably placed to exert independent influence, by virtue of some of the conditions discussed, although lacking in potential in some other respects, especially the capacity to reach beyond the already convinced and motivated audience.

Further reading

Baker, C.E. (2002). *Media, Markets, and Democracy*. Cambridge: Cambridge University Press.

Boyd-Barrett, O. and Rantanen, T. (eds) (1998). *The Globalization of News*. London: Sage.

Eide, M. (2007). 'Encircling the power of journalism', *Nordicom Review,* 28: 21–9.
Gunther, R. and Mughan, A. (eds) (2002). *Democracy and the Mass Media: A Comparative Perspective*. Cambridge; Cambridge University Press.
Hallin, D.C. and Mancini, P. (2004). *Comparing Media Systems*. Cambridge: Cambridge University Press.
Hallin, D.C. and Mancini, P. (2012). *Comparing Media Systems: Beyond the Western World*. Cambridge: Cambridge University Press.
Iyengar, S. (1991). *Is Anyone Responsible?* Chicago: University of Chicago Press.

Online readings

Go to www.sagepub.co.uk/mcquailjournalism for free access to the online readings.

Elvestad, E. and Blekesaune, A. (2008). 'Newspaper readers of Europe', *European Journal of Communication*, 23, 4: 425–47.
Fengler, S. and Russ-Mohl, S. (2008). 'Journalism and the information-attention markets', *Journalism*, 9, 6: 667–90.
Hanitzsch, T. and Mellado, C. (2011). 'What shapes the news around the world? How journalists in 18 countries perceive influences on their work', *International Journal of Press/Politics*, 16: 404–26.
Ravi, N. (2005). 'Looking beyond flawed journalism. How national interest, patriotism and cultural values shaped the coverage of the Iraq war', *International Journal of Press/Politics*, 10, 1: 45–62.
Rosengren, K.E. (1987). 'The comparative study of news diffusion', *European Journal of Communication*, 2, 2: 227–55.
Van Gorp, B. (2005). 'Where is the frame? Victims and intruders in the Belgian press coverage of the asylum issue', *European Journal of Communication*, 20, 4: 487–507.

7 The Accountability of Journalism to Society

Introduction

The previous chapter makes it fairly clear why journalism can expect to feel pressures for accountability. The media systems in which it is embedded play an intimate part in the social, political and economic life of a modern society and it would be unrealistic to expect otherwise, despite the guarantee of press freedom. This is, in any case, a limited guarantee, relating primarily to the legal means used by authoritarian governments for centuries to secure their power, especially advance censorship and punishment after the event for publication.

However, this leaves open the possibility of other forms of control and regulation and room for debate about the boundaries between freedom and control and the means that might be justified to protect society from potential harm. The press is not above the law that secures other rights and freedoms for individuals and organisations. It cannot simply deny responsibility for failings or for consequences that might be held as harmful. The media themselves can even stand to benefit from regulatory structures that protect their interests and are not only restrictive in their purposes. Not least amongst such benefits is the increased trust and influence gained by greater transparency and responsiveness to criticism.

Nevertheless, the situation is a delicate one, where those with power to regulate are often also those who want to exert control for their own ends and sometimes represent the same interests that journalism is supposed to keep an eye on and keep their distance from. All moves to apply regulation are likely to be viewed with suspicion by the media, even when they are a response to widely felt public disquiet. For whatever reason, journalism is not usually rated very highly in public esteem and trust. Public estimations of the quality of the press vary from one country to another and tend to reflect personal experience as well as media system weaknesses. This chapter takes the general position that some forms of accountability and even regulation are necessary and beneficial for media as well as society, but the form they take and the point at which they apply is critical in striking a balance between the interests of society and the ends pursued by journalism.

From these remarks, we can see that issues of accountability are likely to be looked at differently from different perspectives, especially those of: the *political system* (state, government and political parties); the *public*, whether as audience, as a collectivity or as individuals affected by media; interested *third parties* and agencies in the society – political, economic and social; the *media market* and *industry*; and finally, editors and *journalists* themselves. There are inevitable differences of weight attaching to these interests and differing capacity to initiate any form of control. The balance of power and interest varies from time to time and place to place and the relations involved and solutions reached are always dependent on changes in society and in media systems.

Main issues of responsibility and accountability

- What are the most frequently occurring?
- How far are they individual or collective, private or public in scope?
- How far do they relate to harm, and how far to benefit?

Meanings and forms

- What kinds and degrees of responsibility are involved?
- What means and types of accountability?

Processes of accountability

- To whom is accountability owed or by whom is it claimed?
- How is it exercised – by what mechanisms?
- What are the consequences of media change for the existing framework of media of governance?

The main issues of regulation and accountability

The discussion of potential effects from journalism in the preceding chapter provides a guide to the main issues prompting calls for regulation, according to one or other of the different perspectives outlined. The principle of press freedom itself means that the issues are often not clearly established, but there is some predictability about those that most commonly arise, and about the sources of complaint. Leading the way in scrutiny of the press are usually politicians, either as elected office holders concerned about their own standing or as government officials, resentful of any journalism that seems to work against state policy. On both matters, the scope for formal complaint is limited. Politicians claim to look only for accuracy and fairness, as valued also by journalists, but usually want rather more. Governments, in addition, rest their claims on obligations (formal or informal) to respect the justice system and the requirements of national security. Inevitably, there is (or ought to be) a permanent state of actual or latent conflict with journalism over the publication of sensitive information. Such matters aside, politicians and governments can make some claim to democratic legitimacy vis-à-vis unelected journalists.

While there is not much sign anywhere of significant public opinion as a driving force for stricter regulation on political and policy matters, there is plenty of evidence of public concern about threats to security and even more in matters of offence on moral or cultural issues. The principle of freedom alone does not, for a large majority, stand in the way of more control of offensive news content and of unacceptable conduct in its collection. There is also often a body of informed and vocal opinion in civil society seeking to raise standards of journalism. This sometimes relates to an alleged 'trivialisation' and 'sensationalism' of news and to low quality of public information. Such critiques may lead to calls for intervention in media structure as well as more regulation of journalism.

Amongst the self-appointed 'guardians of the public interest' are many critics with well-founded complaints about the performance of news media in matters such as the amplification of prejudice or even hatred directed at various minorities in the society. The victims in such cases are usually not able or inclined to respond or to complain themselves. Prominent amongst complainants are actual or potential victims of harm to reputation or of invasion of privacy. Some protection and redress may be available in law, but often not.

While most issues of accountability relate to specific failures and problems, there is usually a constituency of campaigners seeking a generally better journalism that will keep its own implicit promises of social and cultural benefits, in return for its freedom. Sometimes these pressures for reform have been partly satisfied by the provision of a public service variant of journalism (in broadcasting) that requires a curtailment of professional autonomy but a protection from many market pressures. The emergence of the internet as a main news provider has sparked off demands for an extension of public service structure to online contexts. The main issues of accountability and potential control are summarised in Box 7.1.

Box 7.1 Main issues of journalistic accountability

- Protection of the ultimate interests of the state with respect to its duties of national security and law enforcement
- Matters of morals and norms of society in sensitive areas (violence, sex, crime, religion, etc.), arising from publication
- Securing social and cultural benefits for the public as a whole, by way of full and fair reporting and by enrichment of the public sphere and support for the political system
- Improvement of the professional and ethical quality of journalism, especially in respect of conduct in the collection of information, as well as its quality
- Prevention of harm to individuals in matters of rights to reputation, privacy, and economic interests
- Prevention of direct harm to individuals (e.g. stimulation to self-harm) or society (e.g. inciting disorder) and general harm to society or groups within it (e.g. prejudice or misrepresentation).

Although for the most part we are concerned with effects that are thought to be harmful, some forms of regulation can have the intention of benefiting either society or journalism, or both.

Journalistic responsibility

To speak of responsibility is to speak about duties or obligations. There is little certainty or clarity about what such obligations of journalism might be, notably because of the freedom of the press and also the diversity of press functions in its different branches. As we could see from Chapter 2, there are quite widely varying theories about what journalism might or should contribute to society. For reasons that are well understood, the press as a whole is reluctant to be committed to any specific obligations and they cannot be imposed by law or regulation without diminishing freedom. In effect, aside from cases where a sector of the press (as with public service broadcasting or news organisations committed to serve a cause or value), has a prescribed informational or cultural role, news media can choose and define their own role and degree of responsibility for carrying it out.

Nevertheless, as we have already seen, the wider social context, and the history and traditions of journalism itself, ensure that the press is an object of many expectations and pressures to conform. Many of these are endorsed in some degree by the press institution and are in line with self-chosen purposes. They cannot easily be disregarded. At the very least, news people are usually also citizens of the same country as their audiences, subject to the same laws and also sympathetic in general to the interests, values and opinions of fellow-citizens. Informal pressures of public opinion, patriotism and self-interest attach them to a broad consensus about the public interest. In the light of these remarks, it is helpful to consider responsibilities in any of three categories: those that are assigned (as in the case of public broadcasting or otherwise legally imposed); those contracted (mainly relating to services to clients, advertisers or the audience); or those self-chosen (voluntarily and usually with some ideal or public service in mind).

We might also add that many individual journalists are driven by a personal commitment to truth and justice to adopt and follow strong notions of responsibility for their own professional conduct.

In the end, despite the deniability of most formal accountability, quite a formidable array of 'responsibilities' can be invoked, even when tempered by an overall commitment to the ideal of journalism to report and make public accurately and 'without fear or favour'. The key items are summarised in Box 7.2.

Box 7.2 Potential responsibilities of journalism

- To conform to law on matters varying from state secrets to data collection methods
- To provide information services of high quality at least in respect of accuracy and reliability
- To cooperate as citizens with law enforcement and provide help in national emergency
- To follow rules of conduct in professional or self-regulatory codes
- To remain answerable to one's own conscience, sense of duty or vocation
- To accept rules for conduct in particular circumstances, e.g. in relation to the Justice System and at times of emergency.

The accountability of journalism

According to one theorist, 'The issue of responsibility is ... to what social needs should we expect journalists to respond. The issue of accountability is ... how might society call on journalists to account for their performance of the responsibility given to them' (Hodges, 1986:14). Accountability is the process by which claims against the media are activated, with a view to the satisfaction of complaints, compensation, punishment or remedial action. The conditions of press freedom mean that, where no law is broken, close limits are set to the various forms of accountability that can be found in different media systems.

Normally, accountability only comes into play when some negative consequence of publication occurs or is alleged. It involves an expectation of an account or explanation of conduct when requested for good reasons. Such an account may be given willingly or not and can take various forms. Journalists may be held accountable to a range of different claimants, but especially to their own audience, to those named in or directly affected by news reports and to voices speaking on behalf of society (see below, Lines of accountability). The main elements of an accountability process are as shown in Box 7.3, although not all stages have to be followed in every case. In particular, quite a few complaints can be dealt with quickly by apology or correction and never reach the stage of any procedure, let alone adjudication.

Box 7.3 The accountability process: main elements and sequence

- A claimant
- A claim
- A contested case of publication
- Certain criteria/standards of conduct or performance
- A response to the claim
- A procedure to be followed
- An adjudication.

Many complaints against journalism do not involve formal breaches of any law, although public broadcasting or licensed private broadcasting is often subject to externally imposed conditions and regulations. These requirements usually supplement, rather than replace, the normal obligations of journalists. Of particular importance in public broadcasting is the pressure on broadcast journalists to observe norms of balance and impartiality that are more widely shared in the profession, even if not compulsory (see UK example of broadcast impartiality rules in Appendix §4). Democratic governments may also claim a right to some preferential treatment from journalists in public broadcasting systems on the grounds of fairness and of the public interest (the needs of democratic politics, in particular).

We can differentiate between accountability as defined above and other forms of control. Control proper implies a relation of unequal power, some coercion and an absence of negotiation. Although accountability is primarily considered as being for the public benefit, it also serves the media as a form of feedback from the public. Although rarely welcomed by journalists, it is not necessarily negative in its effects. Some form of accountability and control is an intrinsic element in the media institution. The increased technical complexity and international character of media systems has led to more rather than less regulation of one kind or another, although not necessarily to more accountability for performance.

The main forms of accountability can be distinguished according to a dimension of degree of external compulsion or constraint. More accurately, we can contrast a 'liability' version of accountability with a softer version that depends on 'answerability'. The former is most appropriate for enforcing clear and binding responsibilities, especially where they are legally imposed or specifically contracted. The latter version applies where the issue is not control, but the observance of agreed norms and good intentions.

The liability model presumes that the media can and do cause real harm to individuals or society and can be held responsible and made subject to some form of judicial process, even one adapted to the special circumstances of communication (where direct material harm cannot be proved). The operation of this model puts the media and society in an adversarial relationship and the media are obliged to defend themselves, especially as there can be material penalties if found 'guilty'.

The alternative 'answerability' approach to accountability puts an emphasis on voluntary responsiveness to the interests or wishes of those affected by publication. The emphasis is on explaining, defending and justifying contested publication by way of rational arguments and appeal to higher values of truth and mutual obligations between communicators and society. This presumes good intentions and seeks understanding, reconciliation and, if needed, apology and redress rather than punishment. Where claims and complaints are made against media, there is no demand for material penalties, but for verbal concessions. For the most part this approach deals with the quality of content and standards followed rather than with questions of harm caused.

The choice for one or other model depends on circumstances and the prevailing political culture and social climate, but each has certain advantages and disadvantages. In brief, the liability model is likely to be more effective, but the answerability model is more in keeping with traditions of freedom of expression. The first may have undesirable side-effects, such as a 'chilling' effect on criticism, the second can have constructive side effects and improve relations with clients and public. A summary of the main differences is shown in Table 7.1.

TABLE 7.1 Two accountability models compared

Liability		Answerability
Legal basis	vs	Moral/social basis
Imposed	vs	Voluntary
Formal adjudication	vs	Informal
Adversarial	vs	Conciliatory
Material penalty	vs	Non-material penalty
Reference to harm	vs	Reference to quality

Lines of accountability of journalism

In the absence of assigned public purpose or clear definitions of the role, journalistic accountability is mainly conducted along informal lines, guided by expectations and requirements set by a range of different external partners, supplemented by a number of internal mechanisms. The 'answerability' model is much more common than the 'liability' version. Despite the informality and lack of compulsion, journalists are typically enmeshed in a web of relationships with other persons and agencies. If we leave aside the normal internal responsibilities of the job as determined by owners, managers and editors, as well as limitations set by external 'regulators' on behalf of government and society, journalists are potentially answerable to any of the following kinds of partner:

- The *audience (actual or potential)*, whose expectations cannot ultimately be ignored, even if the accountability relationship with journalists often works indirectly via management.

- Various *lobby and interest groups* that either seek to gain access to, or influence, news channels for their own purposes or keep a watch on what is published and try to counter or correct what they regard as unfavourable reporting.
- Other *social institutions* in the fields of business, law, medicine, policing, education etc., although it applies especially to political agencies. All of these have their own public information needs and seek to shape journalistic coverage of events to further these ends.
- News *sources* are another partner that cannot be ignored and often have an agenda of their own that may sometimes have to be resisted. Sources are often in an exchange relationship with journalists and exert influence, based on information they control.
- There is a wide range of persons and agencies that are *referents* (subjects of reports) in the news, without themselves being sources. While journalists are free to report about specific referents within limits of what is lawful, these in return can have sufficient social, political or economic influence, to be able to claim some degree of answerability on the part of media. Typically, journalists learn to act with discretion on sensitive matters, especially where wealth and power can be deployed.
- Lastly, there are various *clients* of the news media, especially advertisers and others who indirectly 'sponsor' journalistic content and in a sense 'subsidise' it, for commercial reasons. While journalism is supposed to be independent of such interests, there are inevitable pressures to collaborate. Again, lines of accountability are not likely to be formal or direct, but routed by way of the market.

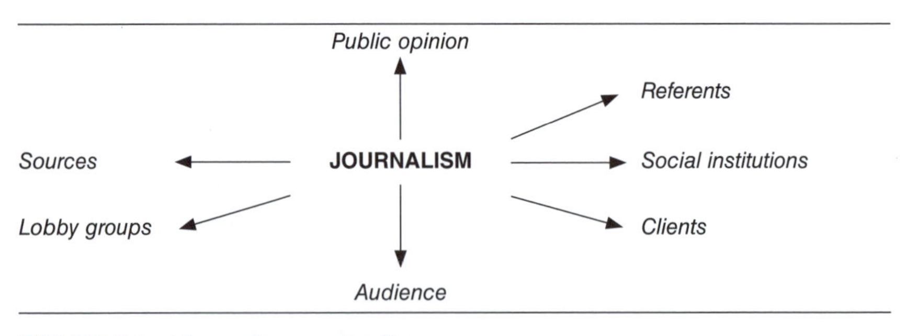

FIGURE 7.1 Lines of accountability

The accountability situation is clearly very complex and varies from case to case and place to place. There is a general need for journalists to reconcile the often conflicting interests of those to whom they owe some sort of obligation (or who claim it), but there is no general pattern to how this will occur. The 'professional ideology' of journalism offers no clear answer to the question of whose interest should take precedence, although it is most likely to indicate public opinion and their own audience. This will depend on the dominant ethos of the news organisation in question. The sociology of news organisations suggests that the choice mainly lies between giving primacy to pleasing the audience, or the management or some external point of reference in society (professional, social or political). In a commercial system, the decisive factor is usually to 'follow the money', rather than any presumed journalistic virtue.

The extent to which a news medium can determine for itself its own degree and kind of accountability depends a good deal on the standing and prestige of the news organisation concerned (not forgetting its economic and political muscle) and the professional standing of the individual journalist. Even so, there is no guarantee that even a well established, authoritative and well financed media organisation can achieve full independence from unwanted pressures. The higher the status or larger the audience reach of the news organisation, the more it is also subject to external pressures or incentives.

Forms of governance and accountability applied to journalism

The term 'governance' refers to all forms of regulation or control and it is helpful to distinguish between its external and internal varieties and also between formal and informal means. External here refers to requirements and pressures that originate outside the media organisation or institution or cannot be challenged, as opposed to constraints imposed by owners, managers or professional bodies of journalism themselves. The difference between formal and informal means is partly one of degree of voluntariness in accepting accountability and partly of the degree of constraint that might be involved (hard versus soft control). In addition, formal controls are codified and applied according to set procedures, while the informal type involves influence and pressure that is not programmed or directly observable.

Where the question of accountability arises it will often be in relation to the authorities or the people of a given locality affected by publication (e.g. region or city), although, for the most part, journalism is also accountable at the national level. Although there are international media without specific national allegiances and such media are multiplying, there is scarcely any supranational authority to which journalism can be held accountable, except within the country which provides the main operating base. For this reason, internet journalism is largely unaccountable (unless an activity of an established news channel), although it may be subject to unpredictable forms of accountability in any national legal jurisdiction that might take an interest in particular cases.

In practice, the internet is probably subject to more arbitrary interference than are established media forms. Its protection under rights of freedom of expression is not usually guaranteed, although it is not free of legal obligations. International journalism is often subject to pressures that arise in its varied audience destinations, without being protected by the freedoms of the national media system, such as they might be.

Leaving aside emerging or uncertain situations, established procedures vary a good deal, according to local conditions of journalistic and political culture. In general, the more libertarian and market-oriented the society, the more likely it is that accountability will be left to market mechanisms or privately originated legal action. In countries that have more 'communication welfare' provisions, there are likely to be more possibilities for appealing to public responsibility, more legal constraints on journalism and more public pressure for journalistic self-regulation. The main dimensions of difference have to do either with the location of accountability – whether external or embodied within the press institution itself – or with the degree of formality of procedures available. It also varies, according to the *locus* (structure, conduct or content). Bertrand (2000) uses the term 'media accountability system' to refer to 'any non-state means of making media responsible to the public'. This covers a variety of types, but refers primarily to self-regulation. The main mechanisms available can be classified in these terms, and described briefly as follows.

Mechanisms of accountability: external

Formal mechanisms of external accountability

- By appeal to constitutional or legal provisions that guarantee press freedom but also recognise certain responsibilities to society and requirements to respect the rights of others.
- The justice system and general law provide some limited possibilities for making claims against the press, with wide variations across national legislations. These relate to specific issues, especially to libel, privacy, freedom of speech, contempt of court, intellectual property, election campaigning, official secrets, public order, human rights, rights

of reply, respect for national symbols and authority, blasphemy and other matters. Although the list of potential matters of accountability is long, in practice, legal action in free democracies against journalism is regarded as generally undesirable and a matter of last resort.

- In some countries there are specific media laws, although these mainly relate to issues of structure, ownership and economy. The standard of news in public broadcasting is sometimes referred to in general in media laws, although enforcement and detailed interpretation is normally left to editorial judgement or to relatively independent media regulatory agencies (see below).
- The main formal and external 'media accountability systems' described by Bertrand (2000) are press councils and complaints procedures that are not fully controlled by the news media themselves or by professional bodies of journalism. The main instruments usually consist of codes of ethics or practice, coupled with set procedures for receiving and judging complaints (see the example of the Irish Press Council code in the Appendix §5).
- There has been a growing trend to establish independent national regulators for all media, often taking over accountability functions from public service media and sometimes providing a base for self-regulatory agencies, especially in respect of electronic news media. Such regulators are intended to stand *between* media and the state, aiming to look after the interests of the public as consumers and citizens. The general trend towards media convergence has increased the pressure for press and broadcasting to be treated on similar terms (Just and Puppis, 2012).
- Governments in a number of countries have occasionally taken the opportunity to launch general public enquiries into journalistic standards, especially where issues of crime or public order are at stake. The era of such enquiries in Europe (e.g the UK Royal Commissions on the Press of 1947 and 1974) was largely confined to the post-war period when a general phase of press concentration seemed to threaten the role of the press in democratic politics.

Informal mechanisms of external accountability

- The media market is probably the most potent (and effective) source of outside pressure on conduct and content. It has the advantage of being non-coercive and self-adjusting but it also has disadvantages. Market criteria of quality are likely to be the most relevant ones but do not cover all aspects of performance. The market (in the form of popular demand or advertiser pressure) is itself sometimes held responsible for some of the alleged failings of journalism, especially in respect of informational quality, good taste and decency.

- It is open to outside pressure groups to organise public opinion on particular issues of journalistic standards or generally on behalf of consumers, especially where there are allegations of bias and discrimination or of potential harm. These activities can involve systematic monitoring of news to provide evidence in support of claims. The main aim is to use unfavourable publicity as a lever of change.
- The media are themselves increasingly exposed to routine assessment, criticism and comment in other media and journalistic performance is not immune to this form of evaluation that can exert pressure for reform or change.
- Education and research in journalism is often carried out by a range of independent, non-profit bodies (including universities). This usually includes some systematic surveillance of journalistic activities on issues of contemporary public interest (for instance, media coverage of war or politics). Publication on aspects of media performance in journalism reviews and scientific journals contributes to accountability. The internet has given rise to a good many initiatives to keep watch on content of an egregious kind, such as relating to sex abuse or stimulation of violence and hatred, in the absence of adequate (or any) editorial control.
- A number of bodies operate internationally to monitor the freedom and human rights of journalists, especially where the domestic political situation is oppressive or where authorities and others use illegitimate means of control (see below, Informal illegitimate mechanisms).The aim is not to criticise the performance of journalism, but to support their freedom of expression. Prominent amongst such bodies, aside from journalists' own international and regional professional organisations, are: Amnesty International; Reporters Without Borders; Index on Censorship; Committee to Protect Journalists; PEN, Article 16.

Box 7.4 External mechanisms of accountability

Formal

- Press or media law
- Other laws that apply

- Press councils with a public component
- Media regulator decisions
- Public inquiries.

Informal

- Pressure groups/public opinion
- Media market
- Journalism education and research
- Media review and criticism.

Mechanisms of accountability: internal

Formal

We can distinguish between lines of accountability that extend 'back', as it were, to the general media governance system, plus the origins and sources of the news-making organisation and those that extend 'forward' to the audience. In the first matter, the predominant form of accountability occurs by way of day-to-day management of news media decision-making, usually via a hierarchy of control from editor to reporter. Typically a news organisation follows a known policy in matters of news selection, editorial opinion, format and style and journalists are accountable to editors for conforming to this policy. Ultimately, all personnel are obliged to answer to the owner or publisher. There are usually formal checks on what is published, in cases where laws concerning libel, confidentiality or copyright or the judicial system might be involved. For an institution often claiming to defend freedom, news media organisations are often remarkably hierarchical, even autocratic in internal management.

As far as accountability relations with the audience is concerned, each media organisation is free to institute a formal process of accountability or not. Practices vary enormously, but it is increasingly seen as good to have some possibility for formal complaint as well as a variety of methods for assessing public reactions, and if necessary responding and correcting. A growing practice is for a medium or channel to appoint its own 'ombudsman' or audience representative and sometimes its own code of practice on sensitive issues. Such forms of accountability are by definition never binding and are entirely within the control of management and owners. They may be designed to serve the interests of the news medium more than the public, as a form of public relations or protection against stronger measures.

Informal

Journalists, like other professionals, are influenced by their colleagues and their work environment in numerous ways. They are 'socialised' into the expectations of the workplace and the culture of the news medium. They compete and cooperate with colleagues and learn what to treat as success or failure. They may discuss or evaluate news decisions on a continuing basis. As individuals, journalists are also members of the society and inevitably pick up reactions and opinions from the public (often in chance personal contacts) concerning the news they publish and the events of the news.

As a result of digitalisation, many journalists have websites or blogs by which they receive direct reactions from the public and a certain limited form of informal accountability is an essential feature of most online news services. One of the consequences of economic pressure is to make journalists more sensitive to public criticism and to seek a firmer relationship with an audience. The revival of the model of paid-for content is one aspect of the case, but the means for improving relations with the audience have been strengthened by the interactive properties of online contact.

A new concept of 'responsiveness' has been coined to describe a variable of openness to the views and reactions of the public. Brants and de Haan (2010) have also shown that the motivations of journalists to be responsive differ. Noticeable is a difference between a 'strategic' motive, where market considerations predominate, and a 'civic' motive, where the aim is a better service to the citizen. In addition, responsiveness can have an 'empathetic' character.

Box 7.5 Main internal mechanisms of accountability

Formal

- Management control
- Editorial and production policies

- Audience and market research
- Complaints via Ombudsman, etc.

Informal

- Socialisation of journalists
- Collegial review and evaluation
- Audience feedback and response
- Personal contacts
- Online dialogue.

Informal and 'illegitimate' mechanisms of control/ accountability

The framework of accountability described above presumes a uniformity of relevant conventions and modes of governance that does not correspond closely with reality. The accountability of journalism is not universally conducted according to guidelines that are themselves compatible with the professional ideals of journalism itself, especially of freedom and impartiality. However, the forms of social control of journalism to be found across many countries are simply too diverse to describe and the framework offered is at least a base from which to recognise deviations. Essentially it is a matter of many different kinds of pressure and many ways of applying it that can be found. The particular pattern depends on the political culture of the times and on the deep historical roots of what is regarded as either customary or tolerable. It is not just a matter of varying degrees of authoritarianism, since this does not take account of the many motives and possibilities for economic influence or for the variety of potential beneficiaries of pressures on journalism.

The different ways in which control can be exercised, not only by the state or its agencies, include the following:

- Control of access to information from official sources by way of 'lobby systems', accreditation of journalists, and freedom (or not) of information. The system of press clubs (or *kisha*) in Japan is an example of an institutionalised grip on publication within the boundaries of legal 'press freedom' (Gamble and Watanabe, 2004).

- The 'politicisation' of journalism itself (and of entire news media), as outlined in Chapter 6, is a widely occurring process that works both to expose and to conceal in predictable and planned ways in countries where 'political parallelism' is the dominant model of media-politics relations.
- Government control of broadcasting networks is commonly found in more authoritarian regimes and not entirely absent anywhere. It inevitably brings some restrictions of a systemic kind. In some cases, print media are also owned by local or regional governments.
- Professional associations of journalists that are effective monopolies (as in some Latin American countries) can lend themselves to various kinds of social control function.
- Despite bans on censorship, the security of the state can justify restrictions on publication on the grounds of over-riding national interest (for instance, the UK system of 'D' notices or the US Patriot Act can lead to some restrictions on the freedom of the press on security grounds).
- Control can also be exercised by giving or withholding certain rewards and benefits that are in the gift of government.
- Where the state is prepared to go beyond the bounds of the defensible, there is a wide range of possibilities for applying sanctions, without resorting to the ultimate of violence. In the case of Russia, where a tradition of 'statism' is long established, recourse may be had to selective application of legal means (e.g. punitive use of tax or safety regulations or using legal actions for defamation as a means of 'chilling' opposition). Economic pressure may also be available by controlling the supply of essential material or causing financial losses in other ways. In the former territories of the Soviet Union that became the CIS, restriction was often blatant and illegitimate (Richter, 2008).

No country is free from one or other instrument of pressure in the hands of the state and sometimes these combine with 'legitimate' market pressures (e.g. arising from the self-interest of monopoly media) to seriously limit press freedom.

Three frames of accountability relationship

We can distinguish three main frames of reference in which accountability takes place, leaving aside processes of market accountability, even though these may provide the most effective constraints on conduct, as well as shaping the choice of responsibilities. Every aspect of content and journalistic conduct is potentially accountable within the organisation in terms of its economic implications. For the most part, accounting is simply a part of the routine evaluation by audiences of their own satisfaction and by media firms of their relative success in the news market. At issue are matters of quality, but also of price and perceived value. Criteria applied also relate to aspects of delivery and service as between different providers and different media. Journalism differs somewhat from other media market commodities in having a wider perceived social and political value and market-based criteria are often contested and resisted by journalists, even if they cannot be ignored by media management.

The three main accountability frames referred to can be named as: political and legal; public accountability; and professional, The first of these applies where there are formal regulations, originating in the political process, to which journalism must comply. These vary from place to place but can apply in the case of such issues as: publication of official or trade secrets; intellectual property; libel and defamation actions; offence to privacy laws; obscenity and pornography; harms specifically attributed to news reports, including incitement to violence, hatred or crime; the integrity of the justice system, including respect for courts and protection of anonymity; and electoral law.

Public broadcasting is always subject to more specific and enforceable regulations extending to matters of content. There are clear procedures to be followed for calling media to account for alleged offences and a set of known penalties, ranging from requirements to publish corrections to fines and imprisonment. This frame typically follows a logic of *blaming* the media for being an actual or potential cause of specific harm, with a discourse that is derived from judicial models. Accountability is primarily external and formal, in the terms described earlier, and usually follows a liability model.

The *public accountability* frame is less clear-cut in the form it takes and is driven in part by pressures from public opinion and in part by a diverging choice of publication goals. Leaving aside requirements on all journalists to avoid causing harm, there are a number of potential benefits and services to the wider society that journalism provides (as summarised above, Box 7.2) for which it often accepts responsibility. The issues arising within this frame have mainly to do with the quality of information and comment made available to the public, especially according to criteria of relevance, diversity, accuracy as well as moral or ethical norms. Apart from the case of public broadcasting, accountability for meeting externally attributed responsibility cannot be enforced, although it may occur as voluntary, or self-regulatory, responses. On occasions, the pressure of general public opinion coupled with political motivation does lead to the establishment of stronger, even statutory forms of regulation, involving forums for complaints, real penalties for transgression and other requirements (e.g. rights of reply). It may be difficult for the press to resist some effective forms of accountability in these circumstances.

The *professional* frame applies to issues of journalistic conduct and quality of content according to craft criteria and ethical norms that have been developed within the institution of the press, according to established tradition and in the particular setting of a news organisation. The most common formal instrument of self-regulation is a code of ethics or conduct, but varied procedures for complaints, response or redress can be found. As with other forms of accountability, merit can be rewarded as well as failings signalled. The general aim of self-regulation is the improvement of performance and protection of the reputation of the profession and practice of journalism. The approach is always according to the model of answerability.

Many questions of professional responsibility are addressed in codes of ethics or news production codes. Codes are usually organised on a national basis, although international codes exist. Many such codes do not explicitly recognise responsibilities to society, but concentrate on the quality of journalism and the protection of the journalist. Laetila (1995) compared the journalistic codes of 31 European countries and concluded that they all more or less agreed on the same ethical principles. These were: truthfulness; the defence of freedom of expression; equality and non-discrimination; fairness in gathering information; respect for sources and referents (thus privacy and dignity); and independence and integrity (e.g. resisting bribery). Sometimes codes refer to the need for loyalty to the employer and respect for state institutions.

The same issue may be handled within more than one of these 'frames of reference', although there is usually a predominant allocation. It is noticeable that the frames operate according to different criteria and logic and the means of accountability that are available. Inconsistencies can be observed between market criteria of performance and those that apply within the professional and public responsibility frames, since high professional quality may not be appreciated by the larger audience and doing good for the society may not be profitable. There are also possible conflicts between meeting commercial goals and requirements of the law, for instance, where there is a strong audience appetite for scandal, sensation and sexual stimulation that conflicts with norms of privacy or decency. The main features of the three frames discussed are summarised in Table 7.2.

TABLE 7.2 Three 'frames' of accountability compared

	Frames of accountability		
	Political/legal	**Public responsibility**	**Professional responsibility**
Main issues	*Structural*	*Public harm/offence*	*Standards*
	Individual harm	*Public benefit*	*Autonomy*
	Property	*Quality*	*Conduct/ethics*
	Justice system	*Opinion*	
Procedure	*Formal*	*Optional*	*Voluntary*
	External	*Irregular*	*Internal*
	Liability-fixing	*Debate*	*Self-regulation*
			Answerability
Benefits/ costs	*Effective*	*Open-ended*	*Undependable*
	Chilling	*Flexible*	*Respects freedom*
	Limited scope	*Relevant*	

Accountability in overview

For reasons given, journalism cannot escape either regulation or accountability in some form or another, although the matter will remain in dispute for reasons both of principle and practice. Despite the potential for self-accountability, it will not provide a remedy in all circumstances where journalists are being 'called to account' nor replace all kinds of limitation and control that conflicts with the letter and the spirit of press freedom. However, enforced accountability, aside from its offence to the spirit of press freedom, can seriously limit the ability of the press to carry out one of its most widely accepted responsibilities – to act as critic, watchdog or even adversary, where called for.

This chapter is based on the view that accountability is not the same as control. It does not extend to cover advance censorship or punishment for what offends authorities. But no freedom from responsibility for the effects of, and reactions to, publication can be guaranteed. So the issue then turns on the degree of pressure to comply with any call for accountability that is made. In practice this will depend on the local circumstances and also on the relative power of the party calling for an account.

The central question raised by this chapter concerns the adequacy of available means of accountability in relation to the various requirements and expectations faced by journalism. It is clear that there are numerous and varied means available but they are far from forming any complete or coherent system. This is as it should be for a free press in a free society. Nevertheless, accountability of some kind is not only inevitable but can be an aid to the press in fulfilling some of its responsibilities. The question of adequacy depends on the root cause of the complaint or critique.

In respect of structure and media system issues, it looks as if few forms of accountability are available. Such problems (e.g. of ownership, concentration) are often deeply rooted in the past and in social-economic forces and in reality there is no 'media system' that can reform itself, since it is a shadowy entity. Nor can democratic governments intervene in any major way except on rare occasions when there is a clear mandate for change, as when despotic governments are overthrown, or at times of fundamental shift in the media for other reasons, otherwise the negative aspects of media structure can only be dealt with by society, if at all, in a piecemeal way, or on a voluntary basis.

In respect of actual or potential public (or even private) harm, there are quite a few forms of accountability that might be effective, although again there is little coherence, with many variations according to circumstances and place. On some matters, public pressure plus political will enable legal measures to be taken to deter or punish harm. For the rest, there is broad scope for the exercise of responsibility by the press via either external or internal means. In relation to expectations of public benefit, there is less chance of enforced compliance and the delivery of such benefits depends on the voluntary acceptance of some public duty by particular news organisations, plus some impetus from professional norms. In addition there can be corporate advantages to be gained from public-spirited behaviour, aside from protection from interference. Public broadcasting, where it exists, is the only certain way of achieving social purposes by way of better media, since this is its raison d'être.

Modern media firms tend to operate their own systems of regulation for their own reasons under the banner of 'corporate social responsibility'. This recognises a need to 'serve society' and to maintain high standards of quality for news audiences. There is a strong element of self-interest in this and the self-regulation of news media cannot be left only to particular firms or the industry as a whole. An independent and more all-embracing source and forum for self-discipline is needed, and has to be created or imagined if it does not seem to exist.

Finally, in the broad area covered by the term 'failings' of the news media, there is also a mixture of accountability measures to hand, especially where it concerns the conduct of journalists (rather than the content produced). Media self-regulation and professional bodies are most likely to be involved. However, a good many alleged 'failings' of the news are likely to evade any effective accountability because they are built into the news process or simply reflect commercial imperatives governing news policy or features of 'news culture'.

In most of the topic areas covered in this chapter, there is little to be said yet about the accountability or regulation of the internet, mainly because it is not regulated or self-regulated in any systematic way. In fact it used to be regarded as not regulable, partly because of its status as a means of private communication, partly because of its marginality, and partly for practical reasons – its lack of any fixed identity or location, except where it is incorporated in the delivery system of an established news organisation. Otherwise accountability of all kinds is rejected by most who publish via the internet.

However, the *de facto* non-regulation of the internet is not, according to most legal opinion, an intrinsic property of the medium, despite difficulties of enforcement. According to Lessig (1999), the freedom enjoyed by the internet up to now is the result of a certain 'architecture' deliberately put in place at the start, but not the only possibility. Other structures are possible and more control is now being exerted, partly for increasing reasons of commerce and national security and partly because of new social and political issues arising. Forbidden uses of the medium can be blocked and also punished.

Conclusion

Voluntary forms of accountability are by definition more consistent with freedom than others, and a diversity of means is better for freedom than an integrated and coherent systems. However, such freedom may have to be traded off for effectiveness. At issue are the ends that accountability is supposed to achieve, a matter that in turn derives from the theory of journalism and its role in society that is in force. In many circumstances, the aims of accountability are simply to reconcile competing interests and bring communication closer to its intended audience. Sometimes, however, the aim is to prevent some specific forms of harm, such as unfair damage to reputation or danger from crime or disorder, in which case voluntary accountability is not likely to work.

Accountability involving liability and material penalties may be more effective but is a step on the way to control and punishment even if not necessarily being incompatible with press freedom as legally defined. Largely left out of this account are the relations of accountability entailed by any media market relationship. Journalists cannot avoid listening and responding to the wishes and complaints of an audience, whether loyal or casual, that also constitutes its body of consumers. This has been described as 'strategic accountability'. The internet has made such feedback loops even more insistent and unavoidable.

Further reading

Bertrand, J.-C. (2000). *Media Accountability Systems*. Brunswick, NJ: Transaction Books.
Dennis, E.E., Gilmore, D. and Glasser, T. (1989). *Media Freedom and Accountability*. New York: Greenwood.
Feintuck, M. (1999). *Media Regulation, Public Interest and the Law.* Edinburgh: Edinburgh University Press.
Hallin, D.C. and Mancini, P. (2012). *Comparing Media Systems: Beyond the Western World*. Cambridge: Cambridge University Press.
Lessig, L. (1999). *Code and Other Laws of Cyberspace.* New York: Basic Books (new edition 2006).
McQuail, D. (2003). *Media Accountability and Freedom of Publication*. Oxford: Oxford University Press.
Trappel, J., Niemenen, H. and Nord, L. (eds) (2011). *The Media Democracy Monitor.* Bristol: Intellect.

Online readings

Go to www.sagepub.co.uk/mcquailjournalism for free access to the online readings.

Brants, K. and de Haan, Y. (2010). 'Three models of responsiveness', *Media, Culture and Society,* 32, 3: 411–28.
Hills, J. (2008) 'What's new? War censorship and global transition', *International Communication Gazette*, 68, 3: 195–216.
McQuail, D. (1997). 'Accountability of media to society: principles and means', *European Journal of Communication*, 12, 4: 511–29.
Richter, A. (2008). 'Post-Soviet perspectives on censorship and freedom of the media: an overview', *International Communication Gazette,* 70, 5: 306–24.

Changing Media Technology: Consequences for Journalism, Press Institution and Relations with Society

Introduction

While the media, and thus the practice of journalism, have always changed with the times, there are turning points at which more fundamental change occurs, as with the industrialisation of print media and, later, the electrification of news transmission. Each of these increased the scale and reach of the activities of the press and also changed the balance of purposes and the potential for various effects on society. The arrival of the mass newspaper also meant a largely new audience, with different tastes and interests, new types of advertising and commercial motivations, new possibilities for journalism to advance political interests and other propagandist purposes.

Broadcasting eventually went further in the same direction, while opening new possibilities for societal control of access to the means of public communication. Change also brought new genres, production formats, and even, in some degree, new content. Broadcasting developed its own journalistic activities but these were, for a long time, subordinate to other purposes of the medium (cultural, entertainment, profit, sport). Television and radio news generally took second place to newspapers and news agencies as 'originators' of news, often following the lead of the printed press as a source in respect of the main issues of the day. Despite this, they quickly reached first place as the main source of news for most people, in many countries. The reason for this primacy lies partly in the much wider reach and popularity achieved, but also in properties of the medium itself: greater verisimilitude, visual and emotional impact, apparently direct and instant transmission.

Main changes in media

- What are the main current changes in technology and systems?
- Why are significant effects expected?

Main potential effects

- What are the implications for journalism as an occupation?
- What effects are expected on the media industry and system?
- What are the implications for the press institution?
- What are the consequences for democratic politics and the public sphere?
- What are the consequences for freedom of expression and of the press?

Longer-term trends

- How might relations between journalism and society be affected?
- Can we expect more or less accountability and control?

The potential of the internet and other new media

It has been argued that, following the latest revolution in (the means of) communication, the paths of media and of journalism will be changing course again in some fundamental ways. The reasons for this lie in characteristics of new online media, plus the enhanced possibilities for mobility of reporting and reception. At the same time, a dramatic reduction in costs of using the telecommunication network for electronic communication of all kinds stimulates change. The characteristics of 'new media' most relevant to changes in the role of journalism are: the opening of access for all to online networks, in principle; the expanded possibility for producing and distributing news content; the interactive potential that differentiates the relation between sender and receiver from the traditional print or broadcast mass media situation of one-way transmission; and the multi-mediality that allows text and pictures to be mixed at will.

While it may not be a unique property of online media, they have created a situation when any person can choose to distribute views and information to a wide public, with little cost. The gateways to transmission are no longer well-controlled by journalists or others and may not even be controllable. The internet has by-passed the former rather effective licensing and supervision arrangements of most terrestrial and satellite broadcasting.

The changes described have led to a diversity of suppliers, distribution platforms and reception opportunities. Reception of mass media (news) is no longer collective in the way it was when a 'mass public' attended the same nightly news on television or shared the same large readership group of a favourite newspaper. The audience is much more individualised and free in principle to create their own personalised package of 'news' and to attend (or not) at their own convenience. There are opportunities for liberated communicators and motivated citizens to come together in new ways. Developments of mobile wireless technology mean that receiving internet content no longer requires a more or less fixed or steady location, and portability may even exceed that of the newspaper (at a price).

These are only some of the main pathways of change, but between them they suggest a number of critical consequences for the traditional newspaper, the institution of the press, the work of journalists, the position of news in media systems and the potential for effects on and in society (of the kind sketched in Chapter 6). The changes entail a re-alignment of links to the wider society that can originate from both sides. These comments, even so, come with the cautionary remark that actual change usually lags a long way behind the potential, and ends up short of it.

Box 8.1 The internet as stimulus to change

- Lower (or no) barriers to access to public space
- Individuation of audience, decline of mass public
- De-location of reception (mobility of audience)
- Multi-mediality becomes the norm
- Interactivity in media use in place of passivity

(Continued)

(Continued)

- Reduced control and regulation
- Increased diversity of suppliers and supply
- A stimulus to globalisation
- Bypassing of the once dominant media of newspaper and broadcasting.

Problematic aspects of media change

For the most part, the potential of new technology and the adaptation of current media systems have been viewed in a positive light, on grounds at least of theories of a democratic and open society (see Chapter 2). Largely positive attitudes have been expressed by journalists as well as press theorists (McGregor et al., 2011). The main promise is of more participation, more active exchange and flow of information in the public sphere. Diversity and equality are promoted and the dangers of monopoly and control by market forces or the state that were inherent in older mass media systems seem to recede. However, aside from the large question of the extent to which the potential of new technology for the benefits mentioned will be either sought or realised, there are also potential losses in departing from established ways in which media have already been harnessed to the needs of democratic society. The following consequences have been predicted in varying degree.

- The 'press institution' becomes even more shadowy and is weakened in influence by the increased diversity of types and sources of 'journalism', while the 'profession' of journalism is 'diluted' by competition from untrained and 'amateur' producers of similar content.
- A weaker press institution combined with de-professionalisation and fragmentation combines to make the accountability of journalism to society harder to achieve.
- There are even doubts about the capacity of society to achieve any effective form of regulation of online media, whether for control or accountability short of blunt censorship.
- The newspaper press in particular, as it declines in the overall media market and the particular media system, begins to lose its position as corner-stone of 'the press' and arbiter of standards of journalism quality. It cannot so easily claim to represent the voice of the 'press' and, for the most part, there is no equivalent successor to this role.

- Some established ideas about the potential effects of the press in society are brought into question, especially those which relate to greater social cohesion, or more susceptibility to hegemonic control (the end of 'mass communication').
- The basic informational needs of a democratic political system and public sphere remain, but the pathways to fulfilling communication needs are more complex and devious, with less clear or certain means of achieving results.
- There is a fundamental uncertainty about whether the much heralded benefits of online media will only serve further to empower an active minority, leaving the mass of citizens relatively worse off in information terms (a widening 'knowledge gap').
- Public and personal networks of communication are no longer distinct and segregated, with the consequences still not yet clear.
- Doubts have been expressed about the reliability and credibility of news on new online sources and the extent to which they can gain the trust of the public.
- The steady commodification (monetisation) of the internet displaces early ties of obligation to the public and society in respect of the potential for an enhanced role in the democratic process.

The issues raised are wide-ranging and the problems signalled will vary from place to place in the way they are manifested. Other large changes are taking place in the world affecting the position and outlook of national societies in such matters.

Box 8.2 Potential downsides of the internet

- Weakening of the press institution
- Erosion of ties to the society
- Decline of the newspaper
- De-professionalisation of journalism
- Lower accountability of journalism
- Public communication benefits in doubt
- New forms of 'knowledge gap'
- Lower trust in, and reliability of, online news
- Increasing 'commercialisation' and superficiality of content.

Initial signs of change

At the time of writing, media structure in most parts of the world is more under the influence of economic than political forces and global circumstances make the immediate future of any major industry less predictable than usual. However, the resulting pressures on news media, especially a decline in advertising and other revenue, have accelerated changes that were long-pending but held in check by inertia. The incursion of online media into the business of the news has been underway for approaching two decades and has passed the experimental phase, with major changes beginning to be apparent. Online opportunities for transmission were initially taken up by established news media, especially newspapers, as an extension of, or complement to, existing operations. They were seen either as potential competition to be kept under control or new opportunities to exploit as older types of news provision declined. We are not out of this phase.

Online news has largely been an extension of existing activities, but with a different and still uncertain business model. While the media experimented, new online operators, especially search engines and service providers started to provide some news as an extra service on their portals. This typically added little to the diversity of news, and nothing to originality. But this alternative supply of journalistic product, beyond the boundaries of the press institution of any national society has steadily expanded and begun to sap demand for traditional press journalism, or so it seems.

The advantages of online news for consumers include the fact that it is usually free, usually more up to the minute, easy to find, and digest. For most practical purposes, short and recent news fulfils daily needs, especially when it can be consulted at will and with full control of time and topic. Online news can also provide in-depth specialised news on certain topics. The shift of news audience from off- to online has so far mainly affected younger people, an audience of particular interest to advertisers and essential to the future of newspapers.

The 'big experiment' is far from concluded, but prospects for shoring up the dominance of the older press business and institution are not promising. Efforts to charge for news content may succeed, but in doing so they transform journalism into a specialist information collection and analysis service for particular groups, especially on financial or political matters. The result is to reduce the society-wide relevance and downgrade the editorial role of the press (as gatekeeper, guardian, commentator and critic). It also tends to reinforce social inequality in information terms.

At the same time, the internet has led to an explosion of new outlets and types of journalism, of a kind which often matches the more subordinate roles of expressing and forming opinion, as well as acting as critic. Overall there seems to be a marked gain from such output, although its actual reach is limited. The volume of news being transmitted by many more channels continues to increase, but without any extra demand for the work of journalists as collectors and sources of original information or as commentators and critics.

One of the early fears was that journalists would cease to be essential as mediators and evaluators of information flow between events/sources on the one hand and the public on the other (the gatekeeper role). There is not much sign of this happening at the source/sender end of the communication chain, since the connections to established journalism are strong and only here are found the resources and organisation to respond to the demands of reporting major events. However, the link to the public may just be less effective since the internet does allow individuals to find and consult their own sources on topics they want to know about. It is likely that selection and mediation will continue much as before, but with less specialist input in the task by professional journalists and supplementation by direct access to source material. It is also the case that our awareness of such source material depends in the first instance on an orientation from journalism. The case of Wikileaks and the mass disclosure of contents of US diplomatic cables in 2010 illustrates the continued relevance of journalism as amplifier, editor, guide and validator of information.

The overall picture presented by emerging media structures, affecting large parts of the world, has not yet been diverted in new directions by technological change. It is arguable that more and more media activities are being taken over by a relatively small number of global firms, thus with more and more vertical integration. The internet is largely controlled by global internet providers, with their own news services. Search engines like Google play an important role in filtering and rank ordering news items without any policy of influence, but with considerable potential for 'agenda-setting' and defining current realities. More powerful sources inevitably have an advantage in shaping the selection process.

Such trends strengthen rather than weaken the need for the professional journalism that has not yet migrated to the net.

Box 8.3 Main trends of internet change

- Development of the internet as a news medium has been pioneered by established print and broadcast news organisations
- Online news platforms are beginning to overtake older media in income and some audience sectors
- There is a large fringe of new suppliers on the internet, but content is largely opinion or advocacy rather than information
- Authority of established news media is being challenged
- The position of the journalist as essential mediator of information and access is weakened, but not fundamentally challenged
- Online news is dominated by a few large global corporations, with little evidence of interference in content, but signs of compliance with local (i.e. national) restrictions.

The internet: liberating promise unfulfilled?

The early days of the internet were marked by great optimism at its liberating and 'de-massifying' potential for civil society and the enrichment of the public sphere. As just remarked, the structures of ownership that have developed have not been encouraging to these trends, except insofar as they helped to expand use and create attachments to new channels of contact. The logic of the system has sought out applications which would eventually be profitable, rather than increase freedom and democracy. Using terms derived from field theory of journalism (see above, Chapter 4), we can say that the economic field has impinged still further on the journalistic one. The same could be probably said of the political field, with politicians seeking to benefit from new ways of mediatising politics and governments trying to control unregulated media channels.

The promises of open access and more freedom remain on the table, but so far the net result for most has not been more diversity of news and opinion from journalistic sources. There has been a general trend to incorporating and re-massifying new uses of communication within and between members of the public. This is probably most evident in the immense and rapid spread of 'social media' worldwide, with accompanying opportunities for advertising, marketing and even propaganda. There is also no doubt that the innovation of the weblog ('blog') represents a genuine expansion of opportunity for freedom of expression, especially in situations where there was most restriction. However, blogs vary greatly in kind and significance. A basic problem is that of securing and keeping an audience and blogs that are successful in terms of reach, especially in a free market system, may seek (or tend) to become institutionalised and lose some essential libertarian features. The semi-institutionalised social media outlet Twitter seems to be colonising what was once the preserve of the blogosphere.

The advance of new media into the provision of news has not obviously affected the nature of news or the overall demand for news. However, it has led to a relative side-lining of what were once major newspapers – especially the prestige quality press and the mass circulation popular press. The former once led and stood up for the press as an institution with a public purpose while the latter made money but was often out of sympathy with the guardians of the sacred role of journalism. The 'prestige' press has less prestige and probably less independence as it ceases to be profitable although it retains some political influence. The popular press can more easily be transformed into something yet more profitable, without provoking unease from political and cultural elites.

The structural trends mentioned, driven primarily by the economic push to exploit new opportunities, have inevitably led to increased commercialisation of the system. In fact this is the driving force and chief logic of change. Although a virtuous term for owners and managers, its consequences for news content divide the journalistic profession and are associated by critics with: lower standards of information and cultural quality; an avoidance of costly news stories without reward from the audience; an avoidance of the 'wrong' sort of controversy, or of 'bad news', that might turn away an audience and/or offend authorities and business clients; using methods of reporting that are dubious or unethical, under the pressure to succeed. The alternatives to 'commercialism' are: journalism with a purpose of its own guided by the ideals and ethics of the profession or by the public conscience of reporters; following assigned public purposes, rewarded by subsidy or in other ways from some disinterested public source.

The era of rise and application of new media has, for reasons independent of technology, been generally unfavourable to public support for, and protection of, media, this both on ideological (or 'principled') grounds or simply as a matter of practicality. The largest changes in this respect followed the end of communist regimes in the former Soviet Union and East Europe after 1990 (Jakubowicz, 2007). In many of the countries involved, the early enthusiasm for freedom, diversity and civic purpose was damped down by economic and sometimes political realities. In Europe generally, public broadcasting has been in retreat and, at the same time, under attack on mixed grounds of ideology and feasibility. Its presence online, even though controversial, has offered some prospects for revival, given survival.

The new online media have not generally created a new independent sector of media in organisation and ownership. The media innovations involved have mainly been extensions of existing structures nationally and internationally. This is in keeping with the logic of convergence which is levelling the playing ground of media regulation and control (as between the technologies) as well as integrating different forms and actual businesses. There is still little firm evidence of any trend to create new regulatory regimes for online media applications. There are an increasing number of difficult issues for would-be regulators or critics (ranging from the perceived menace of major 'leaks' to matters of freedom to communicate and to privacy), but existing laws, rules and procedures are being adapted and applied rather than supplemented by new rules. The general issue of internet 'regulability' (or not) still hangs in the air, although increasingly seems an irrelevance, given the propensity of national authorities to do much as they like and the lack of firm grounds in law or custom for resistance. The practice of journalism is very much affected by this, with potential gains and losses both for employed professionals and freelance or voluntary outsiders.

Box 8.4 The internet and freedom: main points

- Political and economic interests seek to use and control the internet
- Online news lacks traditional safeguards of its independence
- The trend to commercialisation is stronger than one to genuine liberalisation
- No new sector of journalism of any significant extent has emerged, no new public space
- There are no coherent structures of control, but also no guarantees of freedom
- There is a new potential for dissemination of unauthorised information, but the 'mainstream media' may still be necessary for credibility and influence (e.g. the case of Wikileaks)
- Democratic-participant initiatives do co-exist with uses for propaganda and manipulation, and are often tolerated.

Effects of media change on journalism itself

There is no doubt that there has already been a large impact on the work circumstances of journalists and on the wider issue of identity and status as a profession. Most immediately, new technology transformed newsrooms, requiring new skills and ways of working, but here we focus on changes with longer-term consequences for society. One general change with potential effects is in the relationship with news sources. Journalists, like everyone else, have immediate ready access to much information and background material, even if still needing to have some exclusive primary sources and to cultivate relations with insider contacts. But more routine news collecting and processing can be done with less expenditure of time and resources than in the past. Some argue that it can be done better, by way of widespread and active public participation. But the organisation of work (more desk-bound) also means less actual contact with sources, events and places. Several commentators (e.g. Deuze, 2007) have commented on the rise of a new role for the audience member – that of 'prosumer'. With the help of recording devices, plus the internet, many individuals can participate in the production (as well as consumption) of news content by way of their offerings of video clips, opinions, inside information, etc. This can be enriching, but it is a subordinate role and some exploitation may be involved. The way was already opened by various new formats of television documentary and 'reality' shows. Although 'user-generated' content has increased in significance, it does not seem to have much part to play in 'hard news' stories, apart from the contribution of photo and video evidence of happenings.

Even so, the basic pattern of content of online news does not, as noted above, seem to have changed much from the familiar model. Comparative research into old and new forms of news shows that the increased output has not been accompanied by any real innovations of format or actual content. Thus there is little more diversity (aside from the number of channels), as once promised, and little more globalisation of flow. The same, usually official or economically powerful, sources originate most of the news considered important to publish prominently on or offline. The same networks of international communication, as established by the major world press agencies and big media, still operate and lead to the same overall pattern of news attention in the world. News still flows predominantly between the same nexuses of countries as in the past, since the basic factors of supply and demand that structure news flow are not yet affected (Arcetti, 2008).

The same news agendas as in the past are in evidence and are similar between online and offline channels. It looks as if the world will have to change first, before a 'new order' of media is established, and there is no particular reason to expect that when it comes it will be a great advance on what we have. What is still particularly lacking is clear evidence that some of the most distinctive features and potentials of online news-making, especially interactivity, interconnection of people and ready access to channels, can make a long-term difference. Of course, if it does, it will not be of much benefit to journalists or the existing press institution, but will only weaken it further.

More signs of change can be found, if we stop looking for any large paradigmatic shift. The fact of being online and consulted in a different way does make a difference. News has to be presented in fragmentary forms for speedy and fleeting attention even if with possibilities for following up in more depth, by way of hyperlinks. The result is an accentuation of 'sound-bite news', relatively new for the newspaper press, although foreshadowed by the free newspaper (such as *Metro*) for the casual reader on the move. This shifts the balance of probability even more from the 'full standard' of news to the 'fire-alarm' model (see earlier, Chapter 5, The monitorial role and democracy). The typical event-based news of this model lends itself best to the interests of those who 'make' most of the news in the first places, namely large economic players, governments and other authorities. Analysis and interpretation of events is relegated to a later stage, if it happens at all.

Although the interactivity of online media has often been stressed as a transformative benefit and news media claim to welcome audience response, it is not at all certain that it has much control or influence over how contributions are used, compared to other inputs and pressures. It is a double-edged weapon, enhancing the power of management over audiences by way of information about them, without necessarily leading to any dialogue. Journalists may be exposed to public reactions, but may have little time, inclination, or even the freedom to respond.

The efficiency savings, coupled with the economic decline of many newspapers, have led to reduction of work opportunities of the traditional kind. It also implies a more precarious employment situation and less freedom of personal choice. There is an increase in many new kinds of 'information work' that may be available, but it is no longer journalism. The journalist work-force is likely to have a range of new and different skills that reduces an older sense of identity and vocation. Some sources suggest a general trend to a new model in which there is investment in a small number of star reporters or celebrity personalities, with a downgrading of others (Preston, 2009).

Apart from such changes in the nature of the work and in the pre-existing diversity of types of journalism, a new cause of uncertainty originates in the opportunities of engaging in journalistic-type activity outside the boundaries of formal news organisations. The main form of on-line publication that has emerged is the weblog or 'blog', usually a regular output of information and commentary authored by an individual (to begin with) that can be produced by anyone. The resulting 'blogosphere' devoted in one way or another to contemporary events, is comprised of a vast number of websites some of which rise in status, influence and reach by word of mouth or publicity from established media. These new sources sometimes tap into inside information and present an independent voice, but often consist of opinion or gossip with little public impact or particular value. The line between blogging and established journalism is not even a clear one, since journalists quite often contribute their own personal blogs as a separate activity from their main employment.

Various classifications of blogs have been offered but the main division is between individual or 'citizen' journalists and those employed by formal news organisations or who seek to transform a blog into a new regular publication (Domingo and Heinonen, 2008). There is some reason to think that the blog has changed its primary character since it first gained prominence as a new form of journalism. Some evidence suggests that many blogs, if they survive, become 'bureaucratised' and also start to carry advertising (Lowrey et al., 2011). There has also been reference to a process of 'mediatisation' of the internet as it takes on features of established media (Fortunati, 2005). In the context of politics, the term 'normalisation' has been used to refer to a process of incorporation into established routines and strategies of political contenders. All this is not very surprising, but it does change the significance of innovation.

There seems general agreement that the 'blogosphere' has added little to the flow of original factual information, especially as sources are often anonymous and lack verifiability. Under normal conditions of society and events, it looks as if blogs need some recognition from established journalism to have any wide audience. The position of the established media as a 'gateway' to the wider society has not yet been fundamentally challenged in most countries leaving aside circumstances where such 'gateways' were designed to exclude the voice of opposition. However, the new forms of news do further cloud the old issue of what precisely counts as journalism.

Box 8.5 Effects of the internet on journalism

- Greater productivity, but essence of 'news' not changed
- Less secure employment for journalists, more freelance, casual, out-sourcing, a new star reporter system
- New forms of journalism develop
- Status of profession becomes more uncertain
- New competition for the 'blogosphere' audience
- Primary informative role of journalism not challenged by blogosphere
- Gatekeeper role of established media is challenged, but media have power to publicise (or not) new sources
- Rise of 'user-generated content'
- New relationship with sources of power.

The future of the press institution

The idea of an institution has been defined as 'social patterns of behaviour identifiable across the organisations that are generally seen within a society to preside over a particular social sphere' (Cook, 2006:161). In the present context, the social sphere in question is that of public circulation of information and opinion and 'organisations' are the news media. The assumption is made that the news media generally operate according to largely agreed purposes and standards, following rules and procedures that are also widely shared. A second assumption is that the established media are perceived to 'preside' in some sense over this field of social life by themselves, by the general public and also the principal actors in society. Both assumptions are open to question and the delicate structure indicated may well be upset by changes in the means and structure of news provision now under way.

The press institution has supported journalists in their aspirations for professional status reflected in projects for improving ethical and work quality standards. It is also important to the goal of gaining some freedom of action and speech and for protection in carrying out a role that can make enemies or invite undesirable friends. It is not only governments and the law that can pose a threat to journalistic freedom; so do potentially dangerous (even deadly) enemies that reporting the news can make (criminal as well as institutional). The recognition of the press as an institution in society also strengthens the hand of journalists in the face of media proprietors who have power to employ or not employ as well as to determine news policy.

The institution as it emerged in the twentieth century rested on the foundations of associations and unions of journalists, achieved with some struggle, and also associations of press proprietors who came together more as an industry interest group. But their interaction with each other and with governments and the law helped to define a fairly clear field of activity, in which a range of different actors were publicly engaged. The unity of any national case was always limited and there was little consensus as to its extent, given the conflicts of interests and range of different types and goals of journalism. The rise of broadcasting as a news medium, often following different ground rules and with more restrictions and allocated responsibilities, was already a source of fission, before online media made their appearance.

In its function as guardian and standard bearer of a very public occupation, the press institution supports mechanisms of accountability. Authorities, in their dealings with the established media, are restricted in the direct actions they can take and more or less obliged to work through some other non-coercive forms of control, including the press institution. As a result, however, the position of the latter as a means of supporting the press may be compromised. Authorities can offer inducements to conform and impose certain penalties on the non-compliant. The de-institutionalisation of the press can have some liberating consequences.

Box 8.6 The implications of change for the press institution

- The composition of the corps of journalists is more uncertain
- The press institution has little or no authority over much online journalism
- Existing forms and procedures of self-regulation do not apply, meaning less accountability
- The press institution is less effective as an instrument of societal control
- The 'rules of the game' become uncertain for sources, audiences, web journalists and those affected by reporting
- Protection of traditional rights to a free press may be weaker
- There is no unified voice to speak on behalf of online journalism either nationally or in any global forum
- The extension of established media forms to online platforms will limit some of these effects.

The journalism–society relationship

The extensive changes in the production and distribution of news brought about by digitisation and convergence have upset the rather fragile and chance arrangements that have typically emerged for negotiating between the work of journalism and the claims of the wider society. The composition of the corps of 'journalists' as well as the nature of journalism is now much more varied and unclear as a result of the changes mentioned. In the original 'model', only those employed for certain reporting, writing and editorial tasks would have been accounted as journalists. The 'news' has become a tradable commodity largely detached from the context of production, often distributed by agencies who have no other journalistic function and no links of any kind to a press institution or any particular national society. The accountability of journalism depends primarily on its relations with others in the society, especially its audiences, clients and those reported on. It is with these that lines of accountability are drawn (see above, Chapter 7). The trends in journalism already mentioned certainly seem to further undermine the idea of a *unified* press institution both in the sense of a set of consistent principles and good practices and in the sense of an institution of society with widely acknowledged roles of wider benefit for public life.

However, under the emerging circumstances, despite the interactivity that allows stronger ties and real interaction in detail, the ties are often weaker than before and the audience more distant and unknown. This is mainly because contact on the part of the audience is so fleeting and loyalty to any particular journalistic source appears to be in decline, in line with falling newspaper readership and dispersal of attention to many, often mobile, sources. The press institution has depended on quite a strong sense of mutual accountability in the relationship between journalism and society and this sense is threatened by change. These generally pessimistic remarks about the effects of change on the institution do not even take account of the degree to which mainstream journalism is falling into the hands of global media firms and operators for whom the issues mentioned are of little or no concern at all, lacking attachment to any society or community or the profession.

The world of journalism has become fragmented and its link to a particular national base somewhat weakened, although journalism remains essentially national and local in its main orientation to and from society and public. Efforts are increasingly made to establish international norms and standards of freedom and conduct by way of various forms of professional cooperation, with beneficial results (Hafez, 2011). In some regions (for instance the Europe represented in the Council of Europe), common principles are accepted but without any formal process of adjudication or accountability. The United Nations Charter proclaims a standard of freedom with very wide endorsement. A variety of organisations seek to monitor freedom of the press and the welfare of journalists, world-wide (for instance, *Reporters without Borders* and *Index on Censorship*).

A rather similar set of basic journalistic values is formally recognised more or less universally, although with wide variations in the way they are lived up to (Hallin and Mancini, 2012; Hanitzsch et al., 2011; Preston, 2009; Weaver, 2012). Nevertheless, all key battles have to be fought on the home turf. The internationalisation of standards outlined may be more a reflection of the standardisation of the journalistic product brought about by common technology, forms of organisation of production, similar life-styles and participation in the same markets, rather than a matter of converging ideals.

The sense of the press as a social institution amongst (and also servicing) other institutions raises different issues. The primary reference is to the key role that the media have played in the political process for the last 300 years or so. In countries with some form of democracy, the press has quite clearly recognised tasks of reporting to a wider public on the events and issues of the day and the actions and counterclaims of political actors, as well as reporting the views of citizens. In this (once called a 'Fourth Estate') role, there are strong expectations of honesty, diversity and accuracy of news and adequate distribution to all citizens. The arrangements and tasks of the media for achieving these results were clearly known and could be depended on by others. The news media became essential to facilitate the process of politics, including the accountability of politicians and governments to the society and the legitimation of political authority. Here politics covers all matters of public concern that might at some point come within the scope of formal politics. Not much has yet changed in the essential nature of this task.

Even so, the process of 'mediatisation', and the elevation of the media role to near-primacy in the democratic contest for power, has had the effect of distorting the relationship between the media and politics, exaggerating the 'power of the press' (in a way that can be self-fulfilling) and, indirectly at least, shifting press activity from informing to subtle forms of propaganda (presentation counts for more than substance). This shifts the balance of advantage to contenders for power who are 'media-rich' or simply rich enough to buy the right sort of publicity. While it may not be any easier to buy the influential support of journalistic sources with high public esteem, this limitation means less in practice when it is difficult to identify such sources amongst the multitude of voices and news suppliers.

Box 8.7 Consequences of media change for the journalism–society relation

- Forms and procedures for self-regulation are weaker, leading to lower accountability of online media to society
- Ties with audience and community are weaker
- The internet has not taken on the traditional press roles, or those of the 'Fourth Estate'
- The 'rules of the game' have become more uncertain for sources, journalists, audiences and those reported on
- Power in society shifts to media and the media-rich
- Globalisation of journalism is real, but the scope of change is limited.

The question of trust

Research into public trust in the media (press) has shown much variation across countries. In general the press and the occupation of journalism are less well regarded than other better established institutions and in some places a decline over time has been detected, which has nothing to do with the advent of new media as such. However, the reasons for distrust lie partly in a tendency to blame the press for some of the ills of society that it reports. Or it is disliked for its alleged political alliances and tendencies. The press is also much more exposed to public judgement of its own performance than are other institutions and is an easy and regular target of critics. There is evidence to suggest that, for their part, journalists tend to show rather low levels of trust in many major institutions of society. This could simply be a healthy scepticism matching their role as guardians of the public interest, but it could be seen as undermining social cohesion.

Generally, the regulated sector of broadcasting has been more successful at keeping public trust. For example, the results of periodic surveys undertaken across 27 EU states show there to be a significantly higher level of trust in broadcast news in most countries than in the printed press (Eurobarometer, 2010). Television is also overwhelmingly the main source of national political news across the EU. Presumably this is related to the low level of trust in the press – sometimes (as in the case of the UK) this is phenomenally low. An early supposition was that online news would be found less trustworthy than established news. The internet makes available a great deal of information that is intrinsically difficult for anyone to evaluate as to veracity, accuracy and the good faith of the source.

The advantage of older news media forms of supply is that the audience member has some means of estimating reliability or its absence, based on experience and the public visibility and reputation of the sender and some addresses for the direction of complaint. Confidence might be misplaced, but most audiences still seem able to differentiate between sources well enough to make choices for attention. However, as well reputed online platforms have taken over a large share of the news audience, it looks as if they too are generally found reliable. The evidence of *Eurobarometer* shows levels of trust in the internet as a news source to be not very different from those in relation to print media. For the most part, the news diet offered is not different in kind, comes from established agencies and other media and consists of short factual bulletins, without any hidden agenda. In some respects the news has become more 'objective' than it was before. It also conforms more to the 'fire alarm' model (see above, Chapter 5).

Consequences for the 'public sphere'

This concept is probably too ill-defined and contested to make any precise judgement about the changes under way, and the time frame for observing change is much too short, to allow any certainty. When revived for our times by Jürgen Habermas (1962), the public sphere referred to a notional open space between the 'top' and 'basis' of society that was available for the free circulation and exchange of ideas and information, with provision for widespread participation in debate and deliberation. The news media provided for essential elements of these arrangements and to do so would need to be both free and diverse. Habermas raised the alarm at the 'colonisation' of the public sphere by large media firms in pursuit of profits, involving a degradation of quality (sensationalism, tabloidisation, etc.).

Predictions about effects of new media have been divergent. The more optimistic view sees much benefit in the great expansion of intercommunication between citizens using the opportunities offered by email, social media and other *fora* for coming together, for debate and for disseminating new ideas. In effect, the internet has the capacity to create at least a 'virtual' public sphere of its own (Papacharissi, 2002). Instead of there being one public sphere, there could be several, even a 'counter-public sphere' promoting radical change (Milioni, 2009). It has been suggested that the emergence of a new 'network of networks' freely interconnecting all actors and sectors constitutes a 'Fifth Estate', supplementing but not replacing the Fourth Estate' (Dutton, 2009). An essential element of the earlier public sphere concept was the access that should be available for new and diverse voices. It is not altogether certain that 'virtual participation', aside from being very selectively engaged in by those who like the mode is at all the equivalent of real-live participation in debate and action in the presence of others (Goldberg, 2011).

It is hard to deny that the monopoly hold of the established media on the 'gates' of public discussion, in collusion often with powerful 'gatekeepers', has been seriously weakened. There are now many more quite effective points of entry, often for sources that are not inhibited by conventions or iron rules of objectivity or actual laws preventing disclosure. There are many examples of leaks and whistle-blowing that spread from non-institutionalised online sources into the public domain, even if the 'new media' are not immune from reprisal. The major Wikileaks disclosures in 2010, referred to earlier, have provoked a powerful enemy and the story is neither complete nor likely to be replayed again in the same way. As noted above, the established media played a key part in actually disseminating and validating the disclosures.

The interactivity and interconnection made possible by new media allows the formation of movements and groups, especially focused on single issues, and generally helps 'outsiders' in the mainstream political system to garner more popular support on the merits of their cause. There has been much attention to moments of crisis in recent times when mobilisation through online media has been assigned an important role in forming public opinion or actually enabling opposition to unite and turn into action (as in the case of the 'Arab Spring' of 2011).

Many established political systems have shown tendencies to ossification, with loss of followers and declining interest and participation in formal politics. New kinds of more local, specific and also international issues now have a chance to feature in the spectrum of public sphere topics and activities. New forms of political activity have emerged, often adopted reluctantly and clumsily by an older order to political organisations. A new era of public political and social life has not yet dawned, but there is a new sense of possibility and change and many examples of effective intervention.

But reservations are also expressed, leaving aside the probability that a good deal of online activity in the sphere of public information is already penetrated by dominant voices from government and established actors in politics and the economy. The use of online media for any sort of civic or public participation in debate and self-determination is quite limited in its incidence and the new possibilities for engagement are a transfer of action, rather than an expansion of participation into once excluded sectors of society. This is due in part to the fact there is still a 'digital divide', even if not so much in basic access as in the *quality* of uses to which access is put. Active participation requires motivation and competence (and resources) that are still strongly linked to education, occupation and income, still very (or even more) unequally distributed in most societies.

Perhaps the most serious counter-argument to excessive optimism is the very obvious fact that new media are widely and successfully targeted by would-be communicators seeking to harness the power of voluntary interconnection via social media to advance commercial and ideological objectives. Online media provide open access not only to those who are deprived of other means of entry into the public space, but also to those who are already there and wish to defend the ground they hold. The openness, freedom and anonymity of the internet also makes it open to well-financed efforts at management and manipulation of voices and messages posted online, with little chance of defence or redress. Apparently, large-scale public support and approval can be bought without much risk of discovery. Thus the public sphere can be poisoned as well as enriched by deliberate and cynical misuse.

The darkest suspicions about the emerging communication environment have been voiced by those who see a further fragmentation of what has been achieved slowly and with difficulty by democratic change. The downside of the benefits outlined could be a destabilisation of the existing public sphere and its institutional supports. A primary effect of the dispersion of audiences over many new sources of news is to decrease the stock of ideas and information that are held in common and that might be mobilised to achieve wider social change. A tool of expansion adopted by online providers has been to tailor news supply to the personal interests of each consumer, although it is unclear how far this trend has really taken root.

The emerging evidence of relative continuity and stability of news agendas, nationally and internationally suggests that the 'tailored' news supply will be an addition rather than a replacement for the current situation of a shared public space of news. More threatening, however, to the status quo is the competition for other types of media time use and a reduced engagement in public issues. It may become just another minority taste culture to be catered for, of good quality but no longer the basis for collective social action.

Box 8.8 Consequences for the public sphere

- More extensive and more free engagement by citizens in the flow and exchange of information and opinion
- More chance to participate actively in the political process, especially at grass-roots level
- Better interactive connection between political actors and citizens
- More accountability all-round by way of exposure on the web
- Less control of the 'gates' by a few established media
- More chance to mobilise for change at moments of crisis
- Potential still exists for establishing a protected public space for citizens in relation to national or international issues
- New dangers also, as internet use is misused for hidden propaganda
- Generally more fragmentation of a sense of belonging to society and consequent weakening of public sphere (the rise of the 'Daily Me').

In overview

The main issues that have arisen as a result of changes in media technology as introduced at the start of the chapter can now be reviewed, even if the answers are tentative.

On the matter of the *press institution*, it does seem probable that this already rather weak and insubstantial entity has been further undermined (or limited in potential influence) by the changes that have occurred. As a matter of history, its main embodiment and voice was to be found in the traditional mainstream media (especially the newspaper) of the pre-digital age that are struggling to retain their hegemony. The accelerating loss of loyal reading (or viewing) publics weakens the authority with which they can speak or the reach of their influence over the emerging world of news production and flow. It is less clear who can claim to represent the interest and voice of 'the press', even if that concept remains viable.

The health of the press as an institution was rarely the first priority of particular media owners. The predicted decline is not necessarily bad news for freedom of expression, given the pre-existing vulnerability of 'established' media to political and economic pressure. Although a strong press institution has advantages for the quality of public life, by way of more accountability, it can also be seen as a route for more effective control of the press and also a means for media owners to advance their own economic interests. Competition from a less amenable and amorphous internet may be beneficial for democracy.

In a parallel trend, it is probable that the advance of a 'profession' of journalism has not been helped by the extension of the name and role of journalist to untrained and amateur producers of competing content with some similar goals. Even so, there is not a great deal of evidence that the newly enfranchised sector of online communicators do actually produce a great deal of actual news, as opposed to opinion and comment, certainly not in any systematic way. There is some sign that the new forms of 'journalistic' publication are extensions and additions rather than alternatives. However, where regular news flow becomes restricted (by unusual circumstances or government interference), the new channels take on some of the roles of suppressed channels and can provide a home to professional journalism. The internet can be controlled, but with more difficulty and not without it being noticed internationally.

Insofar as we can speak of *fragmentation* and *deprofessionalisation* of journalism and the press, we are likely to find some loss of potential for accountability to society. On the other hand, there are new developments (e.g. new forms of news) and other tendencies at work that may have supportive and innovative consequences for accountability – for instance, by way of more interaction between journalists and media and their publics. There may also be advantages in limiting the influence of a 'profession' that tends to be self-interested, weak in relation to power and limited or distorted in its concept of what is 'good journalism'.

The basis for an assumption of strong and consistent media effects has rested in the past on the fact of uniformity of message and ubiquity of exposure. This applied to 'neutral' effects such as the setting of political public agendas, to unwanted effects of distortion or hidden propaganda, even to beneficial effects such as widespread gaining and sharing of public knowledge and increasing cohesion. Fragmented and more diverse news provision should lead to a less consistent message, less uniform impact and less possibility for propagandists to construct and direct a planned view of events. This adds up to less 'powerful' media as once understood by students of mass communication (Bennett and Iyengar, 2009). It remains to be seen what will happen, but it would be unsafe to under-estimate the capacity of the same powerful vested interests to exploit the potential of new media in new ways for old purposes.

The term 'knowledge gap' was introduced a long while ago to describe the differences in levels of public knowledge amongst different 'strata' of society. The big question concerned how far the mass media, and which one, could help to close this gap. The arrival of online media led at first to the belief that differential access to the new information resources would widen the gap, now termed a 'digital divide'. Gradually as access has expanded, a reverse expectation has been voiced, with the new media seen as potentially more effective than mass media at the task of informing everyone. However, it is gradually being recognised that the fundamental conditions for change are to be found elsewhere than in the media. There almost certainly persists a 'class bias' in access to, and use of, the media. There is no immediate way or prospect for reduction in the inequalities of quality of information received, even when economic and hardware barriers have been narrowed.

Conclusion

No interim balance can possibly be struck between the benefits and costs of ongoing changes, certainly not before the evidence is more definite. Not much has happened yet to suggest that the founding principles of freedom of publication and the corresponding roles for journalism in society need any fundamental revision or extension. Nor is it likely that new forms and arrangements for carrying out these roles will be available or adopted in the foreseeable future. There is a limit to effects from technology and these effects do not necessarily take one in new directions.

Further reading

Domingo, D. and Heinonen, A. (2008). 'Weblogs and journalism: a typology to explore the blurring boundaries', *Nordicom Review*, 29, 1: 3–15.

Kung, L., Picard, R. and Towse, R. (eds) (2008). *The Internet and the Media*. London: Sage.

Livingston, S. and Bennett, W.L. (2003). 'Gatekeeping, indexing and live-event news: is technology altering the construction of news?', *Political Communication*, 20, 4: 363–80.

Online readings

Go to www.sagepub.co.uk/mcquailjournalism for free access to the online readings.

Arcetti, C. (2008). 'News coverage of 9/11 and the demise of the media flows, globalization and localization theories', *International Communication Gazette*, 70, 6: 463–85.

Chang, T.-K., Himelboin, I. and Dong, D. (2009). 'Open global networks, closed international flows', *International Communication Gazette,* 71, 3: 137–59.

Fortunati, L. (2005). 'Mediatizing the net and intermediatizing the media', *International Communication Gazette,* 67, 6: 29–44.

Fuchs, C. (2009). 'ICTs and society: a contribution to the critique of the political economy of the internet', *European Journal of Communication*, 24, 1: 69–87.

Goldberg, J. (2011). 'Rethinking the public/virtual sphere: the problem with participation', *New Media and Society,* 13, 5: 739–54.

Lowrey, W., Parrott, S. and Meade, T. (2011). 'When blogs become orgs', *Journalism,* 12, 3: 243–59.

McGregor, P., Balcytiene, A., Fortunati, L. et al. (2011). 'A cross-regional comparison of selected European newspapers and attitudes to the internet', *Journalism,* 12, 5: 627–46.

Milioni, D. (2009). 'Probing the online counter-public sphere', *Media, Culture and Society,* 31, 3: 409–33.

Papacharissi, Z. (2002). 'The virtual sphere: the internet as public sphere', *New Media and Society,* 4, 1: 9–27.

Singer, J.B. (2003). 'Who are these guys? The online challenge to the notion of professionalisim', *Journalism,* 5, 4: 139–65.

In Conclusion: Striking a Normative Balance

Introduction

Despite enormous changes over the last century or so, the central core of what journalism does or is expected to do for society has not changed all that much over this period, nor is it so very different in essentials across many different national societies today. It is the order of priorities, the standards sought and attained, the cultural and political contexts, the conditions of operation and the perceived needs of society and corresponding responsibilities of journalism that are the main sources of change and variation. These variations are a stimulus to re-assessing the validity and robustness of the guiding ideas that have been outlined in earlier chapters. We begin by sketching the overall institutional framework within which journalism is practised. Linked to this is a reminder of the different levels at which values might be applied by way of guidance or assessment. Answers to the questions posed at the end of Chapter 1 are provided by way of a review of the main themes and issues affecting the relation between journalism and society. The chapter closes with reflections on the prospects for protection or reform of journalism, in respect of the public life of a society.

It is clear that the more idealistic aspirations of journalism are not universally shared or realised and the shortfall can be considerable. At the same time, we recognise that the goals of journalism itself vary, as well as the expectations of others, not only according to the wider context of society, but also according to differences of perspective. The potential benefits of journalism are varied and there are often contrary interests to be served. These thoughts inevitably affect our closing normative reflections. The contents of the book as a whole strongly support the view that journalism is of central significance to contemporary society and that its future cannot simply be left to chance or its current producers alone. However, any hope for protection, or 'improvement', of standards depends, in the first instance, on what is actually wanted as well as needed, and by whom. The question of feasibility of any such change has also to be faced and this depends on issues of social theory and public policy.

A frame of reference for journalism and society

First of all, it is helpful to be reminded of the framework that has been deployed earlier in this book. The notion of journalism as a particular 'field' of institutionalised activity has been adapted from the ideas of the sociologist, Pierre Bourdieu. For us, a 'field' is simply a term denoting the demarcation of journalism from other forms and genres of the public media of communication, other related types of information work and other institutional spheres (such as politics, economics, show business). To demarcate is to differentiate and to set boundaries and, while the boundaries of journalism are rather imprecise, or simply very porous, there is sufficient recognition of journalism as a separate entity to justify this. Thus journalists are primarily engaged in the open dissemination of information about current conditions and events of public relevance, often political in nature, with the 'business' of journalism mainly following market principles.

To speak of journalism as 'institutionalised' means that its activities are purposeful, well-established and governed by systematic procedures, following certain rules and standards. These are largely left to the media organisations and systems (news media) in which the activities take place or to professional associations of journalists, editors and proprietors. The term 'press' is sometimes used (also in this book) to identify the relevant institution, but it can be misleading, not only because it highlights an old medium, the newspaper, but also because many new kinds of journalism have developed outside the older 'mainstream' media and its established rules and procedures.

The institutional character of journalism is also reinforced by an awareness of shared values and purposes and also by recognition from the rest of society. This recognition comes, in the first instance, from other institutions (also fields in their own right) that benefit from the services of journalism. Politics, government, law, business and culture/show business/sport come to mind as 'neighbouring' fields, with a direct interest in what journalists do. The boundary between journalism and these other fields has often been a contested one, not only because of attempts to control and direct the 'power of the press', but also reflecting the overlap and differences of purpose in the task of public information. For instance, journalism has to distance itself from related communication activities, including advertising, marketing, public relations and propaganda (or 'public diplomacy'), all of which deviate from essential values of journalism as providers of impartial information. As journalism and media have become more central to public life, their influence on other fields has increased, notably by way of the process of 'mediatisation'.

Although journalism is not a fully-fledged institution in its own right, it does have some of the relevant characteristics, especially in respect of its claim to independence and the uniqueness of the task it performs 'in the public interest'. As an activity, however, it may be subordinate to the economic interests of news media in market systems or to political pressures in partisan press systems, or to direction in more statist or non-democratic contexts.

At the heart of the matter lies a set of key roles that journalism fulfils for the rest of society, all related to the collection and public distribution of

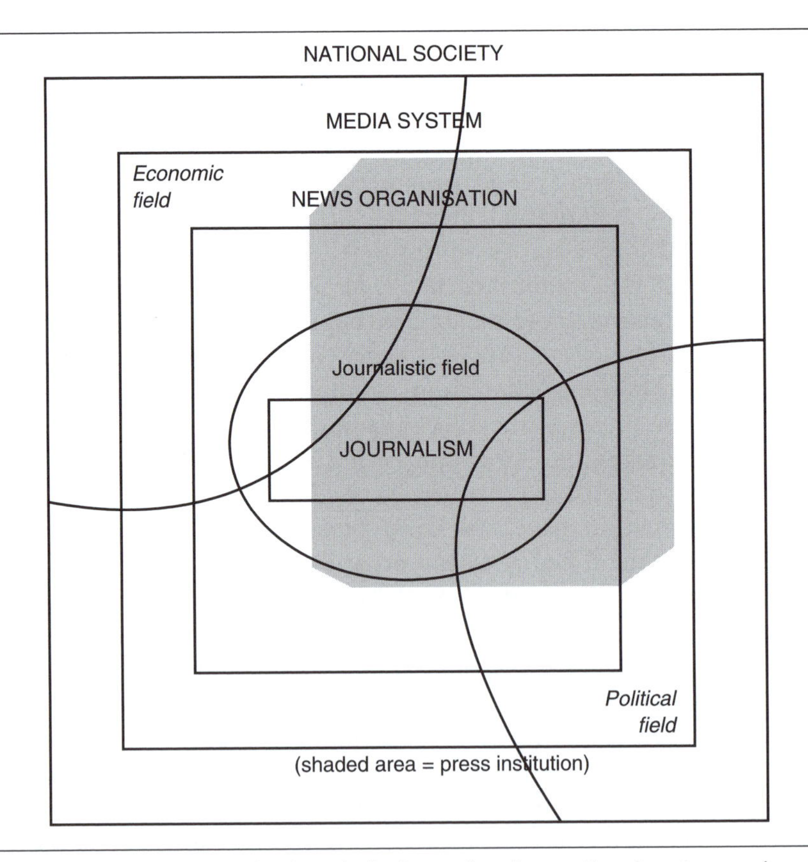

FIGURE 9.1 A framework of analysis: journalism in a national system under overlapping influences

information in the widest sense. Some of these roles are self-chosen, others not. The 'rest of society' is not simply a vague abstraction but consists, in the first instance, of the many producers and consumers of news information. The sources are all those agencies and organisations that need to reach the larger public on their own account or for altruistic purposes. The consumers of news are mainly individual citizens, but also the same organised bodies that act as 'sources'. Journalism is an essential component in the process of 'society speaking to itself' and thus constructing common knowledge, a shared consciousness and memory and a sense of identity. It is equally essential in facilitating and informing the interaction of participants in the many networks making up the complex of social life. Governments and authorities also have a strong interest in journalism as a source of intelligence about the state of opinion of the people as well as by way of the continuous briefing about events. At a more abstract level, the concept of a 'public sphere' that seeks to capture the totality of intercommunication and cooperation of citizens living in the same polity presupposes a ready circulation of current information and ideas of relevance to public decisions.

The various elements mentioned are related to each other as sketched in Figure 9.1. This portrays the practice of journalism as typically carried out within a news organisation, itself a component of a media system, operating within national boundaries. Each national society has a distinctive normative and structural influence and every media system tends to operate under distinctive principles. All such news work pertains to the journalistic field, although there is a significant overlap from both the economic field and the political field, as shown. The autonomy of journalism is always limited or under threat. One extra element (shown by a shaded area) is that of the press institution, also national in character, which is very variable and uncertain in its standing and influence, but which supports autonomy in principle. This sketch does not show changes under way, especially as a result of the internet.

Normative contexts and choices: different levels of application

The practice of journalism in its most widely occurring mode of objectivity aspires to a value-free perspective in reporting on events. Even so, it is inevitably influenced by different value systems and specific value preferences. These values are not usually made explicit and their influence is often unintended and unrecognised by journalists themselves. We can again (see Chapter 1) distinguish between different 'levels' at which (different) value systems operate, in particular the level of: the *society*; the *media system*; the *occupation* or profession; the *personal*. At the first, most general level (society), there are many value systems, often with competing variants, reflecting political, religious, ideological, cultural, humanitarian commitments, all with varying degrees of motivation to find some public expression by way of journalism and with varying degrees of success. Besides this, there is usually a more permanent, consensual set of values relating to patriotism, the national interest, security and social order, all of which tend to shape news selection without acknowledgement.

At the level of the media system, the work of journalism can be influenced by two main sets of value factors: the principles of organisation, control and accountability; and the relative priority attached to the main 'social functions' of the media as sketched in Chapter 4 (i.e. informative, cohesive, critical, cooperative, etc.). In respect of the first, a media system may, for example, be designed (insofar as there is scope and in response to political or public demand) variously to promote social equality (by universal provision requirements), public education, diversity or freedom. The values referred to operate at a long 'distance' from actual news output, but their observance is likely to find some reflection in content. The choices of primary 'function' of the media system are more nebulous, but the corpus of such ideas as a whole is a potential source for journalists in assessing their own role and responsibilities.

This represents the *third level* and journalists, either as individuals or collectively, do often have a definite sense of the options open to them in relation to their own audience and the wider society. The choice will often involve a value preference. Possibly more influential than perceptions of role are the ideas of professional responsibility (in such matters as truth and accuracy, impartiality and fairness, etc.) that have been organised into codes of ethics and conduct for self-regulatory purposes. The 'press institution' often stands behind these influences, but more immediate agents of influence are media employers and associations or unions of journalists. Finally, at the individual level, we return to another (and possibly the main) route by which the values of a society colour the product of journalism, even if professionalism seems to explicitly exclude personalism from news texts. Such personal values are not easy to exclude or entirely conceal. This framework of ideas about value choices will be drawn upon later in the chapter.

Journalism in an information society

Much was written during the latter twentieth century about an emerging 'information society' to encompass varied consequences of a 'communications revolution' based on new technologies and means of transmission.

It was regarded as a further step beyond the 'post-industrial' society, itself the successor to an 'industrial society', based on extraction and large-scale manufacture. The new form of society was also called 'post-industrial' because of a transition to service industry and information-based work instead of physical labour. A new 'information economy' was also recognised as knowledge was applied to increase productivity and provide a new range of consumer goods. The information society goes further, since the focus is now on information itself, not just its application. Journalism may not be a central feature of the transition, but it is inevitably implicated and increasingly affected itself as an occupation and business, as well as being one of the expanding range of information products.

The most relevant core phenomenon of the information society has been the exponential rise in the production and transmission of all forms of information (private and public) by numerous means, primarily as a result of advanced telecommunication and then digitisation, and far out-stripping human capacity to attend to or process. The rise of all forms of public media and of interpersonal connectedness is only one relatively minor feature of the 'information revolution'. Even so, it has played a part in stimulating change and is now increasingly affected in its turn. The impact comes in two main forms – on the one hand the circulation of 'real-world' information is no longer under the control of the news media, since there are many alternative online sources, often more specialised and faster. On the other hand, journalism is challenged by having to process and make sense of the vast supply of data of potential relevance or of interest to the public, easily overwhelmed by the abundance. It is not irrelevant to suggest that journalism in one way or another has acted as cheer-leader for the information society.

Another relevant interpretation of the facts and ideas linked to the information society is that the type of society emerging as a result is better conceived of as a 'network society', at least when viewed from a communications perspective (Castells, 2001). Contemporary societies are increasingly interconnecting by way of many overlapping communication links, some centre–peripheral, others interactive (mobile phones, social media, etc.), many more lateral than vertical. Journalism is infected by network features in several ways: via multiplication of blogs, the trend to 'user' participation and content production, the encouragement of feedback, etc. The network society model also facilitates the formation of contact relations of audiences/users across boundaries that once divided and segregated the media public in rather fixed ways. The process (albeit a slow one) of globalisation of communication is also promoted.

We can envisage the emerging context for journalism as generally threatening the self-sufficiency and autonomy of journalism, except as needed for essential independence and perceived trust, when providing guidance through 'overload' of information. Secondly, journalism will be more openly engaged, responsive and accountable, more likely to participate in public life, nationally and internationally, if only by necessity. Other features will remain, especially as determined by the market, but the product of journalism will probably need to acquire new and varied forms of value. Although still largely contained within the media system, the links with national societies will be less close.

The main normative issues of journalism and society in review

In the following pages, the main conclusions of the book and their normative implications are reviewed and problematic aspects are highlighted.

The contribution of journalism to meeting the needs of society

One of the foundations of social theory of journalism or of the press, or media, is found in various ideas about its eventual functions or purposes for the organised life of society. Abstract theorising of this kind does not take us very far, although there seems to be some agreement about which basic needs are at issue. These mainly comprise:

- The need for much diverse and reliable information about events and conditions affecting the environment of a society and a wide public dissemination, in the interest of change, adaptation and response.
- The general need for a minimum level of consensus and social cohesion, such that a common identity will be supported, along with cooperative activity and effective self-government.
- The facilitation of the work of other institutions of society in all matters that require public communication and the correlation of activities, with primary examples in relation to politics and the economy.

Each of these ideas seems in line with what journalism actually does, although not exclusively and not directly. The aim of facilitating the work of other social institutions is not openly announced in those terms, but easy to recognise in a range of spheres of social life, including sport and, leisure, commerce and business, politics and government. The 'cohesive' function is less self-evident, although it seems plausible, on reflection, that attention to a common supply of news will give some shape to the collective outlook and climate of opinion of a large and otherwise disparate population (e.g. of a city, region or nation). This process is not planned, but reflects the attachment of most journalists to their community and society and its perceived interests and values. Journalism draws heavily on the common stock of culture, symbolism and memory that go to make up an awareness of shared collective identity. In addition to questions of national 'consciousness' and identity, there are matters of active cooperation and interaction within and between the innumerable networks and relationships that exist in social life, formally and informally. Daily journalism is one important source by which these interactive processes are lubricated and integrated by a continued and varied supply of information.

While the news can lead to a shared set of public concerns, it can equally be claimed that news is often divisive in its effects, separating the well- from the minimally-informed and/or also one opinion sector from another depending on the different supply of news from partisan sources' and in different interpretation of 'facts'. For instance, the 'virtue' of supporting minority identity (e.g. as with an immigrant community) can be regarded as detrimental to integration and national unity as well as making a positive contribution. News content is also routinely biased towards covering 'negative' events and problems, crime, conflict and violence. The image of society reflected back to itself and on to the world, is not necessarily a harmonious one. A more fundamental critique of news is that it lacks diversity and that its dominant structure of meaning is consistently inclined towards the views of established powers and elites.

The extent of responsibility and accountability of journalism for the consequences outlined

The principle of freedom of expression and of the press sets a limit to obligations and responsibilities that may be imposed by society. In general, responsibility is freely accepted by the 'press' for the informative aspects of its task. The same applies to avoidance of harm that might be caused by publication, provided that a clear awareness and sound evidence of such effects and awareness of risk is available. Responsibility may or may not be accepted for more controversial matters, especially those relating to the active 'watchdog' role or to the expectation of promoting consensus as determined by authority. In these matters, journalism can claim freedom either to expose and criticise or not to do so and it can decline any obligation to perform a collaborative service, for instance, for the political or business system, or even on grounds of patriotism. Much depends on the possibilities and pressures of the given national environment, on the definition of purpose of the particular news organisation and sometimes also on the personal preference of the individual journalist, if there is any room left over for this.

Accountability inevitably involves some limitation on freedom of action – normal in all social relations but potentially more problematic than usual for journalists since it directly affects their central role. However, there are different kinds and degrees of accountability, with different degrees of acceptability to journalists.

Most acceptable is accountability to their own audiences for standards of service. Least acceptable is being held to account by political or other official authorities for specific acts of publication, although some general public responsibilities are usually accepted. Accountability to commercial clients is often a matter of necessity, as it is to civil claims in law, but also questionable if it impinges on editorial decisions. Normally it is achieved through market mechanisms or the legal system. In practice, some degree of responsiveness to public opinion goes with the territory of journalism as well as a more focused response to the actual audience. Professionalism involves a significant commitment to accountability for conduct and performance, hence the appeal of self-regulation and rejection of external forms of compulsion.

Freedom of the press as a limiting condition of responsibility and accountability

The principle of 'freedom of the press' does not entail total freedom of publication and most formal guarantees of freedom of the press set some conditions regarding the rights of others (see Appendix §2) and the good of society as a whole. In practice, journalism, as a public activity, is only as free to criticise or oppose as permitted, not only by law, but also by custom, culture and its relations with the rest of society. There is an unwritten convention in many countries that the degree of freedom varies according to subject matter. In a liberal model, this means most protection for political speech, religious belief and information in general and least for morally dubious forms of publication, plus gossip of a malicious kind, certain kinds of propaganda and often also advertising in general.

Much also depends in the end on the particular context and the type of publication or journalism involved. In some cases, an adversarial and critical mode is expected (as in the weekly press of opinion) and institutionalised, in others it is not. Broadcast media have not generally been permitted the same degree of freedom of reporting as the newspaper press and this applies especially to critical or adversarial forms of journalism initiated by the medium itself. Requirements of neutrality and objectivity are, by the same token, usually enforced on broadcast journalism by internal self-control. A well-grounded belief that harm might ensue from a particular act of publication can also be a reason for limiting freedom in advance.

However, in general, journalism does not voluntarily accept liability for effects that actually occur as a result of lawful and well-intentioned publication. At most, moral responsibility for consequences might be acknowledged, where effects can be anticipated. Certain kinds of intentional effect (for instance, incitement to violent protest) can be subject to restriction in advance, although most can only be dealt with by warnings or *ex post facto* (but with 'chilling' consequences). The scale of possible effects is also a factor affecting freedom. The smaller the reach and more marginal the media voice, the less effect of any kind will occur and more latitude is allowed on fairly pragmatic grounds, Public expressions of personal views by individuals via media channels can also expect some immunity. The rise of non-institutional, online, media has introduced new uncertainties into these considerations.

In respect of the critical and adversarial role of the press, some broad guidelines apply. One is a rule of proportionality. The more ostensibly egregious the offence or public evil, the more latitude is allowed to journalism to attack. Secondly, the more powerful the object of criticism (and therefore more equipped for self-defence), e.g. a government or large firm, the more leeway for critique is allowed. The potential costs to the news organisation are a disincentive for 'irresponsible' criticism. By the same token, the more powerless, marginal and helpless the objects, the more restrained should be the critique (a matter of ethics) although in practice there are fewer restraints and a high incidence of this abuse. Another general rule (also of prudence) is that the stronger the terms of any critique, the firmer grounds as evidence or argument there have to be.

Press publication is generally much more constrained than personal expression, because the consequences are likely to be greater and more people affected. More scrutiny is given to what is published (and thus has more impact and also a more permanent form) than to what is spoken, and more conditions apply. Moreover, it takes much more than written law to secure the right in practice. Threats to freedom do not come only from the state, but also from political, economic and even criminal sources. There is much evidence of routine self-censorship in response to pressures and of many failures to actually make use of the freedoms that are available for the purposes that are supposed to justify it (e.g. holding power to account). It is a right or privilege that is valued, but the responsibilities that go with it are frequently neglected. The caution and predictability of most journalism most of the time has been widely remarked on.

The relation between journalism and democracy

Journalism is often thought of as promoting the rise of democracy and it has certainly become both necessary to it and intrinsically interconnected with it. The age of democracy has also been an age of journalism and the two have always supported each other. The main reason lies in what journalism does – providing essential information on issues of the day to citizens that enables them to make informed choices and judgements concerning policies and politicians. It also meets the needs of politicians and other agencies to communicate extensively with citizens. It plays a vital role in the formation and dissemination of opinion.

Nevertheless, journalism is also often well-established in non-democratic societies and its democratic credentials are not unchallengeable. It is a service produced and sold for different purposes (of its own and others) in a variety of markets. For the owners of media industries, service to democracy is only one purpose amongst many others. Moreover even its service to democracy is not disinterested, or always with positive consequences for the democratic process. Non-democratic and autocratic regimes and movements also use journalism for their purposes. There is a journalistic bias towards democracy, arising from a historic commitment to truth, freedom and equality, but systems and structures can blunt and deflect professional and ethical purpose.

The status of journalism as profession or occupation

It is neither possible, nor essential, to give a firm answer one way or another to the question of journalism's status as a profession, but the process of considering it can be revealing. Certainly there is a strong aspiration to professional status amongst the ranks of paid journalists – those who operate within the boundaries of the 'press institution'. However, there are different versions of what professionalism might entail. For a minority it involves a dedication to truth in the service of a more just and well ordered society according to chosen values. For a larger section of the press it means a commitment to supplying original and reliable information in depth on significant issues of public concern. For others, it is more a question of achieving high levels of public attention and popularity from as wide an audience as possible, usually within a commercial framework and exercising creative skills in doing so.

The common ground is an acceptance of at least minimal rules of objectivity and reliability in respect of factual information and a view of the public as primary beneficiary. Much more variable is the acceptance of accountability for goals and performance. Long-standing obstacles to professional status are also to be found in: limited autonomy; subordination to commercial imperatives; a lack of any institutional or professional monopoly over the roles of public informant, critic or entertainer. More recent trends may even have worked against professional standing and unity, especially the opening up of new media channels for access by many new voices and groups, with no control of standards or purposes, and no processes of accountability. There is evidence of casualisation, and sometimes 'deskilling' of journalistic work as a result of economic pressures on the traditional media organisations that provided a home for journalism in the past. On the other hand, the complexity of the 'information society' places new demands on the skills of journalism for handling large volumes of raw information.

The journalistic role as self-perceived

The version of 'functions' of journalism with which this review of issues opened is quite abstract and general. Empirical inquiry amongst practising journalists has given firmer foundations to ideas about the tasks and purposes of journalism in the wider society. The findings largely confirm the theoretical view of the functions of journalism as sketched, but are easier to relate to actual practice. Role perceptions divide fundamentally according to a few basic dimensions, especially along a scale from active and critical to neutral observer and reporter. These choices reflect a more fundamental division between a view of journalism as an altruistic and socially responsible profession (a 'sacerdotal' image) and a pragmatic one that identifies it as a provider of services to customers and clients according to demand. These services can be about gossip, diversion and social identification rather than about factual, useful information or deep analysis. Mixed versions are of course possible, and are, in fact, normal.

In countries without firm democracies or orderly government, the watchdog and adversary roles are typically much weaker or even absent and preference goes to the role of objective information provider, even if the reality often departs from this in the direction of collaboration with a ruling regime or in deference to criminal pressures. Even providing objective information can be regarded as an act of defiance and thereby dangerous to engage in. In developing countries, the wish or obligation to contribute to planned change has a clear place alongside dissemination of information. The general pattern seems quite predictable and reflects 'national news cultures' that vary between countries, usually along lines that relate to reigning democratic principles (or their absence).

Freedom for journalists is viewed from within as primarily a matter of politics and the state, although financial and economic constraints and organisational requirements also shape the prospects for autonomy. The main elements of purpose mentioned above do not exhaust all possibilities, especially those relating to political opposition and partisan advocacy. The rather ubiquitous (and often predominant) 'sensationalist' and commercial purposes of much journalism do not receive due attention in these reported self-perceptions. The public face, as presented to researchers also conceals other less desirable aims and practices of journalism, especially related to propaganda, public relations and concealed forms of advertising.

The 'power of the press'

This phrase is both familiar and quite misleading, since one can really only speak of 'influence' in this context. Genuine power involves availability of force or compulsion as well as direct impact, whether intended or not. Journalism is not typically a source of power on its own account, but an *instrument* that can be used by or on behalf of real power holders, or even *against* them, again either as an instrument of opposition or an independent critic. At most, the larger effects of journalism in society will be indirect and gradual. In the mainstream version of professional journalism, the news is assembled and transmitted without motives of influence in any specific direction. The primary aims of journalism, as most generally practised, are to interest and inform and not to make propaganda and punish, not even to advocate or criticise, even if information made public does get drawn into these processes that other agencies in society engage in. It is also the case that news media have considerable freedom on day-to-day matters to choose their focus of attention and the terms of reporting. Many of the short-term and immediate effects mentioned can be cumulative and significant. The 'power to publicise' can easily lead to the amplification of bad news for some, harm to reputation, prejudice and misinformation, from a variety of causes.

The potential influence of journalism (or 'press' or 'media') is, thus, considerable and the media in general have moved from a peripheral to a central position in society's power processes and relations. None of the parties involved can afford to ignore or neglect their assistance or resistance. It is quite evident from the behaviour of holders of power in contemporary society, that media are regarded as tactical instruments for gaining, using and keeping power and are acted on accordingly. The reasons have largely been explained, since both the current stock of public 'knowledge' of events and circumstances and the direction and balance of the prevailing climate of opinion are often dependent on what people learn from news media. Such 'knowledge' is open to varied interpretation and, once disseminated, is no longer neutral, but value-laden and contributes to specific attitudes and opinions. Journalists also, albeit without a conscious political aim, act as 'gatekeepers' giving access and directing attention to voices and persons who do have some real power and often some purpose of their own. Thus the news 'sets the agenda' of issues on which power will be focused at the current moment, and signals who the decision-makers are and what they think.

In a democracy especially, the allocation of power is legitimately dependent on the balance of preference and judgement of 'the people' and this is intensely fought over in modern political life, using the immense resources of media expertise and channels of public communication. While outcomes are typically unpredictable and slow to appear, there are also certain critical moments and events when the contribution of journalism can and does make a crucial difference. No serious power player can afford to leave it to chance.

The conditions that will determine the relative influence of the press have been outlined in Chapter 6 and several of these are met quite often, especially as a result of media concentration, political and other pressures and factors in the production of news that reduce diversity. Other possibilities for power-related effects that occur in the form of resistance or opposition have already been mentioned. The existence of a free press and the undoubted (soft) power of (bad) publicity can have a strong cautionary effect on government and authority that depends ultimately on public opinion. A press united in determined opposition can be a hard opponent to take on, even if a rare occurrence. Journalism is often seen accordingly as an important defence against the abuse of power, by virtue of its capacity and willingness to publicly expose failings and misdeeds on the part of all who exercise public power. The continued scrutiny of power-holders is often described as a 'watchdog' or 'checking' function.

The 'power of the press' can be knowingly abused as well as harnessed to the positive purposes of holding power to public account. Examples include the targeting of individuals to induce fear and compliance, or freely allowing news to be used for grey propaganda, on behalf of interest, faction or ideology.

Critical Theory usually views the mainstream news media as acting on behalf of state or ruling class interests as a means of hegemonic control on behalf of the state or a ruling class elite, often without a deliberate intention to do so. The theory holds that such a system of dominance is a fundamental condition of industrial society. The evidence of systematic bias on the part of news media seems to support this view, but it is not the only interpretation of the evidence and the argument risks being circular and self-confirmatory.

Accountability is achieved via exposure by trusted news sources, when based on convincing evidence. This is the start of a process that has to be completed by citizens and civic organisations and the theory rests on an assumption of democratic self-government. Necessary conditions for fulfilling this function include the independence and diversity of journalism, freedom of publication and the courage to face the consequences of offending the powerful. Journalism facilitates the role of other agencies of accountability (e.g. in politics and civil society) in the first instance. The 'watchdog' image is popular in the mythology of journalism, but other models have been suggested, including the 'lap-dog', the 'guard-dog' or the 'attack-dog'.

An ideology of 'objective news'?

The news, as the main product of journalism, should, if professional beliefs are fulfilled, consist essentially of information about current events, chosen on grounds of significance and relevance according to criteria of truth and objectivity. This means information that aims to be factual, accurate, balanced, verifiable and reliable. This outcome cannot be guaranteed, but it can be approached by way of a number of widely understood and appreciated practices, especially in relation to checking facts, citing sources, evidence and witnesses and adopting an attitude of impartiality and neutrality in respect of the interpretation of the 'facts'. The journalist should, ideally, be a neutral and detached recorder of 'reality'. Theoretically, this style of news maximises its truth value. Its core defining feature is the reduction of uncertainty for the attentive news 'reader'.

Belief in the efficacy of objectivity has often been challenged by critics. Journalists are sometimes accused of adhering to an ideology of their own in this respect rather than accepting the limitations of the objective mode. News is a cultural and organisational product, shaped by a set of factors that often conflict with the informational criteria just mentioned. Some of these factors relate to the requirements and limits of technology and organisation, others to the cultural background of news of producers or of the intended audience. Not least influential are the requirements of 'media culture', with its attention-gaining and personalising imperative and its tendency to 'mediatise' all phenomena encountered. Journalism does, in its own way, seek to 'reflect' the reality of society as it might appear to an unattached observer, with only limited attempts to interpret or to evaluate, but the result is inevitably partial, superficial and unintentionally misleading.

The 'reality' can only be recorded and reproduced selectively, and this results in an over-emphasis on what is abnormal or dramatic, the heights and depths, neglecting what is routine and unremarkable. It is not possible to eliminate all value judgements from the news selection process, only to conceal or disregard their influence. Other characteristics and requirements of news are incompatible with the strict notion of objectivity, especially its story-telling form and devices to attract and keep an audience. Just as problematic can be the relation between journalism and sources on whom it depends for new or insider information. Significance and relevance are inevitably influenced by the interests of these sources. In addition, the ties of ownership that bind much journalism to large media enterprises, with their own economic and sometimes political interests, call into question the claim (or capacity) to be genuinely impartial. Journalism is extremely vulnerable to pressures and limitations endemic in the 'system'.

Towards a universal normative theory of journalism?

This account of journalism and its practitioners reveals some common ground, especially in the shared informational needs of all modern societies, and the vulnerability of all such provision to established sources of power. There is plenty of evidence of similarity, across countries, in the actual product of journalism (the 'news') at any given point in time, and there is broad agreement amongst journalists about their primary role. However, the diversity of national circumstances makes it hard to be able to speak convincingly of any universal 'theory of journalism'. There are too many varieties of journalism and conflicts of purpose and understanding concealed by the apparent consensus on the 'main tasks' in broad terms. The basic requirements of a democratic political system and public sphere provide the firmest and most widely acknowledged basis for the principles that sustain the central role of *public informant*. This role, in turn, requires a commitment to truth, as far as attainable and to a measure of neutrality and good faith in the selection of information for wider dissemination and of opinions voiced or given access in relation to events. However, democracy is still not firmly established world-wide and is open to different, sometimes conflicting, interpretations.

Equally current, at least in democracies, is the view that journalism does or should play an essential part in a process of 'public accountability', meaning holding those who exercise power accountable to the public. For the most part, journalists do not see it as their task to act as accuser or judge, but they do enable others to act in this way via the provision of information and evidence and by the expression of supportive opinion. This position appeals as much to the pragmatically minded as to the altruistic wing of journalism since it leads to saleable news as well as legitimising scandal and gossip relating to the rich, powerful and celebrity elite on grounds of service to the 'public good'. This further demonstrates the ambiguity of the public good concept. It can justify both total liberty and over-cautious respect for authority. In the end, pragmatism rules. However, the reality is that in many countries the conditions of independence and freedom do not exist in sufficient degree to enable the press to hold power to account.

The virtues (values) that have informed and guided journalism in its more altruistic moments and manifestations have been noted at various points in this book. Despite the limits to universality, there is increasing evidence of a wide recognition amongst journalists of much the same set of values, even if practical realisation is limited by 'reality'. Most commonly found, at least in aspiration, are the values listed in Box 9.1.

Box 9.1 Values of journalism

- Attachment to truth and reason
- An attachment to justice in respect of the law, to social justice in respect of distribution of the wealth of society and to fairness in family and personal relations
- Care for the powerless and exploited and for society's victims in general, as well as the victims of chance misfortune
- Supporting and showing loyalty and attachment to a wider community, embodied in the immediate audience, but extending further and deeper to community, nation and beyond
- Showing courage in exposing wrong-doing and standing up to pressure to ignore or suppress information
- Exercising professional skills in the communication arts
- Attachment to independence of position and autonomy of action as institution, organisation, and practitioner.

Sometimes these values are notable by their absence from news as published. The contrasts and inconsistencies reflect the diversity of goals of journalism as well as the fact that 'reality' and human failings always impinge on idealistic motivations. In any case, the normal or average is not what matters most (even when it can be calculated and compared), but individual journalists actually living up to the values just summarised, when it matters. Society needs an effective journalistic presence and performance which, in turn, requires recognition and protection of the press institution as well as structural provisions to ensure conditions for operation (diversity, freedom, etc.) plus support for forms of accountability that are effective without being oppressive.

There is yet another point at which normative considerations arise – where they impinge on everyday activity and in a less ambiguous way. This concerns the ethics and norms of conduct affecting the collection of information, relations to sources and how information is then used. Codes of conduct set out rules and guidelines on a number of sensitive issues (see examples in the Appendix §3). These are subject to 'policing' by colleagues, supervisors and occasional more formal procedures. Conformity is often secured initially through practical experience and informal socialisation at work. External forms of accountability such as press councils and the ombudsman system may apply a selection of the same standards in adjudicating on complaints from the public and others affected. There is evidence of a high degree of formal acceptance of much the same ethical and professional rules across media systems, although observance and enforcement are very variable. There is also scope for self-regulation to develop and be effective, even without any structural change in systems.

The consequences of ongoing changes in media technology and structure for normative relations between journalism and society

The direction and strength of change are not yet clear enough to know or foresee the consequences. But there are some grounds for expecting some of the following trends:

- Traditional news media forms (newspapers and broadcasting), are declining and also adapting to new forms of online publication, but so far without fundamental changes of aims, practices or norms. So there is continuity. A less complete and less uniform distribution of general news is one likely outcome, with implications for equality and diversity.

- The already loose 'press institution' is becoming looser and less clearly bounded. Individual news organisations are smaller and less integrated, with more casualisation of work, and a less common purpose. Accountability to society is less easy to implement. The role of holding governments to account is less likely to be adopted.
- The trends to monopoly that have sometimes threatened press freedom may have slackened somewhat, as a result of more competition and open access for new and different voices. However, journalism itself may be losing its place as a core component of an expanding media industry. New forms of conglomeration may threaten the social role of journalism.
- The internet is accelerating trends to globalisation of news supply, more likely to weaken than strengthen the social role of the press and the possibilities for accountability in any national context.
- The position of the press as the main 'gate-keeper' for what is admitted to the public domain is being challenged by alternative non-institutional online sources. The major 'Wikileak' of confidential US communications in 2010 exemplifies this trend, but also confirms the continuing role of the press as a disseminator and a vital source of validation of the information leaked.
- The forces of legal and state power have not been weakened and are directing more attention to online media of all kinds, which turn out not be so immune to control as once supposed and, in general, have no clear protection of their rights.
- No transformation of an essentially 'mass communication' model of public communication has yet occurred, despite more interactivity, participation and an opening to more sources of content. Journalism is largely on the sidelines of this whole process and new online forms are being adapted to old purposes.
- The question of the degree of public *trust* that attaches to journalism still needs to be asked. Early fears were that online news would not have the same credibility as traditional forms, because it is not backed by a dedicated institution and the resources of the historic press media. The initial evidence does not seem to support this expectation and, in reality, a great deal of online news still comes from the same sources as before.
- The many new forms of journalism that have flourished in the first decade or two of the internet age are already forcing a modification

of the 'dominant' version of 'professional' journalism, as 'unmotivated' and objective current information. The consequences are still limited in extent and the potential effects on the journalism–society relationship are still unrealised.

- Newer, online, forms of journalism are developing a familiar dual 'structure', taking further the current division between a commercial 'mainstream', majority, media supply and a committed or critical, alternative, minority press. There is still a potential for the expansion of a more 'professional', and also a more socially committed, journalism that is currently marginalised in commercial structures.
- It is most probable that benefits to democracy will have, as always, to come 'from below', by the active use and expansion of new possibilities and by defence of freedoms that now exist. Political and other forces 'from above' will seek to marginalise and hold back further change and reverse some freedoms gained.
- Numerous niches and cracks in the hegemony of dominant media have been opened up for many minorities and political movements excluded from power and voice in society. The advantages of the internet in allowing access without direct regulation are real and even quasi-authoritarian regimes seem prepared to tolerate what they cannot easily suppress, as long as reach and impact are marginal. Moreover, such access offers a ready opportunity for surveillance of dissidence.
- Although journalism has usually played a progressive role in the political upheavals of the long 'age of democracy', at moments of dramatic change (such as the Russian Revolution or the 'Arab Spring') it is events and underlying realities that determine outcomes. It remains to be seen whether or not the 'new media' can make any greater difference, by way of new channels and forms of journalism.

This review suggests that technology and industry changes have both positive and negative potentials. Which will predominate need not be completely a matter of chance, hence our closing attention to the challenges faced by public policy and the journalism profession.

What can be done? Reflections on the chances for better journalism

It is not too surprising to reach the conclusion that journalism fails, on a wide front, to live up to its aspirations and potential, but limited success does not invalidate the whole enterprise. Journalism cannot on its own change or stand against the world of which it is an integral part, only provide information channels and motivation for society itself to initiate change. Limits are set by the particular circumstances of each society as well as by the diversity of perspectives and interests involved. Ideas of what might count as 'improvements' often differ as between those that might be variously labelled as: priests; politicians; professionals; profit-seekers; and public. Moreover, the means to achieve change are not equally available.

In considering what practical options there are for protection or improvement, we need to take account again of the different 'levels' in the overall social process of journalism that were identified earlier in this chapter and book. This division helps to specify the main contexts in which normative problems arise, the different kinds of values and means that might serve towards the defence or advance of 'good journalism' (as viewed in terms of social roles and effects).

At the *level of* ***society*** and the ***media system***, taken together, the context of operation of journalism is characterised by widely varying social and economic conditions that change only slowly and cannot be manipulated. Likewise, the cultural and political contexts are an outcome of long and complex national histories that exert a powerful influence. Even after fundamental change, the shadow of the past is long. The history of Russian media, for instance, indicates some continuity with the tsarist era, despite one revolution and a second one, of sorts, 70 years after the first. Although new laws and principles can be established, an underlying climate of opinion about the role of journalism in society, affecting rulers, public and journalists themselves, cannot be so quickly changed.

The situation, in general terms, is not so different in other long-established national societies where political cultures have deep historical roots (see Hallin and Mancini, 2012; Mugham and Entman, 2002). The deep ideological attachment to free market principles in the US and elsewhere does not, for instance, seem to weaken in the face of evidence of poor public information provision. There is not much prospect of journalism becoming any less 'national' or 'local', despite the globalising and universalising effects of technological and other changes. Nor are societies attached to consensual or communal forms of social life and governance inclined to welcome more freedom of expression or new adversarial and investigative ideals of reporting, however much basic press freedoms are guaranteed in law.

Nevertheless, contemporary journalism, world-wide, does seem to be guided by much the same broad range of purposes or primary functions: the informative; the integrative; the transformative; and the cooperative. The convergence effects of technology and global markets have reduced the differences that exist between national media systems and exerted pressure towards shared principles of operation that have a basis in values, such as those of freedom, truth, diversity and order. Given the political will, there is an opportunity at the level for public policy initiatives that will lead to better outcomes, even if not necessarily 'better journalism' from all points of view. The potential is for interventions in media structure that will strengthen these values of press performance, on behalf of the society as a whole. There are many examples in the twentieth century of such interventions that have either succeeded or have had a realistic chance of doing so. These include: the instituting of public broadcasting; the limitations on ownership concentration; the content rules for protection of children and others; the use of subsidies to promote different types of media and more universal provision; societal pressures towards co- and self-regulation and accountability, etc. In the coming time, the internet, as the latest medium, should become the main object and beneficiary of positive support, although the signs in this respect are not very hopeful.

The most important requirement at the level of media system is to protect and advance genuine diversity in all aspects of news and information. This should be manifested in a plurality of channels, ownership, content and access for sources and audiences. A necessary condition is an acceptance of the principle of public intervention directly or by way of forms of regulation that also respects basic freedoms, not an impossible goal. Neither media owners nor journalists can achieve much on their own in this matter, even if committed to the principles outlined.

Despite the resistance of market and other forces in society, the current phase of media system governance has been marked quite widely by the appearance of new independent offices for the regulation of media at national level that promote change as well as exert control. Not only is planned change in media systems possible (they change anyway), it is arguable that improvements in professional practice that depend in the end on the news media and journalists themselves will also require supportive attention to media structures on the part of society. For the most part this will involve pressure for improved accountability and self-regulation, but also practical encouragement for innovations designed to advance the values mentioned, especially those of freedom and diversity.

The specific means and forms for the improvement of media structures need themselves to be consistent with the basic values mentioned, especially that of independence. The justification for any proposed change must lie in a concept of the 'public interest', but one revised in the light of its alleged ambiguity. An alternative, more general, but more inclusive term, might better serve the purpose, namely the idea of the 'common good' or 'general good'. This can be given meaning, as democratically decided, by its intended beneficiaries and by society at large. The lessons of theory and performance suggest that a broad goal of promoting social, cultural and informational development (and greater equality) for the majority could provide a viable starting point and a foundation for a variety of arrangements designed to meet the information needs of citizens and social actors, as an alternative, or in addition to, what a purely market system can achieve.

There are various possibilities for innovation of media structures as evidenced by diverse arrangements already in place. The opening up of cyber-space also offers new opportunities for quite a few forms of publishing arrangements, some of which would be suitable for journalism. One such innovation would be the creation of guaranteed and protected public 'spaces' for wider public participation, without major direct costs or need for profits. A proposal for a 'civic commons' has been launched which envisages an enduring structure and an agency designed to promote access and facilitate public deliberation – a meeting place for diverse networks in the public sphere (Coleman and Blumler, 2009). The need for something of this kind grows stronger as the once-promising 'social media' networks are increasingly monopolised and monetised in sophisticated and even exploitative ways for the benefit of owners, remote from any notion of serving the public sphere. An older model is suggested by the sector of the press serving particular political and religious movements and paid for by its own public, a model open to revival by way of online business models (based on subscription). Another model, tested on a limited scale is the formation of independent trusts that operate one or more media outlets on a not-for-profit basis. Key criteria for alternative arrangements would be effective accountability to users and society and participation in policy-making by an audience or sector of the public served.

In respect of these and other possible suggestions for improving the position of journalism, it has to be recognised that the climate for change is very hostile in the most fundamentally 'liberal' countries and likely to be one of suspicion in environments prone to authoritarianism.

At the ***level of journalism practice*** (occupation and role), there are clearly opportunities for improvement that lie within the scope of a press institution or a journalistic profession, as well as the management of particular news media. The account of journalism given in this book lends support to the view that journalism has distinctly idealistic elements of its own as well as making an essential contribution to society's efforts to realise certain general purposes. The scope for self-determination is typically limited and uncertain, but it is the freedom to make choices and judgements at this level that probably has most significance for the practitioner and the most creative and valuable outcomes.

There are alternative conceptions of the values that journalism seeks to uphold and the values may sometimes be corrupted or distorted. The pursuit of social order and harmony can turn into oppressive conformism; the inclination to criticise government and politics can lead to a negative and rancorous social and political climate; patriotic attachment to a national interest can end as narrow ethnocentricity and prejudice; targets for investigative reporting can be vulnerable or trivial, sparing the powerful.

The contrast between aspirations and expectations on the one hand and the limitations and failings of journalism on the other is real enough, although not very surprising and not untypical of most human endeavours with noble aims. Journalism may well have a higher proportion of mundane tasks to fulfil than most similarly placed occupations, such as scholarship, education, literature, the arts, or even politics. It has to earn a living without subsidy and its relationship to society is more directly influenced by material circumstances.

In the suggested division according to levels at which values relevant to performance may be applied, the 'base' level is that of the ***journalist as an individual person*** rather than as a member of a profession or occupation. There remain some issues of purpose and values still to be determined by journalists individually, often on an ad hoc basis, although the scope for self-determination is typically limited and uncertain. The motivations for personal choice are diverse (aside from career ambitions), ranging from an aspiration to achieve the ideals of the profession (as in exposing corruption or wrong-doing on the part of the powerful) to fulfilling some more personal aim of public enlightenment or social good. This is where conscience and a personal value system can influence conduct and transcend the limitations of the system and external pressures. The most socially significant and remembered instances of journalism are quite likely to originate in such individual aspirations rather than in organisational tasks or professional routines, although a supportive work environment is also needed. The idea of journalist as hero, that finds some expression in our culture, is more likely to depend on the example of those who are motivated in this way rather than the professional celebrities that the system rewards.

Last word

It is clear from these summary remarks that relations between journalism and society, while they might seem open and unconstrained, aside from certain necessities, are subject to many forms and degrees of normative influence, leaving aside any formal regulation that might apply and the working of personal conscience. Journalism is a fundamentally normative activity, both in the respects outlined but also in the difficulties an open-minded and honest journalist would have in observing and making sense of reality without reference to some of the values outlined, even while making an effort to adopt a neutral position. In sum, the conception of journalism as a 'calling' that is sometimes claimed on behalf of other secular occupations, as noted above, is not entirely far-fetched.

The circumstances where the highest ideals of journalism are put to severe test are not normally to be wished for and not at all the norm for the occupation, but also not all that rare. It is hard to think of any other group or profession whose members are still being imprisoned, tortured or executed just for doing their work well. Journalism is not a saintly occupation, but it has a continuing supply of martyrs to celebrate or mourn, even though martyrdom is not a professional requirement.

Further reading

Cammaerts, B. and Carpentier, N. (eds) (2007). *Reclaiming the Media*. Bristol: Intellect.

Capella, J.N. and Jamieson, K.H. (1997). *The Spiral of Cynicism: The Press and the Public Good*. New York: Oxford University Press.

Castells, M. (2001). *The Internet Galaxy*. Oxford: Oxford University Press.

Coleman, S. and Blumler, J.G. (2009). *The Internet and Democratic Citizenship*. Cambridge: Cambridge University Press.

Davis, N. (2011) *Flat Earth News*. London: Vintage.

Just, N. and Puppis, M. (eds) (2012). *Trends in Communication Policy Research*. Bristol: Intellect.

Online readings

Go to www.sagepub.co.uk/mcquailjournalism for free access to the online readings.

Curran, J., Iyengar, S., Lund, A.B. and Salovaaria-Moring, I.(2009). 'Media system, public knowledge and democracy: a comparative study'. *European Journal of Communication*, 24, 1: 5–25.

Hafez, K. (2011). 'Global journalism for global governance? Theoretical views, practical considerations', *Journalism*, 12, 4: 83–93.

Josephi, B. (2005) 'Journalism in the global age between normative and empirical', *International Communication Gazette*, 67, 6: 575–90.

Appendix: Selected Documents Relating to Rights and Obligations of News Media

§1 Examples of international norms

Declaration of the Rights of Man 1789

Approved by the National Assembly of France 1789

(Excerpts)

Article 4

Liberty consists in the freedom to do everything that injures no-one else; hence the exercise of the natural rights to each man has no limits except those that assure to other members of society the enjoyment of the same rights. These limits can only be determined by law.

Article 11

The free communication of ideas and opinions is one of the most precious of the rights of man. Every citizen may, accordingly speak, write and print with freedom, but shall be responsible for such abuses of this freedom as shall be defined by law.

United Nations

Universal Declaration of Human Rights

Adopted by the UN General Assembly 1948

Article 19

Everyone has the right to freedom of expression, this right includes the rights to hold opinions without interference and to seek, receive and impart information and ideas through any media and regardless of frontiers.

European Convention on Human Rights

Effective from 1953 and currently endorsed by 47 member states of the Council of Europe. Its implementation depends on the European Court of Human Rights, also a body of the Council of Europe.

Article 9

Freedom of thought, conscience and religion

1. Everyone has the right to freedom of thought, conscience and religion, freedom to change religion or belief and freedom, either alone or in community with others and in public or private, to manifest religion or belief in worship, teaching, practice and observance.
2. Freedom to manifest one's religion or belief shall be subject only to such limitations as are prescribed by law and are necessary in a democratic society in the interests of public safety, for the protection of public order, health or morals, or for the protection of the rights and freedoms of others.

Article 10

Freedom of expression

1. Everyone has the right to freedom of expression. The right shall include freedom to hold opinions and to receive and impart information and ideas without interference by public authority and regardless of frontiers. This Article shall not prevent States from requiring the licensing of broadcasting, television or cinema enterprises.
2. The exercise of these freedoms, since it carries with it duties and responsibilities, may be subject to such formalities, conditions, restrictions and penalties as prescribed by law and are necessary.

UNESCO Media Declaration

Declaration on fundamental principles concerning the contribution of the mass media to strengthening peace and international understanding, to the promotion of human rights and to countering racialism and incitement to war.

Adopted by the 20th General Conference of UNESCO, 1978.

(Excerpts)

This resolution was adopted in the context of the time, a late stage of the 'Cold War' and a world even more divided economically than now. It was regarded by some member states as too controversial and too politicised for UNESCO. The primary difficulties were with the implications that states should have the right to supervise the work of foreign journalists and block reporting with negative implications for countries concerned. This was held to contravene the principle of 'Free Flow of Information', itself a politically loaded concept. Nevertheless, the Resolution was and remains significant for giving clear expression to principles relevant to global news flow.

Article I

The strengthening of peace and international understanding, the promotion of human rights and the countering of racialism, apartheid and incitement to war demand a free flow and a wider and better balanced dissemination of information. To this end, the mass media have a leading contribution to make. This contribution will be the more effective to the extent that the information reflects the different aspects of the subject dealt with.

Article II

1 The exercise of freedom of opinion, expression and information, recognised as an integral part of human rights and fundamental freedoms, is a vital factor in the strengthening of peace and international understanding.

2 Access by the public to information should be guaranteed by the diversity of the sources and means of information available to it, thus enabling each individual to check the accuracy of facts and to appraise events objectively. To this end journalists must have freedom to report and the fullest possible facilities of access to information. Similarly, it is important that the mass media be responsive to concerns of peoples and individuals, thus promoting the participation of the public in the elaboration of information.

3 With a view to the strengthening of peace and international understanding, to promoting human rights and countering racialism, apartheid and incitement to war, the mass media throughout the world, by reason of their role, contribute to promoting human rights, in particular by giving expression to oppressed peoples who struggle against colonialism, neo-colonialism, foreign occupation and all forms of racial discrimination and oppression and who are unable to make their voices heard within their own territories.

4 If the mass media are to be in a position to promote the Principles of this Declaration in their activities, it is essential that journalists and other agents of the mass media, in their own country or abroad, be assured of protection guaranteeing the best conditions for the exercise of their profession.

Article III

1 The mass media have an important contribution to make to the strengthening of peace and international understanding and in countering racialism, apartheid and incitement to war.

Article V

In order to respect freedom of opinion, expression and information and in order that information may reflect all points of view, it is important that the points of view presented by those who consider that the information published or disseminated about them has seriously prejudiced their effort to strengthen peace and international understanding, to promote human rights or to counter racialism and incitement to war be also disseminated.

§2 Examples of national legal enactments relating to rights and obligations of the press

Several examples are given, to show something of the range of variation in scope and formulation. The essential principles underlying all examples are much the same, although much is left to interpretation and/or more detailed exposition in other places. Notable is the ambiguity, silence, or simply uncertainty about which media forms enjoy the full degree of protection promised.

Constitution of the United States of America

First Amendment (1791)

Congress shall make no law respecting an establishment of religion, or prohibiting the free exercise thereof; or abridging the freedom of speech or of the press; or the right of the people peacefully to assemble, and to petition the government for a redress of grievances.

Basic law of the Federal Republic of Germany

Freedom of Expression

1 Every person shall have the right freely to express and disseminate his opinions in speech, writing and pictures without hindrance from generally accessible sources. Freedom of the press and freedom of reporting by means of broadcasting and film shall be guaranteed. There shall be no censorship.

2 These rights shall find their limits in the provisions of general laws, in provision for the protection of young persons, and in the right to personal honour.

Constitution of the Russian Federation

(Relevant excerpts)

Chapter 2. Rights and Liberties of Man and Citizen

Article 17

1 The basic rights and liberties in conformity with the commonly recognised principles and norms of the international law shall be recognised and guaranteed in the Russian Federation and under this Constitution.

2 The basic rights and liberties of the human being and citizen shall be inalienable and shall belong to everyone from birth.

3 The exercise of rights and liberties of a human being and citizen may not violate the rights and liberties of other persons.

Article 23

1 Everyone shall have the right to privacy, to personal and family secrets, and to protection of one's honor and good name.

2 Everyone shall have the right to privacy of correspondence, telephone communications, mail, cables and other communications. Any restriction of this right shall be allowed only under an order of a court of law.

Article 29

1 Everyone shall have the right to freedom of thought and speech.

2 Propaganda or campaigning inciting social, racial, national or religious hatred and strife is impermissible. The propaganda for social, racial, national or religious or language superiority is forbidden.

3 No-one shall be coerced into expressing one's views and convictions or into renouncing them.

4 Everyone shall have the right to seek, get, transfer, produce and disseminate information by any lawful means. The list of information constituting the state secret shall be established by federal law.

5 The freedom of the mass media shall be guaranteed. Censorship shall be prohibited.

The Netherlands: Constitution

Chapter 1. Fundamental Rights

Article 7 [Expression]

1 No-one shall require prior permission to publish thoughts or opinions through the press, without prejudice to the responsibility of every person under the law.

2 Rules concerning radio and television shall be laid down by Act of Parliament. There shall be no prior supervision of the content of a radio or television broadcast.

3 No-one shall be required to submit thoughts or opinions for prior approval in order to disseminate them by means other than those mentioned in the preceding paragraphs, without prejudice to the responsibility of every person under the law. The holding of performances open to persons younger than sixteen years of age may be regulated by Act of Parliament in order to protect good morals.

4 The preceding paragraphs do not apply to commercial advertising.

Sweden: The Freedom of the Press Act

Sweden can claim to have the earliest formal legal guarantee of Freedom of the Press (1766). The present text is notable for its detail on several points.

Chapter 1. On the Freedom of the Press

Article 1

1 The freedom of the press means the right of every Swedish subject, without hindrance by a central administrative authority, or other public body, to publish any written matter, and not to be prosecuted thereafter on grounds of the content of such matter than before a court of law, or to be punished therefore in any case other than a case in which the content is in contravention of an express provision of law, enacted to preserve public order without suppressing information to the public.

2 In accordance with the principles set forth in Paragraph 1) concerning freedom of the press for all, and in order to ensure the free interchange of opinion and enlightenment of the public, every Swedish subject shall be entitled, subject to the provisions set forth in the present Act for the protection of individual rights and public security, to publish his thoughts and opinions in print, to publish official documents and to make statements and communicate information on any subject whatsoever.

3 All persons shall likewise be entitled, unless otherwise provided in the present Act, to make statements and communicate information on any subject whatsoever, for the purpose of publication in print, to the author or to any person who shall be considered the originator of material in such a publication, to the responsible publisher or editorial office, if any, of any publication, or to an enterprise which professionally purveys news or other information to periodical publications.

4 All persons shall, furthermore, be entitled, unless otherwise provided in the Act, to procure information and intelligence for the purpose of its publication in print, or for the purpose of making statements or communicating information in the manner referred to in Paragraph 3).

Article 2

1 No publication shall be subject to scrutiny before printing, nor shall the printing thereof be prohibited.

2 Furthermore, no central administrative authority or other public body shall be permitted on grounds of the content of a publication to take any action not authorized under this Act to prevent the printing or publication of the material, or its circulation among the public.

Article 3

1 No person shall be prosecuted, convicted under penal law, or held liable for damages on grounds of abuse of the freedom of the press, or complicity therein, nor shall the publication be seized or confiscated other than in the manner and in the cases specified in this Act.

Article 4

1 Any person entrusted with passing judgment on abuses of freedom of the press or otherwise ensuring compliance with this Act shall constantly bear in mind that freedom of the press is fundamental to a free society, direct his attention more to illegality of subject matter and thought than to illegality in the form of expression, to the aim rather than the manner of presentation, and, in case of doubt, to acquit rather than to convict.

Article 5

1 The present Act shall apply to all material using a printing press.

2 The term published matter includes pictures, even where there is no accompanying text.

Article 6

Printed matter shall not be considered as such unless it is published. Printed matter shall be deemed to have been published when it has been delivered for sale or disseminated by some other means.

§3 Voluntary codes of conduct and ethics adopted by associations of journalism

American Society of Newspaper Editors (ASNE) Statement of Principles

ASNE's statement of principles was originally adopted in 1922 as the 'Canons of Journalism'. The document was revised and renamed 'Statement of Principles' in 1975.

Preamble

The First Amendment protecting freedom of expression from abridgement by any law, guarantees to the people through their press a constitutional rights and thereby places on newspaper people a particular responsibility.

Thus journalism demands of its practitioners not only industry and knowledge but also the pursuit of a standard of integrity proportional to the journalist's singular obligation. To this end, the American Society of Newspaper Editors sets out this Statement of Principles as a standard encouraging the highest ethical and professional performance.

Article I – Responsibility

The primary purpose of gathering and distributing news and opinion is to serve the general welfare by informing the people and enabling them to make judgments on the issues of the time. Newspapermen and women who abuse the power of their professional role for selfish motives or unworthy purposes are faithless to that public trust. The American press was made free not just to serve as a forum for debate but also to bring an independent scrutiny to bear on the forces of power in the society, including the conduct of official power, at all levels of government.

Article II – Freedom of the Press

Freedom of the Press belongs to the people. It must be defended against encroachment or assault from any quarter, public or private. Journalists must be constantly alert to see that the public's business is conducted in public. They must be vigilant against all who would exploit the press for selfish purposes.

Article III – Independence

Journalists must avoid impropriety and the appearance of impropriety as well as any conflict of interest or the appearance of conflict. They should neither accept anything nor pursue any activity that might compromise or seem to compromise their integrity.

Article IV – Truth and Accuracy

Good faith with the reader is the foundation of good journalism. Every effort must be made to assure that the news content is accurate, free from bias and in context, and that all sides are presented fairly. Editorials, analytical articles and commentary should be held to the same standards of accuracy with respect to facts as news reports. Significant errors of fact, as well as errors of omission, should be corrected promptly and prominently.

Article V – Impartiality

To be impartial does not require the press to be unquestioning or to refrain from editorial expression. Sound practice, however, demands a clear distinction for the reader between news reports and opinion. Articles that contain opinion or personal interpretation should be clearly identified.

Article VI – Fair Play

Journalists should respect the rights of people involved in the news, observe the common standards of decency and stand accountable to the public for the fairness and accuracy of their news reports. Persons publicly accused should be given the earliest opportunity to respond. Pledges of confidentiality to news sources must be honoured at all costs, and therefore should not be given lightly. Unless there is clear and pressing need to maintain confidences, sources of information should be identified.

These principles are intended to preserve, protect and strengthen the bond of trust and respect between American journalists and the American people, a bond that is essential to sustain the grant of freedom entrusted to both by the nation's founders.

§4 National regulation of broadcast news

Nearly everywhere news distributed by broadcasting has been limited in various ways and degrees. The purpose is often to apply standards of objectivity and impartiality, as in the example given. Currently, regulations (or codes of practice) of this kind are usually either applied by the broadcasting body concerned or by an independent Regulator.

UK: Ofcom Code for Broadcasting

This text has its origins in paragraphs of the legislation enacted in the 1950s to allow commercial television to operate in the UK alongside the public broadcaster, the BBC. Essentially they are a formalisation of the same internal guidelines that applied and still apply to the BBC.

Section Five: Due Impartiality and Due Accuracy and Undue Prominence of Views and Opinions

(Relevant legislation includes, in particular, sections 319 (2) and (d), 319 (8) and Section 320 of the Communications Act 2003 and Article 10 of the European Convention on Human Rights.)

(This section of the code does not apply to BBC services funded by the licence fee, which are regulated on these matters by the BBC Trust.)

Principles

To ensure that news in whatever form, is reported with due accuracy and presented with due impartiality.

To ensure that the special impartiality requirements of the Act are complied with.

Rules

MEANING OF 'DUE IMPARTIALITY'

'Due' is an important qualification to the concept of impartiality. Impartiality itself means not favouring one side over another. 'Due' means adequate or proportionate to the subject and nature of the programme. So 'due impartiality' does not mean an equal division of time that has to be given to every view, or that every argument and every facet of every argument has to be represented. The approach to due impartiality may vary according to the nature of the subject, the type of programme and channel, the likely expectation of the audience as to content, and the extent to which content and approach is signalled to the audience. Context, as defined in Section Two, Harm and Offence of the Code, is important.

DUE IMPARTIALITY AND DUE ACCURACY IN NEWS

5.1 News, in whatever form, must be reported with due accuracy and presented with due impartiality.

5.2 Significant mistakes in news should normally be acknowledged and corrected on air quickly. Corrections should be appropriately scheduled.

5.3 No politician may be used as a news reader, interviewer or reporter in any news programme, unless, exceptionally, it is editorially justifiable. In that case, the political allegiance of that person must be made clear to the audience.

SPECIAL IMPARTIALITY REQUIREMENTS: NEWS AND OTHER PROGRAMMES

Matters of political or industrial controversy and matters relating to current public policy.

MEANING OF 'MATTERS OF POLITICAL OR INDUSTRIAL CONTROVERSY AND MATTERS RELATING TO CURRENT PUBLIC POLICY'

Matters of political or industrial controversy are political or industrial issues on which politicians, industry and/or the media are in debate. Matters relating to current public policy need not be the subject of debate but relate to a policy under discussion or already decided by a local, regional or national government or by bodies mandated by those public bodies to make policy on their behalf, for example non-governmental organisations, relevant European institutions, etc.

THE EXCLUSION OF VIEWS AND OPINIONS
(Rule 5.4 applies to television and radio services.)

5.4. Programmes in the services (listed above) must exclude all expressions of the views and opinions of the person providing the service on matters of political or industrial controversy and matters relating to current public policy (unless that person is speaking in a legislative forum or a court of law).

THE PRESERVATION OF DUE IMPARTIALITY
(Rules 5.5 to 5.12 apply to television programme services, national radio and national digital programme services.)

5.5 Due impartiality on matters of political or industrial controversy and matters of current public policy must be preserved on the part of any person providing a service (listed above). This may be achieved within a programme or over a series of programmes taken as a whole.

§5 Independent self-regulation of the press at national level

In a number of countries, some very limited regulation of the printed press has been instituted, usually with a statutory basis, but depending on voluntary cooperation of organs of the press. The Irish example fits this model.

The Press Council of Ireland: Code of Practice

Preamble

The freedom to publish is vital to the right of the people to be informed. This freedom includes the right of a newspaper to publish what it considers to be news, without fear or favour, and the right to comment upon it.

Freedom of the press carries responsibilities. Members of the profession have the duty to maintain the highest professional and ethical standards.

This code sets the benchmark for those standards. It is the duty of the Press Ombudsman and Press Council of Ireland to ensure that it is honoured in the spirit as well as in the letter, and it is the duty of publications to assist them in this task.

In dealing with complaints, the Ombudsman and Press Council will give consideration to what they perceive to be in the public interest. It is for them to define the public interest in each case, but the general principle is that the public interest is invoked in relation to a matter capable of affecting the people at large so that they may legitimately be interested in receiving, and the press legitimately interested in providing, information about it.

Principle 1 – Truth and Accuracy

1.1 In reporting news and information, newspapers and magazines shall strive at all times for truth and accuracy.

1.2 When a significant inaccuracy, misleading statement or report or picture has been published, it shall be corrected promptly and with due prominence.

1.3 When appropriate, a retraction, apology, clarification, explanation or response shall be published promptly and with due prominence.

Principle 2 – Distinguishing Fact and Comment

2.1 Newspapers and magazines are entitled to advocate strongly their own views on topics.

2.2 Comment, conjecture, rumour and unconfirmed reports shall not be reported as if they were fact.

2.3 Readers are entitled to expect that the contents of a publication reflects the best judgment of editors and writers and has not been inappropriately influenced by undisclosed interests. Wherever relevant, any significant financial interest of an organization should be disclosed. Writers should disclose significant potential conflicts of interest to their editors.

Principle 3 – Fairness and Honesty

3.1 Newspapers and magazines shall strive at all times for fairness and honesty in the procuring and publishing of news and information.

3.2 Publications shall not obtain information, photographs or other material through misrepresentation or subterfuge, unless justified by the public interest.

3.3 Journalists and photographers must not obtain information and photographs through harassment, unless their actions are justified in the public interest.

Principle 4 – Respect for Rights

Everyone has constitutional protection for his or her good name. Newspapers and magazines shall not knowingly publish matter based on malicious misrepresentation or unfounded accusations, and must take reasonable care in checking facts before publication.

Principle 5 – Privacy

5.1 Privacy is a human right, protected as a personal right in the Irish Constitution and the European Convention on Human Rights, which is incorporated into Irish law. The private and family life, home and correspondence of everyone must be respected.

5.2 Readers are entitled to have news and comment presented with respect for the privacy and sensibilities of individuals. However, the right to privacy should not prevent publication of matters of public record or in the public interest.

5.3 Sympathy and discretion must be shown at all times in seeking information in situations of personal grief or shock. In publishing such information, the feelings of grieving families should be taken into account. This should not be interpreted as restricting the right to report judicial proceedings.

5.4 Public persons are entitled to privacy. However, where a person holds public office, deals with public affairs, follows a public career, or has sought or obtained publicity for his activities, publication of relevant details of his private life and circumstances may be justifiable where the information revealed relates to the validity of the person's conduct, the credibility of his public statements, the value of his publicly expressed views or is otherwise justified by the public interest.

5.5 Taking photographs of individuals in public places without their consent is not acceptable, unless justified by the public interest.

Principle 6 – Protection of Sources

Journalists shall protect confidential sources of information.

Principle 7 – Court Reporting

Newspaper and magazines shall strive to ensure that court reports (including the use of photographs) are fair and accurate, are not prejudicial to the right to a fair trial and that the presumption of innocence is respected.

Principle 8 – Prejudice

Newspapers and magazines shall not publish material intended or likely to cause grave offence or stir up hatred against an individual or group on the basis of their race, religion, nationality, colour, ethnic origin, membership of the travelling community, gender, sexual orientation, marital status, disability, illness or age.

Principle 9 – Children

9.1 Newspapers and magazines shall take particular care in seeking and presenting information or comment about a child under the age of 16.

Principle 10 – Publication of the Decision of the Press Ombudsman/ Press Council

10.1 When requested or required by the Press Ombudsman and/or the Press Council to do so, newspapers and magazines shall publish the decision in relation to a complaint with due prominence.

References

Altschull, J.H. (1984). *Agents of Power. The Role of the News Media in Human Affairs*. New York: Longman.

Arcetti, C. (2008). 'News coverage of 9/11 and the demise of the media flows, globalization and localization theories', *International Communication Gazette*, 70, 6: 463–85.

Baker, C.E. (2002). *Media, Markets, and Democracy*. Cambridge: Cambridge University Press.

Bardoel, J. (1996). 'Beyond journalism: between information society and civil society', *European Journal of Communication*, 11, 3: 283–302.

BBC (2007). *World Service Poll: World Opinion on Press Freedom.*

Becker, L., Vlad, T. and Nusser, N. (2007). 'An evaluation of press freedom indicators', *International Communication Gazette*, 69, 1: 5–28.

Bennett, W. L. (1990). 'Towards a theory of press–state relations in the US', *Journal of Communication*, 40, 2: 103–25.

Bennett, W. L. (2003). 'The burglar alarm that just keeps ringing: a response to Zaller', *Political Communication*, 20, 2: 131–38.

Bennett, W.L., Lawrence, R.G. and Livingston, S. (2007). *When The Press Fails.* Chicago: University of Chicago Press.

Bennett, W.L. and Iyengar, S. (2008). 'A new ear of minimal effects? Changing foundations of political communication', *Journal of Communication*, 58(4): 707–31.

Benson, R.D. (2006). 'News media as a journalistic field. What Bourdieu adds to new institutionalism and vice versa', *Political Communication,* 23, 2: 187–202.

Benson, R.D. and Neveu, E. (eds) (2005). *Bourdieu and the Journalistic Field.* Malden MA: Polity Press.

Berkowitz, D. (ed.) (1997). *The Social Meanings of News.* Thousand Oaks, CA: Sage.

Bertrand, J.-C. (2000). *Media Accountability Systems.* Brunswick, NJ: Transaction Books.

Blumler, J.G. (ed.) (1992). *Television and the Public Interest.* London: Sage.

Blumler, J.G. and Gurevitch, M. (1995). *The Crisis of Public Communication.* London: Routledge.

Bourdana, S. (2010). 'On the values guiding the French practice of journalism', *Journalism*, 3: 293–310.

Boyd-Barrett, O. and Rantanen, T. (eds) (1998). *The Globalization of News.* London: Sage.

Brants, K. (1998). 'Who's afraid of infotainment?', *European Journal of Communication,* 13, 3: 315–35.

Brants, K. and de Haan, Y. (2010). 'Three models of responsiveness', *Media, Culture and Society,* 32, 3: 411–28.

Brodasson, T. (1994). 'The sacred side of professional journalism', *European Journal of Communication*, 9, 3: 227–48.

Broersma, M. (2009). 'The unbearable limitations of journalism. On press critique and journalism's claim to truth', *International Communication Gazette,* 72, 1: 21–34.

Cammaerts, B. and Carpentier, N. (eds) (2007). *Reclaiming the Media.* Bristol: Intellect.

Campus, D. (2010). 'Mediatization and personification of politicians in France and Italy: the case of Berlusconi and Sarkozy', *International Journal of Press/Politics,* 16, 1: 215–35.

Capella, J.N. and Jamieson, K.H. (1997). *The Spiral of Cynicism: The Press and the Public Good.* New York: Oxford University Press.

Castells, M. (2001). *The Internet Galaxy.* Oxford: Oxford University Press.

Chalaby, J. (1996). 'Journalism as an Anglo-American invention', *European Journal of Communication*, 11, 3: 303–26.

Chang, T.-K., Himmelboin, I. and Dong, D. (2009). 'Open global networks, closed international flows', *International CommunicationGazette*, 71, 3, 137–59.

Christians, C., Glasser, T., McQuail, D., Nordenstreng, K. and White, R. (2009). *Normative Theories of the Press.* Champaign, IL: University of Illinois Press.

Coleman, S. and Blumler, J.G. (2009). *The Internet and Democratic Citizenship.* Cambridge: Cambridge University Press.

Commission on Freedom of the Press (1947). *Report.* Chicago: University of Chicago Press.

Cook, T. (2006). 'News media as a poitical institution', *Political Communication,* 23, 2: 159–72.

Curran, J., Iyengar, S., Lund, A.B. and Salovaaria-Moring, I. (2009). 'Media system, public knowledge and democracy: a comparative study'. *European Journal of Communication*, 24, 1: 5–25.

Dahlberg, L. (2011). 'Reconstructing digital democracy: an outline of four "positions"', *New Media and Society*, 13, 6: 855–72.

Dahlgren, P. (1995). *Television and the Public Sphere.* London: Sage.

Davis, N. (2011). *Flat Earth News.* London: Vintage.

Dayan, D. and Katz, E. (1992). *Media Events.* Cambridge, MA: Harvard University Press.

Dennis E.E., Gilmore, D. and Glasser, T. (1989). *Media, Freedom and Accountability.* New York: Greenwood.

Deprez, A. and Raeymaeckers, K. (2009) 'Bias in the news? Belgian press coverage of the First and Second Intifida', *International Communication Gazette,* 72, 1: 91–110.

Deuze, M. (2002). 'National news cultures', *Journalism and Mass Communication Quarterly,* 79, 1: 134–49.

Deuze, M. (2005). 'What is journalism? Professional ideals and ideology of journalists reconsidered', *Journalism,* 6: 442–64.

Deuze, M. (2007). *Media Work.* Cambridge: Polity Press.

Domingo, D. and Heinonen, A. (2008). 'Weblogs and journalism: a typology to explore the blurring boundaries', *Nordicom Review*, 29, 1: 3–15.

Downing, J.D.H. (2001). *Radical Media: Rebellious Communication and Social Movements.* Thousand Oaks, CA: Sage.

Dutton, W.H. (2009) 'The Fifth Estate emerging through the network of networks', *Prometheus*, 27, 1: 1–15.

Eide, M. (2007). 'Encircling the power of journalism', *Nordicom Review,* 28: 21–9.

Elvestad, E. and Blekesaune, A. (2008). 'Newspaper readers of Europe', *European Journal of Communication*, 23, 4: 425–47.

Entman, R.M. (1993). 'Framing: towards clarification of a fractured paradigm', *Journal of Communication,* 43, 4: 51–8.

Ettema, J. and Glasser, T. (1998). *Custodians of Conscience: Investigative Journalism and Public Virtue.* New York: Columbia University Press.

Eurobarometer (2010). Standard Survey EB 74.

Fengler, S. and Russ-Mohl, S. (2008). 'Journalism and the information-attention markets', *Journalism,* 9, 6: 667–90.

Fortunati, L. (2005). 'Mediatizing the net and intermediatizing the media', *International Communication Gazette,* 67, 6: 29–44.

Fuchs, C. (2009). 'ICTs and society: a contribution to the critique of the political economy of the internet', *European Journal of Communication*, 24, 1: 69–87.
Gamble, A. and Watanabe, T. (2004). *A Public Betrayed*. Washington, DC: Regnery.
Gans, H.J. (1979). *Deciding What's News*. New York: Vintage.
Glasser, T.L. (ed.) (1999). *The Idea of Public Journalism*. New York: Guilford Press.
Goldberg, J. (2011). 'Rethinking the public/virtual sphere: the problem with participation', *New Media and Society*, 13, 5: 739–54.
Graber, D. (2003). 'The Rocky Road to New Paradigms: Modernizing News and Citizenship Standards', *Political Communication*, 20: 145–48.
Graber, D., McQuail, D. and Norriss, P. (eds) (2005). *The Politics of News: News of Politics*, 2nd edition. Washington, DC: Congressional Quarterly.
Gunaratne, S.A. (2002). 'Freedom of the press: a world system perspective', *Gazette*, 64, 4: 342–69.
Gunther, R. and Mughan, A. (2002). *Democracy and the Media: A Comparative Perspective*. Cambridge: Cambridge University Press.
Habermas, J. (1962/1984). *The Structural Transformation of the Public Sphere*. Cambridge, MA: MIT Press.
Habermas, J. (2007). 'Political communication in media society', *Communication Theory*, 16, 4: 411–26.
Hafez, K. (2011). 'Global journalism for global governance? Theoretical views, practical considerations', *Journalism*, 12, 4: 83–93.
Hall, S. (1977). 'Culture, media and the ideological effect', in J. Curran and M. Gurevitch (eds), *Mass Communication and Society*. London: Arnold, pp. 315–48.
Hallin, D.C. and Mancini, P. (2004). *Comparing Media Systems*. Cambridge: Cambridge University Press.
Hallin, D.C. and Mancini, P. (2012). *Comparing Media Systems: Beyond the Western World*. Cambridge: Cambridge University Press.
Hanitzsch, T. (2007). 'Deconstructing journalism culture: towards a universal theory', *Communication Theory*, 17: 367–85.
Hanitzsch, T. et al. (2011). 'Populist disseminator, detached watchdog, critical change agent: professional milieus, the journalistic field and autonomy in 18 countries', *International Communication Gazette*, 73, 6: 477–94.
Hanitzsch, T. and Mellado, C. (2011). 'What shapes the news around the world? How journalists in 18 countries perceive influences on their work', *International Journal of Press/Politics*, 16: 404–26.
Hardt, H. (1991). *Critical Communication Studies*. London: Routledge.
Hardt, H. (2003). *Social Theories of the Press: Early German and American Perspectives*. Malden, NJ: Rowman and Littlefield.
Herman, E. (2000). 'The propaganda model: a retrospective', *Journalism Studies*, 1, 1: 101–11.
Hills, J. (2008). 'What's new? War censorship and global transition', *International Communication Gazette*, 68, 3: 195–216.
Hjarvard, S. (2008). 'Mediatization of Society', *Nordicom Review*, 29: 105–29.
Hocking, W.E. (1947). *Freedom of the Press: A Framework of Principle*. Chicago: University of Chicago Press.
Hodges, L.W. (1986). 'Defining press responsibility: a functional approach', in D. Elliot (ed.), *Responsible Journalism*. Beverly Hills, CA: Sage, pp. 13–31.
Hutchins, R. (1947). Commission of Freedom of the Press. *A Free and Responsible Press*. Chicago: University of Chicago Press.
Iyengar, S. (1991). *Is Anyone Responsible?* Chicago: University of Chicago Press.

Jakubowicz, K. (2007). 'The East European/post-communist model', in G. Terzis (ed.), *European Media Governance. National and Regional Dimensions*. Bristol: Intellect, pp. 305–15.

Janowitz, M. (1975). 'Professional models in journalism: the gatekeeper and advocate', *Journalism Quarterly*, 52, 4: 618–26.

Josephi, B. (2005). 'Journalism in the global age between normative and empirical', *International Communication Gazette*, 67, 6: 575–90.

Just, N. and Puppis, M. (eds) (2012). *Trends in Communication Policy Research*. Bristol: Intellect.

Keane, J. (1991). *The Media and Democracy*. Cambridge: Polity.

Kim, H.S. (2012). 'War journalism and forces of gatekeeping during the escalation and de-escalation of the Iraq War', *International Communication Gazette*, 7, 4: 323–41.

Klaehn, J. (2002). 'A critical review and assessment of Herman and Chomsky's "Propaganda Model"', *European Journal of Communication*, 17, 2: 148–82.

Kung, L., Picard, R. and Towse, R. (eds) (2008). *The Internet and the Media*. London: Sage.

Laetila, T. (1995). 'Journalistic codes of ethics in Europe', *European Journal of Communication*, 10, 4: 527–46.

Lasswell, H.D. (1948). 'The structure and function of communication in society', in L. Bryson (ed.), *The Communication of Ideas*. New York: Harper, pp. 32–51.

Lemert, J.B. (1989). *Criticising the Media*. Newbury Park, CA: Sage.

Lessig, L. (1999). *Code and Other Laws of Cyberspace*. New York: Basic Books (new edition 2006).

Lichtenberg, J. (1991). 'In defense of objectivity', in J. Curran and M. Gurevich (eds), *Mass Media and Society*. London: Edward Arnold, pp. 216–31.

Livingston, S. and Bennett, W.L. (2003). 'Gatekeeping, indexing and live-event news: is technology altering the construction of news?', *Political Communication*, 20, 4: 363–80.

Lowrey, W., Parrott, S. and Meade, T. (2011). 'When blogs become orgs', *Journalism*, 12, 3: 243–59.

Luhmann, N. (2000). *The Reality of the Mass Media*. Cambridge: Polity Press.

Marliére, P. (1998). 'Rules of the journalistic field', *European Journal of Communication*, 13, 2: 219–34.

McCombs, M. and Shaw, D.L. (1993). 'The evolution of agenda-setting theory: 25 years in the marketplace of ideas', *Journal of Communication*, 43, 2: 58–66.

McGregor, P., Balcytiene, A., Fortunati, L. et al. (2011). 'A cross-regional comparison of selected European newspapers and attitudes to the internet', *Journalism*, 12, 5: 627–46.

McManus, J.H. (1992). 'What kind of commodity is news?', *Communication Research*, 19, 6: 767–85.

McManus, J.H. (1994). *Market-Driven Journalism*. Thousand Oaks, CA: Sage.

McManus, J.H. (2009). 'The commercialization of news', in K. Wahl-Jorgenson and T. Hanitzsch (eds), *Handbook of Journalism Studies*. London: Routledge, pp. 218–233.

McQuail, D. (1992). *Media Performance: Mass Communication in the Public Interest*. London: Sage.

McQuail, D. (1997). 'Accountability of media to society: principles and means', *European Journal of Communication*, 12, 4: 511–29.

McQuail, D. (2003). *Media Accountability and Freedom of Publication*. Oxford: Oxford University Press.

McQuail, D. (2006). 'The mediatization of war', *International Communication Gazette*, 68, 2: 107–18.

Meyer, T. (2002). *Mediated Politics*. Cambridge: Polity Press.

Milioni, D. (2009). 'Probing the online counter-public sphere', *Media, Culture and Society*, 31, 3: 409–33.

Mill, J.S. (1869/1956). *On Liberty*. Oxford: Oxford University Press.

Nerone, J. (1995). *Last Rights: Revisiting Four Theories of the Press*. Urbana, IL: University of Illinois Press.

Noelle-Neumann, (1984). *The Spiral of Silence*. Chicago: University of Chicago Press.

Norstedt, S.S., Kaitatzi-Whitlock, S. Ottosen, R. and Riegert, K., (2000). 'From the Persian Gulf to Kosovo: war journalism and propaganda', *European Journal of Communication*, 15, 3: 383–404.

Papacharissi, Z. (2002). 'The virtual sphere: the internet as public sphere', *New Media and Society*, 4, 1: 9–27.

Park, R. (1940/1967). 'News as a form of knowledge', in R.H. Turner (ed.) *Social Control and Collective Behavior.* Chicago: Chicago University Press, pp. 32–52.

Pasti, S. (2005). 'Two generations of Russian journalists', *European Journal of Communication*, 20, 1: 89–116.

Pasti, S., Chernysh, M. and Svich, L. (2012) 'Russian journalists and their profession', in D. Weaver and L.Wilhoit (eds), *The Global Journalist in the 21st Century: News People Around the World*. New York, Routledge.

Patterson, T.E. (2005). 'Political roles of the journalist', in D. Graber, D. McQuail and P. Norris (eds), *The Politics of News: News of Politics*, 2nd edition. Washington: CQ Press, pp. 23–39.

Peterson, T. (1956). 'The social responsibility theory', in Siebert, F.R. et al. (eds), *Four Theories of the Press*. Urbana, IL: University of Illinois Press, pp. 73–104.

Preston, P. (ed.) (2009). *Making the News: Journalism and News Cultures in Europe*. London: Routledge.

Quandt, T. and Singer, J.B. (2009). 'Convergence and cross-platform content production', in K. Wahl-Jorgenson and T. Hanitzsch (eds) *Handbook of Journalism Studies*. London: Routledge, pp. 130–46.

Ravi, N. (2005) 'Looking beyond flawed journalism. How national interest, patriotism and cultural values shaped the coverage of the Iraq war', *International Journal of Press/Politics,* 11, 1: 45–62.

Richter, A. (2008). 'Post-Soviet perspectives on censorship and freedom of the media: an overview', *International Communication Gazette,* 70, 5: 306–24.

Robinson, J.P. and Levy, M. (1986). *The Main Source*. Beverly Hills, CA: Sage.

Rosengren, K.E. (1987).'The comparative study of news diffusion', *European Journal of Communication*, 2, 2: 227–55.

Schudson, M. (1998). 'The public journalism and its problems', in D. Graber, D. McQuail and P. Norris (eds), *The Politics of News, The News of Politics*. Washington, DC: CQ Press, pp. 132–49.

Schultz, J. (1998). *Reviving the Fourth Estate*. Cambridge: Cambridge University Press.

Schulz, W. (2004). 'Reconstructing mediatization as an analytic concept', *European Journal of Communication*, 19, 1: 87–102.

Shoemaker, P.J. and Cohen, A.A. (2006) *News Around the World: Practitioners, Content and the Public*. New York: Routledge.

Siebert, F.R., Peterson, T. and Schramm, W. (1956). *Four Theories of the Press*. Urbana, IL: University of Illinois Press.

Singer, J.B. (2003). 'Who are these guys? The online challenge to the notion of professionalism', *Journalism*, 5, 4: 139–65.
Singer, J.B. (2007). 'Contested autonomy: professional and popular claims on journalism norms', *Journalism Studies*, 8: 79–95.
Strömbäck, J. (2005). 'Democracy and norms for journalism', *Journalism Studies,* 6, 3: 331–45.
Strömbäck, J. and Danilova, D.L. (2011). 'Mediatization and media interventionism', *International Journal of Press/Politics,* 16, 1: 30–49.
Thompson, J. (1995) *The Media and Modernity*. Cambridge: Polity Press.
Thussu, D. (2000). 'Legitimizing humanitarian intervention', *European Journal of Communication,* 15, 3: 45–61.
Thussu, D. (2007). *News as Entertainment*. London: Sage.
Tichenor, P.J., Donahue, G.A. and Olien, C.N. (1970) 'Mass media and the differential growth in knowledge', *Public Opinion Quarterly*, 34: 158–70.
Trappel, J., Niemenen, H. and Nord, L. (eds) (2011). *The Media Democracy Monitor.* Bristol: Intellect.
Tuchman, G. (1978). *Manufacturing the News*. New York: Free Press.
Tunstall, J. (1971). *Journalists at Work*. London: Constable.
Van Gorp, B. (2005) 'Where is the frame? Victims and intruders in the Belgian press coverage of the asylum issue', *European Journal of Communication*, 20, 4: 487–507.
Vartanova, E. (2012). 'The Russian media model in the context of post-soviet dynamics', in D. Hallin and P. Mancini (eds), *Comparing Media Systems: Beyond the Western World.* Cambridge: Cambridge University Press, pp. 119–142.
Vasterman, P. (2005). 'Media Hype: Self-reinforcing news waves, journalistic standards and the construction of social problems, *European Journal of Communication*, 20, 4: 508–30.
Wahl-Jorgenson, K. and Hanitzsch, T. (eds) (2009). *Handbook of Journalism Studies.* London: Routledge.
Waisbord, S. (2000). *Watchdog Journalism in South America*. New York: Columbia.
Waisbord, S. (2007). 'Democratic journalism and statelessness', *Political Communication,* 24, 2: 143–60.
Weaver, D. (ed.) (1999). *The Global Journalist*. New York: Hampton Press.
Weaver, D. and Wilhoit, C.G. (1986) *The American Journalist*. Bloomingdale: University of Indiana Press.
Weaver, D. and Wilhoit, L. (eds) (2012) *The Global Journalist in the 21st Century*. New York and London: Routledge.
Weber, M. (1948). 'Politics as a vocation', in H. Gerth and C.W. Mills (eds) *Max Weber Essays*. London: Routledge.
Westerstahl, J. (1983). 'Objective news reporting', *Communication Research*, 10, 3: 403–24.
Westerstahl, J. and Johansson, F. (1994). 'Foreign news: values and ideologies', *European Journal of Communication*, 9, 1: 71–89.
Wright, C.R. (1960). 'Functional analysis and mass communication', *Public Opinion Quarterly*, 24: 606–20.
Wu, H.D. (2003). 'Homogenity around the world? Comparing the systematic determinants of news flow between developed and developing countries', *International Communication Gazette*, 65, 1: 9–24.
Zaller, J. (2003). 'A new standard of news quality: burglar alarms for the monitorial citizen', *Political Communication,* 20, 2: 109–30.
Zeno-Zencovitch, V. (2008). *Freedom of Expression*. London: Routledge.

Index